ARTHUR OF BRITAIN

BY

E. K. CHAMBERS

CAMBRIDGE : SPECULUM HISTORIALE
NEW YORK : BARNES & NOBLE, INC

Originally published by Sidgwick & Jackson, Ltd.: 1927

Reprinted, by arrangement, with supplementary bibliography in 1964

for

SPECULUM HISTORIALE

42 Lyndewode Road, Cambridge

PRINTED IN GREAT BRITAIN
BY LOWE & BRYDONE (PRINTERS) LTD., LONDON

Arturi regis ambages pulcherrimae.

DANTE
De vulgari eloquentia

ADDENDA TO BIBLIOGRAPHY

R. S. Loomis, *The Development of Arthurian Romance* (London, 1963).

N. Tolstoi, 'Nenius, chapter 56', *B.B.C.S.* xix, 118-26.

H. Pähler, *Anglistik: Strukturuntersuchungen zur Historia Regum Britanniae des Geoffrey of Monmouth* (Bonn, 1958).

G. L. Brooks and R. F. Leslie, *Layamon's Brut*, *E.E.T.S.*, 1963.

R. N. Illingworth, 'Celtic Tradition and the Lai of Guigemar', *M.Ae*, xxxi, 176-187.

J. Marx, 'Observations sur la structure du roman gallois de Peredur', *E.C.* x, 88-108, and cf. *E.C.* ix, 92-105.

R. S. Loomis, *The Grail: from pagan myth to christian symbol* (Cardiff, 1963).

H. Adolf, *Visio Pacis: Holy City and Grail* (Pennsylvania, 1960).

J. A. W. Bennett, *Essays on Malory* (Oxford, 1963).

R. Bromwich, 'Scotland and the earliest Arthurian tradition', *B.B.S.I.A*. xv, 85-95.

K. H. Jackson, *The International Popular Tale in Wales* (Cardiff, 1961).

CORRIGENDA

Correct p. 303, ch. 1, line 16: B.B.C.S. viii to read vii.

      p. 313, line 1: T.H.S.C. 1956 to read 1936.

      p. 315, line 4: M.Ae. xxvii to read xxvi.

      p. 320, line 1: R.P. vii to read viii.

CONTENTS

*The extracts from Chronicles in the Rolls
series are made with the permission of the
Controller of H.M. Stationery Office.*

CHAPTER I

THE EARLY TRADITION

THERE are many names in the long bead-roll of England's memory. But none should stir the historic imagination more deeply than that of Arthur, the legend-hung champion of a dying order, through whom we reach back, beyond the advent of the chill barbarians from the north, to the slow spread of Mediterranean civilization by the shores of the Atlantic, and to that *pax Romana*, of which this island was the ultimate outpost.

Arthur first meets us, fully equipped and a Christian warrior, in the enigmatic pages of Nennius. The tale of Vortigern, that queer blend of chronicle, hagiography and folk-lore, has been told. Nennius turns to a later phase of the Saxon invasion. Hengist is dead. His son Octha has established a realm in Kent.

Of him sprang the kings of the Kentishmen. Then Arthur fought against them in those days with the kings of the Britons, and it was he who led their battles. The first battle was at the mouth of the river which is called Glein. The second, third, fourth and fifth were upon another river, which is called Dubglas and is in the region of Linnuis. The sixth battle was upon the river which is called Bassas. The seventh battle was in the wood of Celidon; it is Cat Coit Celidon. The eighth battle was on the castle Guinnion, wherein Arthur bore the image of St Mary the ever-virgin upon his shoulders, and the pagans were turned to flight on that day, and there was a great slaughter of them by virtue of our Lord Jesus Christ and by virtue of St Mary the Virgin his mother. The ninth battle was fought in the City of the Legion. He fought the tenth battle on the bank of the river which is called Tribruit. The eleventh battle was on the mount which is called Agned. The twelfth battle was on the mount of Badon, wherein fell nine hundred and sixty men in one day at a single onset of Arthur; and no one overthrew them but he alone, and in all the battles he came out victorious.

I have followed what is generally considered the best manuscript, *Harleian MS* 3859, of the eleventh or early twelfth century. A *Vatican MS*, of much the same date, adds that many of the British kings were of higher rank than Arthur. This and other manuscripts also give to the battle of Mount Agned the alternative names of Cat Bregoin, Breguoin or Bregomion. And some thirteenth-century manuscripts add glosses, which attempt to explain the name of Arthur, claim that the relic of the Virgin was preserved in Wedale, and tell us that Arthur brought it from a journey to Jerusalem, with a model of the true Cross, through which he achieved his victories.[1]

For all the twelve battles, with one exception, Nennius is the sole authority. That exception is the battle of the *Mons Badonicus*. Of this we know from a much earlier writer, Gildas, who was himself born on the very day of the battle. A little before 549 Gildas included in his *De Excidio Britanniae*, as a

[1] *Record* iv.

preface to the *admonitiuncula* against contemporary British wickedness of which that treatise mainly consists, a short historical account, fantastic in its earlier stages, of the Roman domination in the island, of the troublous times which succeeded, of the Saxon invasion, and of its progress up to his own day.[1] He tells how the Britons, harried by Picts and Scots, wrote a letter for aid to *Agitius, ter consul.* By Agitius must be meant Aetius, the lieutenant of the Emperor Valentinian in Gaul, whose third consulate fell in 446. The letter was in vain. But some of the Britons maintained a guerilla warfare and, after contests lasting 'through many years,' the aggressors withdrew. A period of prosperity and even luxury followed, marred by the internecine feuds, displeasing to God and to Gildas, of chieftains. Then the Scots came back. The Britons, led by a *superbus tyrannus*, took the unwise step of calling in a body of Saxons. These turned against them, brought reinforcements, and endeavoured to occupy the country for themselves. At first they blazed from sea to sea. The 'colonies' were overthrown. Many of the Britons were slain; others became serfs; others fled to the hills and forests, or to lands beyond the seas. At last head was made against the invaders under the leadership of Ambrosius Aurelianus, a man of modest position, but survivor of a noble Roman family, whose degenerate descendants were still in the land when Gildas wrote. A victory of Ambrosius stemmed the flood, and thereafter, says Gildas, came a time during

[1] *Record* ii.

3

which now the natives and now their enemies had the upper hand, up to the year of the *obsessio Badonici montis*. This was a heavy slaughter of the Saxons, and ushered in a period of peace, which still prevailed. The battle took place, if I read Gildas aright, exactly forty-four years and one month after the activities of Ambrosius. But some treat this period as extending from the battle to the writing of the *De Excidio*. Gildas, it will be seen, says nothing of Arthur, although he certainly does not say that the victory of the *Mons Badonicus*, as well as the initial victory, was won by Ambrosius. On the other hand, Nennius gives no direct account of Ambrosius, and it is only from incidental references in the story of Vortigern that we can gather the persistence of his fame.

Vortigern rules in Britain, and is harassed by the proximity of the Picts and Scots, by Roman pressure, and by dread of Ambrosius. We are not told what he has to anticipate from this quarter. Then come Hengist and Horsa. Vortigern enlists their help against the Scots, and is led by his love for Hengist's daughter Rowena into giving them dangerous concessions of land. They prove treacherous. Vortigern consults his *magi* and is advised to build a fortress. He cannot do so because the masonry crumbles away by night. A boy, supposed to be fatherless, is found for a sacrifice. But he has the gift of prophecy, and reveals a pool beneath the site, wherein the conquest of a white by a red dragon symbolizes a final victory of the Britons over the Saxons. When asked his name the boy replies, 'I am called Ambrosius,' to

4

which the writer, or perhaps a scribal gloss, adds, *Embreis Guletic ipse videbatur.*[1] And when the boy goes on to say that his father was a Roman consul, it may be inferred that behind the wild narrative lies the record of Gildas. Nennius goes on to relate victories over the Saxons, won not by Ambrosius, but by Vortimer the son of Vortigern, and terminated by Vortimer's death. Thereafter the invaders slay Vortigern's counsellors at a conference, and acquire the lands of the East, South and Middle Saxons. Interspersed in the progress of the Saxon story are passages of a distinct one, in which Vortigern commits incest with his daughter, is reproved by St Germanus, and at the prayer of the saint is destroyed in a tower by fire from heaven. As authority for this Nennius cites a *liber beati Germani* and adds that he knew other versions of Vortigern's end. And now we come to Ambrosius again, for Nennius tells how, after Vortigern's death, his son ruled in the South Welsh districts of Buelt and Gwerthrynion by the gift of Ambrosius, 'who was king among all the kings of the British race.' After the death of Vortigern St Germanus returns to the continent. At this point Nennius inserts a narrative of St Patrick's career in Ireland, and then resumes his account of the Saxon invasion with the passage on the settlement of the Kentish kingdom and on the battles of Arthur already quoted.[2] If the whole story hangs together,

[1] On Guletic cf. p. 176.
[2] The *Vatican MS* puts the *Vita Patricii* after, instead of before, this passage.

5

it would seem that Nennius thought of Arthur as a contemporary or immediate successor of Ambrosius.

But who or what was Nennius, and what reason is there to suppose that his precise and even statistical description of Arthur's campaigns rests upon any veritable foundation of tradition or record? There is no reason to doubt the existence of Nennius, although only the faintest trace of him can be found outside the *Historia Britonum* which goes under his name. It is not indeed ascribed to him in all the manuscripts. Some are anonymous; others, by explicable misunderstandings, bear the name of Gildas or that of a certain anchorite Mark. But several preserve prefatory matter, in which Nennius claims the authorship, and speaks of himself as the disciple of one Elbodugus. He was Elfodd, bishop of Bangor in North Wales, who died about 811, and a composition date for the work of Nennius in the earlier part of the ninth century would fit in well enough with certain time-references in the *Historia Britonum*. Probably Nennius himself was of South rather than North Wales, for we find appended to the *Historia* notices of certain *mirabilia* or natural marvels of this country. And in two of these Arthur meets us again.[1]

There is another marvel in the district which is called Buelt. Here is a pile of stones and on the top of the heap is a single stone with the foot-print of a dog in it. When they hunted the pig Troynt, Cabal, who was the dog of the warrior Arthur, set his foot-print in the stone, and Arthur afterwards made a heap of stones beneath the stone in which

[1] *Record* iv.

6

his dog's foot-print was, and it is called Carn Cabal. And men come and bear off the stone in their hands during the space of a day and a night, and on the morrow it is found upon its heap.

There is another marvel in the district which is called Ercing. Here is a burial-place beside a well, which is named Licat Anir, and the name of the man who was buried in the mound was called Anir. He was the son of the warrior Arthur, and he himself slew him there and buried him. And men come and measure the mound, sometimes six feet in length, sometimes nine, sometimes twelve, sometimes fifteen. However you measure it on one occasion, you will never find it of the same measure again, and this I have myself tested.

Early in the ninth century, then, Arthur was not merely a national British hero; he was also the centre of popular aetiological myths in South Wales and in Ercing, which is Herefordshire. How much farther back does the tradition go? It is difficult to say. Doubtless the *Historia Britonum* was largely an assemblage of earlier and in places disparate material. Nennius, both in his preface and from time to time in the course of the treatise, cites as his authority a *vetus traditio seniorum nostrorum*. It was written, not oral, at least in part, for he once speaks of *veteres libri veterum nostrorum*. He also claims to have used *annales Romanorum*, the chronicles of Jerome, Eusebius and Prosper, and *annales Scottorum Saxonumque*. And, as already noted, he cites a *liber Germani*. There is a further reference to this *liber* in a rubric at the beginning of a text of the *Historia Britonum* preserved in *Chartres MS* 98. This is the earliest manuscript, variously dated from the ninth to the eleventh century, and contains a version of the *Historia* which differs considerably from that found in the Harleian and other texts. The rubric runs, *Incipiunt exberta [experta* or *excerpta?] fili Urbagen de libro sancti Germani inuenta et origine et genelogia Britonum*. Opinions differ as to the relation of the *Chartres MS* to the work of Nennius. It has recently been held that they show a common Latinity, and that the *Historia* in its various recensions is wholly a treatise of the ninth century, based upon Gildas, Bede, and a *liber Germani*, with many confusions and inventions due to Nennius himself.[1] There is, however, not much in common between Nennius and Bede, except the use of the name Vortigern, which seems to have the same meaning as the *superbus tyrannus* of Gildas; and it is difficult to prove that either writer knew the work of the other. The view which has generally prevailed, and which still seems to me the most plausible, is that the *Chartres MS* represents, not a version of Nennius, but an earlier *Historia*, which he used as a source, and which is in fact his *vetus traditio*. It was no doubt itself a composite work. The early sections are based partly upon sixth and seventh-century attempts to derive an origin for the Frankish and British nations from Biblical genealogies and the legends of Rome and Troy, and partly upon the accounts of the Roman domination given by Gildas and the Latin chronicles. These sections have in the *Chartres MS* already under-

[1] F. Liebermann in *Tout Essays* (1925).

gone a clumsy revision. Then follow, as in Nennius, the juxtaposed stories of Vortigern and the Saxons and Vortigern and Germanus. The latter of course came from the *liber Germani*. St Germanus of Auxerre is known to have visited Britain in 429 and again not long before his death between 444 and 450. We may safely take the *liber* to have been a *Vita* of the saint, more fabulous in character and later in date than the fairly historical *Vita*, written by one Constantius about 480, which still survives. Did this also contain the Hengist story? Probably not. The two narratives remain independent throughout, and it is not *prima facie* likely that the *Vita* of a saint would have contained quite so much incident with which its hero was not concerned. Moreover, the Hengist story, although written from a British point of view, shows a knowledge of Saxon names and genealogy, and probably owes something to a Saxon source. The chances are that matter from such a source has been dovetailed by the author of the early *Historia* into matter from the *liber*. Against this, the absence of any reference to another authority in the Chartres rubric need not weigh much.

But we have not yet a name or a date for the author of the early *Historia*. The natural interpretation of the Chartres rubric would be that he was a son of Urbagen. A proper name may have slipped out. Conceivably this gives a clue; for Nennius tells us, in passages probably not derived from the early *Historia* itself, that Urbgen, the Urien of Welsh legend, was one of the British kings who fought against the Northumbrians at the end of the sixth century; and also that Run map Urbagen was the name, presumably before baptism, of St Paulinus, the chaplain of Aethelberga of Kent, who baptized King Edwin and his Northumbrians in 627, became Archbishop of York, fled from Northumbria to Kent on the death of Edwin, and died there in 644. There is no confirmation of the statement that St Paulinus, who came from Rome to join St Augustine, was of British parentage. But if he was, and if he interested himself in British history, he would be in a very good position to combine native and Saxon sources. A document of the first half of the seventh century would serve well enough for the *vetus traditio* of Nennius. It is not necessary to assume that the *Chartres MS* represents the early *Historia* just as it was originally written. There is one passage, indeed, which cannot be earlier than the abbacy of Slebine at Iona in 752–67. But this reads like an interpolation, and in fact Nennius does not use it.

The ascription of the early *Historia* to St Paulinus, and with it the seventh-century date, must remain uncertain. I doubt whether it bears much upon the emergence of Arthur. When Nennius in his turn began to work upon the *Historia*, he seems to have rewritten the opening sections very freely. On the other hand, he incorporates the two Vortigern stories practically *verbatim*, so far as the *Chartres MS* goes. Unfortunately this is only a fragment. But we may reasonably suppose that the early *Historia* continued to be the main source of Nennius, at least as far as the return of Germanus to Gaul. Nennius has added something of his own towards the end, and conceivably he inserted from Welsh traditions of Snowdon the passage about Ambrosius and the red and white dragons. Here the *arx Guorthigirni* is put in North Wales; the account of Vortigern's end, for which Nennius cites the *liber Germani*, puts it in South Wales. The discrepancy may be due to the disparate origin of the pre-Nennian *Historia* itself. In any case the earlier reference to Vortigern's dread of Ambrosius is in the pre-Nennian version. We come now to the sections in Nennius which follow the return of Germanus. It is very doubtful whether in any of these we are still in touch with the early *Historia*. The varying place of the *Vita Patricii* in the manuscripts suggests that it is an insertion. The section on Arthur ends with a rapid transition to Ida, king of the Northumbrian Angles from 547; and the notice of Ida leads in turn to a series of Anglo-Saxon royal genealogies, followed by a more detailed account of the North British kings who fought against them, and of the bards who sang in their days. The genealogies are related to others found in manuscripts of Anglo-Saxon origin, and one of these has a curious misdating of the *Adventus Saxonum*, possibly taken from another passage of Nennius or from the early *Historia*. This historical matter may have originally ended in 679; in its present form it goes up to 796. It cannot therefore come from the early *Historia*, if that is really not later than the first half of the seventh century. It seems to be derived from a North British

11

document, partly based on Anglo-Saxon material, but Northumbrian and not, as in the early *Historia*, Kentish. On the whole, it is likely that Nennius himself added this section, together with a list of the cities of Britain and the account of the *mirabilia* of the country, which conclude his treatise. What then of the Arthurian section itself? This has a head-link connecting it with Hengist and a tail-link connecting it with Ida. It can hardly belong to the North British document. The battles are clearly described as related to the Kentish and not the Northumbrian invasion. On the other hand, it would be rash to take it for granted that it came from the early *Historia*. It too may have been contributed by Nennius, with the Arthurian *mirabilia*, from South Welsh sources familiar to him. It will be seen from later chapters that the balance of evidence points to a southern rather than a northern area, alike for the development of the story of Arthur and for his historical activities, although this area was probably not South Wales, but Dumnonia across the Severn.

The tradition, then, makes Arthur a warrior of the late fifth century or early sixth. And the tradition itself emerges conceivably with the Filius Urbagen in the seventh, but more probably with Nennius at the beginning of the ninth. It is of purely British *provenance*. Bede, in the eighth century, and the early compilers of the *Saxon Chronicle*, at a later date than Nennius in the ninth, say nothing of Arthur, although they know of Vortigern, a Vortigern without his trappings of romance and folk-lore, and

Bede repeats from Gildas the account of Ambrosius and the *Mons Badonicus.*[1] Obviously the English writers were not much concerned to record the names and exploits of those British chiefs who won victories against them. The next notices of Arthur belong to the tenth century. They come again from the Harleian manuscript of the *Historia Britonum* already quoted. Into this, between the Northumbrian history and the *mirabilia* of Britain, has been inter-polated a brief chronicle of events ranging from the middle of the fifth century to the middle of the tenth, together with a set of Welsh genealogies. The chronicle is generally known as the *Annales Cambriae.*[2] The latest entry is that of the death of a prince of South Wales in 956. The compiler probably worked soon after that date, and frequent notices of the ecclesiastical affairs of St David's suggest that he dwelt in that diocese. The outlook, however, is not purely Welsh; both English and Irish events are often noted. Some of the earlier entries are apparently derived from an eighth-century source which also underlies various sets of Irish annals, such as the *Annals of Tigernach* and the *Annals of Ulster*. Others repeat statements of the *Historia Britonum* itself, the ascription of the Northumbrian baptisms to Run filius Urbgen, for instance. The form of the document is an odd one. The dates are calculated, not from any pagan or Christian era, but from an unspecified *annus i*, and spaces are left for 533 years in all, against only some of which historical entries are

[1] *Record* iii.　　　　　　[2] *Record* v.

13

given. It has been suggested that the compiler
worked upon a table arranged in accordance with the
532 years' cycle devised by Victorius of Aquitaine in
457 to illustrate the incidence of Easter. But what
was his *annus i*? The first eight years are left blank,
and the earliest entry, for *annus ix*, is of the change
in the date of Easter accepted by Leo I for the
Roman church in 455. This points to 447 as the
annus i, and although most scholars have taken it to
be 444 or 445, I think that 447 receives confirmation
from a short introductory *computus* or chronological
calculation which is prefixed to the *Annales* proper.
This, although with a digression to which I must
refer presently, is in substance a measurement of
time, firstly from the Passion, taken with Victorius
as 28, to the coming of the Saxons, which is here put
in 428, being the fourth year of Vortigern; and
secondly from the coming of the Saxons to the
consulate of Decius and Valerianus, which is said to
be an interval of sixty-nine years. There is no such
consulate, and no significance for British history in
the sixty-nine years' interval. The error is obvious,
but the correction less obvious. Many attempts have
been made at it, but I feel little doubt that the
computist is really aiming at 446, that year of the
third consulate of Aetius, in which, as we have seen
from Gildas, the British provincials made their last
appeal to Rome. It is fairly easy to read *Aetium* for
Decium and *xix* years for *lxix*; both terminal years, as
elsewhere in the *computus*, being counted in the
interval. No doubt the colleague of Aetius in 446

14

was not Valerianus but Symmachus. One chronicler, however, gives the name in error as Valentinianus, and of this Valerianus is a possible corruption.[1] I must leave over for later discussion the question as to why the computist put the *Adventus Saxonum* before instead of after the appeal to Aetius. The present point is that, if the *computus* leads up to 446, the *Annales*, to which it is a prelude, begin naturally enough in 447.

There are two Arthurian entries in the *Annales*. The first is for the year 518, on my reckoning:

The battle of Badon in which Arthur bore the cross of our Lord Jesus Christ for three days and three nights on his shoulders, and the Britons were victorious.

The second is for 539:

The battle of Camlann in which Arthur and Medraut fell.

Here are famous names in Arthurian romance, about which the *Historia Britonum* told us nothing. It has been suggested that some of the earlier entries in the *Annales*, which concern Elfodd, the master of Nennius, and the paschal controversies in which Elfodd was interested, may have been derived ultimately from Nennius himself, and if so, it might be natural to group the Arthurian entries with these. On the other hand, the annalist seems to have altered the character of the supernatural protection which Nennius gives Arthur at the battle of Guinnion, and transferred it to the battle of Badon. On the whole, it does not seem safe to press the tradition of the

[1] *Chronicle of Marcellinus* (*M.G.H. Chronica Minora*, ii. 82).

Annales Cambriae upon Arthur farther back than the second half of the tenth century. The *computus*, as distinct from the *Annales*, says nothing about Arthur. But it does, in the digression already mentioned, add a word about Ambrosius. It was twelve years, it tells us, from the reign of Vortigern to 'the *discordia* of Guitolinus and Ambrosius, which is Guoloppum, that is Catguoloph.' The meaning of *cat* is battle, and one is tempted to find here the name, unrecorded by Gildas, of the battle in which Ambrosius made head against the Saxons, and to translate it into a battle of Wallop in Hampshire. But we know nothing of this Guitolinus and the sense of *discordia* is uncertain.

The eleventh century contributes nothing to our formal chronicle of Arthur, although we may see reason to believe that before its close he had become a notable figure of literary and still more of oral legend. Certainly when we meet him in the pages of the greatest of the twelfth-century historians, William of Malmesbury, he has taken on a singular new aspect. William's *Gesta Regum*, completed in 1125, contains two passages about Arthur.[1] The first is in its natural place, as part of the account of the Saxon invasion.

On the death of Vortimer, the strength of the Britons grew faint, their diminished hopes went backwards; and straightway they would have come to ruin, had not Ambrosius, the sole survivor of the Romans, who was monarch of the realm after Vortigern, repressed the overweening barbarians through the distinguished achievement of the warlike Arthur. This is that Arthur of whom the trifling of the Britons talks

[1] *Record* xii.

16

such nonsense even to-day; a man clearly worthy not to be dreamed of in fallacious fables, but to be proclaimed in veracious histories, as one who long sustained his tottering country, and gave the shattered minds of his fellow-citizens an edge for war. Finally, at the siege of Mount Badon, relying upon the image of the mother of the Lord which he had sewn upon his armour, he made head single-handed against nine hundred of the enemy and routed them with incredible slaughter.

The second passage is incidental to an account of an archaeological discovery during the reign of William the Conqueror, a generation or so before the historian's own day.

At this time was found in the province of Wales called Ros the tomb of Walwen, who was the not degenerate nephew of Arthur by his sister. He reigned in that part of Britain which is still called Walweitha. A warrior most renowned for his valour, he was expelled from his kingdom by the brother and nephew of Hengist, of whom I spoke in the first book, but not until he had compensated for his exile by much damage wrought upon them, worthily sharing in the praise of his uncle, in that they deferred for many years the ruin of their falling country. But the tomb of Arthur is nowhere beheld, whence ancient ditties fable that he is yet to come. The tomb of the other, however, as I have said, was found in the time of King William upon the sea shore, fourteen feet in length; and here some say he was wounded by his foes and cast out in a shipwreck, but according to others he was killed by his fellow-citizens at a public banquet. Knowledge of the truth therefore remains doubtful, although neither story would be inconsistent with the defence of his fame.

When William of Malmesbury wrote, then, the name of Arthur had already become linked with that

of Walwen, the Gawain of romance. Arthur's tomb
was still unknown, and this fact was believed by the
critical historian to explain certain fables of the second
coming of Arthur which he regarded as Celtic
childishness. The existence of these fables is the
singular new fact in the development of the tradition
to which I referred above. It can be confirmed, and
perhaps even localized, from another source. In
the year 1113 certain canons of Laon paid a visit
to England, which is described in a narrative by
Hermann de Tournai, probably written in 1146.[1]
They had with them a shrine containing the miracle-
working relics of Our Lady of Laon, and their object
was to raise funds for the rebuilding of their cathedral.
From Exeter they made their way to Danavexeria,
by which is apparently meant Devonshire, and here
they were told that they were upon the very land of
the famous King Arthur, and were shown Arthur's
Chair and Arthur's Oven. They came to Bodmin
and here a dispute arose between one of their company and a man with a withered arm, who came to
seek healing at the shrine. 'Just as the Britons are
wont to wrangle with the French on behalf of King
Arthur,' says Hermann—presumably he means the
Britons of Brittany—so the cripple maintained that
Arthur still lived. The dispute grew into a brawl;
an armed crowd gathered, and bloodshed was with
difficulty averted. Our Lady of Laon was offended,
and the paralytic was not healed.

William of Malmesbury, as a scientific historian,

[1] *Record* xi.

attempts to combine his sources. He takes the Ambrosius of Gildas and the Arthur of Nennius, and treats them as contemporaries, working together after the fall of Vortimer. Perhaps he also knew the *Annales Cambriae*, since he assigns the wearing of the image of the Virgin to the siege of Badon and not that of Guinnion, although he does not accept the substitution of a cross. But he says nothing about Camlann or Medraut. A somewhat different reconstruction appears in the *Historia Anglorum* of Henry of Huntingdon, who inserts an account of Arthur, taken from Nennius, between two episodes of 527 and 530 respectively, taken from the *Saxon Chronicle*.[1] The first version of the *Historia* dates from 1129, but the unsatisfactory modern text obscures the modifications made in later years.[2] Certainly Henry of Huntingdon was destined to learn much about Arthur after 1129. And so we come to Geoffrey of Monmouth.

[1] *Record* xiii (*a*).
[2] F. Haverfield in *Athenaeum* for 6 April 1901.

CHAPTER II

GEOFFREY OF MONMOUTH

No work of imagination, save the *Aeneid*, has done more to shape the legend of a people than the *Historia Regum Britanniae* of a writer who describes himself in his prefatory epistles as Gaufridus Monumetensis. Monmouth has since given its name to a county, but in the twelfth century this county was still the Welsh district of Gwent, and Monmouth was a Norman settlement around a castle built at the confluence of the Mynvy or Monnow and the Wye. Before the coming of the Normans Gwent had been debatable land. Saxon penetration had extended westward beyond the old line of the Wye and Offa's Dyke. But in the days of Edward the Confessor Gruffydd ap Llywelyn, organizing for once the scattered forces of Welsh nationality, had in his turn crossed the Wye, and raided the English earldom of Hereford, until he was driven back by Earl Harold and fell to a plot in 1063. Under the Conqueror, the Norman William Fitz-Osbern, lord of Breteuil, became Earl of Hereford, and brought order into the marches. He built a line of castles, of which Monmouth was one, down the Wye, and from this base conquered or reconquered Gwent to the line of the Usk. An outlying castle was built at Caerleon on Usk, the site of the old

Roman Castra Legionis at Isca. In 1075 William's son Roger rebelled, and the earldom of Hereford was suppressed. Monmouth was given to the Breton Wihenoc, who also held lands in Devonshire. He founded at Monmouth a priory of the Benedictine abbey of St Florent, near Saumur on the Loire, became himself a monk at St Florent, and left Monmouth to the heirs of his brother Baderon. The house of Baderon were still its lords under Henry I; but by this time Norman domination had spread from Gwent over the whole of South Wales, and the great magnate of the marches was Henry's bastard son Robert of Gloucester, who had married the heiress of Robert Fitz-Hamon, the founder of the castle of Cardiff, and had been made Earl of Gloucester about 1122.

Geoffrey, as we shall see, was attached to Robert of Gloucester, and presumably his epithet *Monumetensis* indicates that he was born at Monmouth or brought up in the priory. But the extent of his relations with South Wales is very uncertain. The Welsh chronicle known as the *Brut y Tywysogion* or *Brute of the Princes*, itself a continuation of the *Historia* and alleged to be based on the work of Geoffrey's contemporary Caradoc of Llancarfan, treats him as a Welshman. The earliest reference, in the fourteenth-century *Strata Florida Brut*, only tells us that he became Bishop of Llandaff (an error for St Asaph) in 1152, and died at mass in 1154. But the *Gwentian Brut*, a compilation of the fifteenth or sixteenth century, is more detailed.

In [1152] Galfrid, son of Arthur, family priest (*offeiriad teulu*) of William son of Robert, was made bishop; but he died in his house at Llandaff, before he entered on his functions, and was buried in the church there. He was a man whose like could not be found for learning and knowledge and all divine excellencies. He was a foster-son of Uchtryd Archbishop of Llandaff, his uncle by the father's side; and for his learning and excellencies an archdeaconry was conferred upon him in the church of Teilo at Llandaff, where he was the instructor of many scholars and chieftains.

Very little credence can be given to this. The manuscripts of the *Brut y Tywysogion* are late and the tradition from Caradoc of Llancarfan probably apocryphal. Moreover, there is clearly a confusion with another Geoffrey. Uchtryd Archdeacon of Llandaff succeeded Urban as bishop, not archbishop, of Llandaff in 1140, and he had a nephew Geoffrey, who was a priest and canon of St Peter's, Gloucester, in 1146. This, however, cannot be our Geoffrey, who did not take priest's orders until 1152. And if the Uchtryd connection fails, that with Llandaff becomes at least dubious. It is surely a fantastic suggestion which, on the ground of supposed stylistic resemblances to the *Historia*, ascribes to Geoffrey of Monmouth, rather than to yet a third Geoffrey, a brother of Bishop Urban, the compilation about 1150 of the cartulary and the lives of St Dubricius and others in the *Liber Landavensis*. These lives are intended to support a Llandaff counter-claim to the St David's claim, as against Canterbury, of metropolitan jurisdiction over the Welsh church. Geoffrey, in the *Historia*, pointedly refrains from encouraging either

claim, and puts his quite unhistorical Welsh arch-
bishopric at Caerleon. As a matter of fact, most of
the external records which we have of Geoffrey's
earlier career as an ecclesiastic relate him, not to
Llandaff, but to the neighbourhood of Oxford in the
diocese of Lincoln. Here he appears as a witness to
not less than seven charters, ranging from 1129 to
1151, and concerned with the monastic houses of
Oseney, Godstow and Thame, and the canonical
house of St George in Oxford castle. He is described
as Galfridus Arthur, sometimes with the academic
prefix *magister*, and among his fellow witnesses are
Walter Archdeacon of Oxford and a certain Ralph
of Monmouth. He may well have taught at Oxford,
and it is not an improbable conjecture that he was
himself a canon of St George's before that foundation
came to an end in 1149. That he was known, not only
as Geoffrey of Monmouth, but as Geoffrey Arthur,
is confirmed by references of his contemporaries, as
well as by the *Gwentian Brut*. It is less likely, so
early as 1129, to be a nickname due to the *Historia*
than a patronymic. The name Arthur was rare,
although not unknown, in Wales; there is the
plausible alternative that he was the son of some
Breton follower of the house of Wihenoc and
Baderon. Geoffrey is of course a Norman name. The
few and approximately dated Monmouth charters
which have been preserved yield it rather frequently,
in various spellings. Our Geoffrey can hardly be a
Goffredus *Parvus*, who was prior about 1120–40.
He might be a Gaufridus *scriba* (c. 1120). Somewhat

later comes a Gaufredus *capellanus*, but the presence of a Gosfredus or Galfridus d'Espiniac renders any inference hazardous. The evidential value of an oriel window, popularly called 'Geoffrey of Monmouth's,' in the ruins of Monmouth priory is discounted by its late perpendicular architecture.

We must think then of Geoffrey as probably rather of Breton than of Welsh blood, as brought up in a Norman environment, on the Welsh marches, but far back from any active Welsh life, and as connected by origin with the political domination of Robert of Gloucester, and by profession with the ecclesiastical circle of Oxford and Lincoln. It was in fact to Alexander Bishop of Lincoln that his first work was dedicated. It was not his first bit of writing. He had already, he tells us, made a beginning with the *Historia*, when the prevalence of rumours about Merlin led Alexander and others to call upon him for a Latin translation of that prophet's British utterances. We have no independent tract from Geoffrey containing the *Prophecies*. But they occupy the seventh book of the *Historia*, and to them are prefixed the short introduction which I have cited and an epistle to Alexander.[1] Geoffrey assigns the *Prophecies* to the reign of Vortigern and uses them to elaborate the explanation given by the boy Ambrosius of the red and white dragons on Mount Snowdon. But he calls the boy *Merlinus, qui et Ambrosius dicebatur*, gives him a daemonic father, for the possibility of which he cites Apuleius, and treats

[1] *Record* xiv (*a*).

him as distinct from Aurelius Ambrosius, who afterwards reigns. The *Prophecies* are long and obscurely
wrapped up in symbolical imagery from the animal
world. Oracular utterances are always more precise
in dealing with the past than with the future, and in
the earlier passages of Merlin's harangue it is possible
to trace allusions to historical events as known to or
conceived by Geoffrey. These are not in all cases
covered by the narrative of the *Historia* itself, and in
fact they extend beyond the scope of the *Historia* to
the Norman reigns. Arthur is foretold as follows:

She that is oppressed shall at last prevail, and shall resist
the fierceness of the strangers. For the Boar of Cornwall
shall bring succour and shall trample their necks beneath his
feet. The islands of the ocean shall be subdued to his power,
and he shall possess the forests of Gaul. The house of
Romulus shall dread his fierceness, and his end shall be
doubtful. In the mouth of the peoples shall he be celebrated,
and his deeds shall be food unto the tellers of tales.

Arthur is given six inheritors of his rule, although
the *Historia* itself only makes out five. And then we
get certain events of the later struggle with the
Saxons, the coming of the Normans, the slaying of
William Rufus, the dominion of Henry I, called the
'lion of justice,' the tragedy of the White Ship. And
with Henry I the clearly historical allusions stop. One
to his death is absent from many manuscripts of the
Historia and is doubtless an addition or interpolation.
Others, which were taken, even in the twelfth century,
to point to the reigns of Stephen and Henry II, are
generally vague, and are at most examples of intelli-

gent anticipation. Thus a king who will overthrow
the walls of Hibernia naturally suggests Henry II,
but an expedition against Ireland had been a project
soon after the Conquest. And thereafter all is
oracular. We can dimly see a foreshadowed combination of the Celtic peoples and expulsion of the
aliens. Cadwallader shall call unto Conan, and shall
receive Albany into his fellowship. The fountains
of Armorica shall flow and shall be crowned with the
diadem of Brutus. Cambria shall be filled with joy
and the oaks of Cornwall shall wax green. Then the
zoological images get thicker and thicker. There are
a Goat of the Castle of Venus, and a Lioness of
Stafford, and an Ass of Wickedness, and a Serpent
of Malvern, and a Boar of Totnes, and a Hedgehog
laden with apples, and a Heron from the Forest of
Calaterium. Whether there have been further interpolations, to which prophecies are obviously liable,
it is difficult to say, in our present knowledge of the
text of the *Historia*. If not, Geoffrey is probably
letting his imagination revel. The themes are at
least as much English as Celtic. They end with an
astrological chaos. Stilbon of Arcady shall change his
shield, and the helmet of Mars shall call unto Venus.
The Virgin shall mount upon the back of the
Sagittary, and shall darken her maidenly honour.
The chariot of the moon shall disturb the Zodiac,
and the Pleiades shall be turned to weeping.

It is clear that the *Prophecies* must originally have
become known in an independent form. The evidence
for this is the use made of them by Ordericus Vitalis

in the twelfth book of his *Historia Ecclesiastica*.[1]
After recording the death of Robert Duke of
Normandy at Cardiff on 10 February 1134, Ordericus stops his narrative to call attention to the
fulfilment of much of the prophecy of Ambrosius
Merlin to King Vortigern, from which he will give
certain points 'which seem relevant to our own time.'
He does not name Geoffrey, but describes Merlin as
a contemporary of St Germanus, for whose visit to
Britain and other happenings to the Britons Ordericus refers his readers to the books of Gildas, by
whom he doubtless means Nennius, and Bede. He
then narrates the episode of the red and white dragons,
with a curious variation by which the red dragon
becomes the Saxon and the white one the British
symbol. And he adds that, after explaining this
portent, the seer went on to foretell the destiny of
the northern islands in symbolical language. Here
he gives, as a *lectiuncula* taken *ex libello Merlini*, a long
passage on the Norman domination and the ultimate
expulsion of the invaders, almost precisely as we
have it in the *Historia*, but without the interpolation
on the death of Henry I. Ordericus, indeed, was
writing before that death, which took place on
1 December 1135. For he adds a comment. Much
of the prophecy is destined to bring joy or sorrow to
those yet unborn. But parts of it will be intelligible
to those who know the histories of Hengist and
Catigirn, Pascent and Arthur, Aethelbert and
Edwin, Oswald and Oswy, Cadwal and Alfred, and

[1] *Record* xv.

27

of other English and British princes, down to the days of Henry and Griffith, 'who yet await the doubtful lot of forthcoming events, divinely ordained for them by the ineffable decree.' He must, then, have had the *libellus Merlini* before him at some date between the death of Robert of Normandy and that of Henry I. It is possible that the *libellus* did not give the *Prophecies* exactly as we find them in the *Historia*. That Ordericus quotes nothing from Geoffrey's final rigmarole proves little. But the version in the *Historia* contains no very clear allusions to most of the string of princes whom he specifies, or to Gruffydd ap Cynan, who organized Welsh nationality against Henry and outlived him. Further, there is a curious passage at the end of the remarks of Ordericus which suggests that even he may have known more than one version. He has quoted the passage about the sons of William the Conqueror, as we have it in the *Historia*, with the somewhat obscure phrase about Robert of Normandy, *Alter vero sub umbra nominis redibit*. And now he gives the gloss: *Alter (id est: Rodbertus dux) sub umbra carceris, stemma pristini nominis (id est: ducis) gerens, peribit*. As an interpretation, this seems very far-fetched. Surely the natural meaning of Geoffrey's words is that the shadow of Duke Robert's name will return in Robert of Gloucester. Is Ordericus trying to combine two texts of what Geoffrey wrote, the first of which ran *Alter vero sub umbra carceris peribit*? The twelfth book of the *Historia Ecclesiastica* does not seem to have been completed as a whole before 1136 or 1137, and it is possible therefore that Ordericus might have revised it with Geoffrey's *Historia* before him. To the date of Geoffrey's *Historia* I must return. In any case it seems clear that there was some reference to Robert of Normandy's death in the *libellus*. The limits of dates for the issue of this, as well as for the reference to it by Ordericus, will therefore be 10 February 1134 and 1 December 1135.

Ordericus dismisses the *libellus* with the statement that he could explain much more of it, were he to apply his knowledge to a commentary upon Merlin. One wishes that he had done so. Merlin, however, inspired other interpreters, none of whom necessarily go back to the original *libellus*. The sentences on Henry I are quoted and expounded, again without the interpolation on his death and without mention of Geoffrey, by Suger, the French statesman and abbot of St Denys, in his life of Lewis the Fat, written before 1152.[1] Much of Geoffrey's prose was paraphrased in Latin hexameters, adapted as regards some of the unhistorical part to the outlook of his own day, and fitted with an exposition, by one John of Cornwall, who dedicated his work about 1155 to Bishop Robert de Warelwast of Exeter. And about 1167–83 a long commentary, printed under the title *Prophetia Anglicana* in 1603, was compiled by the famous *Doctor universalis*, Alain de Lille.[2] These bear more upon the long history of pseudo-Merlinic political prophecy than upon Geoffrey, or at any rate upon Geoffrey's Arthur.

[1] *Record* xvi.   [2] *Record* xxii.

And so to the *Historia Regum Britanniae*. As in many other branches of Arthurian study, one is hampered by the absence of an adequate edition. Those current contain a 'vulgate' text, based with imperfect help from manuscripts upon the sixteenth-century editions of Badius Ascensius (1508, 1517) and Jerome Commelin (1587). Nearly two hundred full manuscripts are known, of which about fifty are of the twelfth century. The British Museum is rich with thirty-seven; Oxford has twenty-six and Cambridge thirty-two. One now at Leyden (*MS Lat.* 20) can be identified as having been at Bec before 1154 from a description in the catalogue of the abbey library, compiled by Robert of Torigny. Critical work on the manuscripts is still in its infancy, and in these circumstances speculation as to the original form of the *Historia* and any revision which it may have undergone can only be tentative. But the vulgate may serve as the basis for a short structural analysis, which is necessary to show the relation of Geoffrey's account of Arthur to the general nature of the *Historia*. The framework of the structure is derived from the *Historia Britonum* of Nennius, who like Geoffrey begins with Brute and ends with Cadwallader. But the meagre outlines of Nennius are hardly recognizable under the elaboration of detail with which they have been clothed by Geoffrey.

The *Historia* is divided by its editors into twelve books. But for the consideration of subject-matter and method it may be better treated as falling into six sections. These are (1) the Conquest of Albion

(Bk i); (2) the Pre-Roman Kings (Bks ii, iii); (3) the Roman Domination (Bks iv–vi. 3); (4) the House of Constantine (Bks vi. 4–viii); (5) Arthur (Bks ix–xi. 2); (6) the Saxon Domination (Bks xi. 3–xii). In the first section Geoffrey takes up Brutus, the eponymous founder of Nennius, and tells a story of his expulsion from Italy, his wanderings in Greece, Africa, and Gaul, and his final arrival at the destined shore. It is obviously a literary exercise on the Virgilian model, and it is helped out by some etymological fancies. Thus Geoffrey found Corineus among the heroes who fell when Turnus attacked the Trojan camp (*Aen.* ix. 571), and made him the chief comrade of Brutus, in order that he might give a name to Cornwall. The second section contains brief genealogical annals narrating the fortunes of the island down to the coming of Caesar. There is nothing even quasi-historical, except the assertion of a British origin for Brennus, the Senonian Gaul who took Rome in 390 B.C. Geoffrey is still working out his etymologies. We get Locrine (Loegria), Camber (Cambria), Albanact (Albania), Humber, Sabrina (Severn), Ebraucus (Eboracum, York), Leil (Carlisle), Leir (Leicester), Lud (Ludgate). Of the Celtic Llyr and Lludd Geoffrey shows no knowledge. Belinus, a 'ghost-name' due to confusions of Orosius and the *Historia Britonum*, serves to father the Saxon Billings-gate. Other names Geoffrey must have got from a set of Welsh genealogies of tenth-century princely houses, probably very similar to those which accompany the text of Nennius in *Harleian MS* 3859, and

31

in which many of the same names occur. And all
the names he has brought together into a quite
imaginary filiation of dynasties, and fitted with
stories drawn from very diverse sources. The episode
of Leir and Cordelia is a version of a far-travelled
folk-tale; and the myth of Daedalus is adapted to
serve the turn of Bladud. In the third, the Roman,
section Geoffrey derives a little more help from such
fragments of historical knowledge as have filtered to
him through Latin writers. He knows something of
Caesar's invasions and the resistance of Cassivellaunus, and of the conquest by Claudius; something
of Cunobelinus, his and Shakespeare's Cymbeline,
but nothing of his greater son Caratacus, for whom
he finds a substitute in Arviragus, a northern
chieftain named incidentally by Juvenal, and nothing
of Boadicea. He knows of Severus and his wall, but
not of Hadrian and his. He knows of Vespasian, of
the insurrection of Carausius, of the death of Constantius in Britain and the fame of his son Constantine the Great, although he has no justification
for treating Constantine's mother Helena as a
British lady. He knows of the fourth-century tyrant
Maximus, whom he calls Maximianus, and of the
fifth-century tyrant Gratian, and from Gildas he
knows of the final extinction of Roman rule and of
the appeal of the Britons for help from Agitius. As
before, he pieces his misconceptions of these, with
the help of his literary ingenuity, into dynastic
annals. Etymology gives him 'old King Cole,' the
eponym of Colchester; ecclesiastical legend Lucius,

the supposed introducer of Christianity. He gets a Marius from an inscription at Carlisle, and an Octavius from some unknown source, involving a confusion between the Welsh district of Ewias near Monmouth, and the Saxon kingdom of the Gewissae. And with Octavius begins a connected story in which the historical adventures of the tyrant Maximus on the continent are mixed up with dubious tales about a Caradoc of Cornwall and a Conan Meriadoc who becomes King of Armorica, and with the hagiographical legend of St Ursula.

To these episodes I shall have to return in the next chapter, when I come to discuss Geoffrey's material. They serve to introduce the fourth section of the *Historia*, upon the house of Constantine, from which Arthur sprang. The analysis must now be more detailed. After the failure of the appeal to Agitius, Archbishop Guethelin, presumably the Guitolinus of the introductory *computus* to the *Annales Cambriae*, applies for aid to Aldroen of Armorica, a descendant of Conan Meriadoc. Aldroen sends his brother Constantine to Britain. Constantine marries a Roman wife, reigns for ten years, and is knifed by a Pict. He leaves three sons, Constans, a monk at Winchester, Aurelius, and Uther Pendragon. There is again an historical element to be traced. Constantine was another tyrant emperor of the West, and he had a son Constans, who was a monk. But this was forty years or so before the appeal to Agitius, and it is Geoffrey who links Constantine to Arthur. Vortigern, who, like Octavius, is made a chieftain—

Geoffrey calls him '*consul*,' which is his translation of 'earl'—of the Gewissae, persuades the Britons to elect Constans, then plots his assassination by Picts, and becomes king himself. Then follows the long story, much elaborated in Geoffrey's usual fashion from Nennius and Bede, of Vortigern's negotiations with the Saxons, of the battles of Vortimer, of the coming of St Germanus, and of Vortigern's tower of refuge, into which, as already told, is inserted the long prophecy of Ambrosius Merlin. Geoffrey introduces a hero of his own in Eldol Earl of Gloucester, who attempts to stem the treacherous massacre of Britons by Saxons at a conference with Vortigern. Oxford or the martyrology of Gloucester gave him St Aldate, his Bishop Eldad, who buries the victims in the churchyard of the monastery of Abbot Ambrosius (Amesbury), hard by Kaercaradauc, 'which is now called Salisbury.' And the Ambrosius of Gildas, so shadowy in Nennius, is plain enough as Aurelius in Geoffrey's pages. His *rôle* of prophet has been handed over to Merlin, but he lives as the destined avenger of the house of Constantine upon Vortigern. At the crowning of Constans he was carried with his brother Uther to the protection of Budecius of Armorica. Now he returns, and with Eldol burns Vortigern in the castle of Genoreu upon Doward Hill near Monmouth. Geoffrey has transferred the death of Vortigern to his own neighbourhood from Caer Gwrtheyrn further west on the Taff, where Nennius put it. Aurelius is enthroned and makes successful war

34

against the Saxons with the valorous aid of Eldol.
They are driven into the north of the island. The
country is now settled. In memory of the great
massacre Merlin brings the Giants' Dance from
Ireland, and rears it up near Amesbury. Samson
becomes Archbishop of York and Dubricius of
Caerleon. Then Aurelius is poisoned, at the time of
a great comet, by a Saxon emissary of Vortigern's son
Pascentius. He is buried in the Giants' Dance, and
Uther Pendragon reigns in his stead. The Saxons
rise again, and Uther in his turn repels them.
And now Geoffrey launches into romance. At the
feast which celebrates his victory Uther falls in love
with Igerna the wife of Gorlois Duke of Cornwall.
He picks a quarrel with her husband, who puts
Igerna in Tintagel and himself in Damelioc. By the
sleight of Merlin, Uther enters Tintagel in the
likeness of Gorlois, and in this adventure is conceived Arthur. Uther then slays Gorlois in battle,
weds Igerna and has, besides Arthur, a daughter
Anna, who weds Loth of Lodonesia, Earl of Leicester.
When Uther grows old and feeble, the Saxons rise
again. He defeats them, but they poison him, and
he too is buried in the Giants' Dance.

Arthur is the theme of the fifth section. He is
crowned, being then fifteen, by Archbishop Dubricius
at Silchester, and his first task is to grapple with the
inevitable Saxons, who are led by Colgrin and
Baldulf. They are defeated by Arthur near the river
Douglas and by Cador Duke of Cornwall between
the sea and York. Here Colgrin is besieged. The

siege is raised on the arrival of reinforcements under Cheldric from Germany. Arthur in his turn calls in his nephew Hoel, son of Dubricius of Armorica, and wins battles at Lincoln in Lindsey and in the forest of Caledon. The Saxons promise to return to Germany, but instead sail round to Totnes, raid up to the Severn sea, and besiege Bath. Here Arthur, with his sword Caliburn, forged in the isle of Avallon, his lance Ron, and his shield Pridwen, painted inside with the image of the Virgin, has a great victory. The Saxons are driven to Thanet and there surrender. No more is heard of them until the end of the reign. Arthur now turns against the Picts and Scots, reduces Alclud, wins three battles, beleaguers the fugitives on the islands of Loch Lomond, beats off a relieving host under Guillamur King of Ireland, and finally reduces the northern enemy to vassalage. He shows the wonders of Lomond to Hoel and describes those of another lake in Moray and of a third in Wales. I stop to note that in these episodes Geoffrey is evidently working upon the list of Arthur's battles in Nennius, although he does not name them all, assigns one only instead of four to the river Douglas, and distributes the localities according to his geographical fancy. In placing Arthur's charmed shield, not at Guinnion but at Badon, he follows William of Malmesbury. The wonders of the islands are similarly taken from the *mirabilia* of Nennius, who does not, however, connect these particular *mirabilia* with Arthur. All this is very characteristic of Geoffrey's attitude towards his sources.

Arthur and Hoel return to York for Christmas. Arthur re-establishes the baronage and churches of Britain, and makes his chaplain Pyramus Archbishop of York in place of Samson, who had fled and is later said to be Archbishop of Dôl in Brittany. He assigns the three Scottish kingdoms of Albany, Moray and Lothian to the three brothers Augusel, Urian and Loth. The sons of Loth are Gawain (*Walgannus, Walwanus*) and Mordred. Arthur then marries Guinevere (*Guanhumara*), a lady of noble Roman family, brought up in the chamber of Duke Cador of Cornwall. In the next year he conquers Ireland and Iceland and receives the homage of the Kings of Gothland and the Orkneys. There is peace in the islands for twelve years. Arthur's court becomes the most famous in the world, and no man, however noble, thinks himself of any account unless his raiment and warlike equipment follow the model of Arthur's *milites*. Arthur conceives the ambition of subduing all Europe. He conquers Norway and gives the crown to Loth, whose son Gawain, then twelve years of age, is a lad in the service of Pope Sulpicius. He invades Gaul, slays Flollo, the Roman tribune under the Emperor Leo, in single combat, and after nine years masters the whole of the country. He gives Normandy to his butler Bedivere (*Beduerus*) and Anjou to his steward Kay (*Cheudo*).

Arthur wears his crown at a great Whitsuntide festival in Caerleon, and Geoffrey furnishes a long nominal list of those present; the archbishops, the earls (*consules*) of the great cities, the lesser warriors, for whom once more Geoffrey draws upon the Welsh genealogies, the vassal kings of Wales, Scotland, Cornwall, Brittany, of the conquered islands and the European provinces. Among the latter it is of particular interest to find the twelve peers of Gaul, and it is easy to see that Geoffrey is fashioning Arthur's court upon that of Charlemagne. The feast itself is conducted on twelfth-century lines, with a feudal homaging and a banquet and a tournament in honour of the ladies. 'For none was thought worthy of a lady's love, unless he had been three times approved in the bearing of arms. And so the ladies were made chaste and the knights the better by their loves.' At the close Dubricius resigns the see of Caerleon for an hermitage. The king's uncle David takes his place, and Teilo (*Chelianus*) of Llandaff succeeds Samson at Dôl. Then an embassy is announced. Twelve grave men, bearing branches of olive in their hands, bring a summons to Arthur from Lucius Hiberius, *procurator* of the republic, to appear before the senate at Rome. Arthur, spurred on by Cador of Cornwall and Hoel of Brittany, accepts the challenge, and recalls how before his time Belinus and Brennus had taken Rome and Constantine and Maximian had worn its crown. He makes ready for a campaign. Britain is left in the charge of Guinevere and Mordred. Arthur crosses to the continent, and on board has a dream of a bear vanquished by a fiery dragon from the west. He is delayed by an episodic adventure on St Michael's Mount, where he slays a Spanish giant who has

ravished Helena, the niece of Hoel. The tomb of
Helena was there in Geoffrey's day. This recalled
the memory of an earlier contest of Arthur upon the
Mons Aravius with the giant Ritho, who had made
a cloak of the beards of fallen kings and bade Arthur
contribute his. But Arthur slew him. The war with
the Romans in Gaul is described in great detail.
Bedivere and Kay and Ider the son of Nu are
among those who fall on the side of the Britons. But
Boso Earl of Oxford and above all Gawain prove
mighty champions, and in the end Arthur, who is
himself conspicuous with Caliburn on the field,
remains victorious. He is preparing to pass into
Italy, when news comes of the treachery of Mordred,
who has taken the crown of Britain and wedded
Guinevere. Arthur returns. Mordred has called in
Cheldric with an army of Saxons, and Scots, Picts
and Irish. There is a battle at Richborough, in
which fall Gawain and Augusel, who is succeeded
by his nephew Ywain (*Eventus*) son of Urian.
Mordred is driven back to Winchester, and Guinevere takes the veil in Caerleon. After a defeat at
Winchester, Mordred retreats again to Cornwall and
awaits Arthur on the Camel (*Cambula*), presumably
the Camlann of the *Annales Cambriae*. Here he is slain,

And the famous (*inclytus*) Arthur too was wounded to the
death, and being born thence for the healing of his wounds to the
island of Avallon resigned the diadem of Britain to his kinsman
Constantine, son of Cador Duke of Cornwall, in the five hundred and forty-second year from the incarnation of our Lord.[1]

[1] *Record* xiv (*a*).

In the final post-Arthurian section of the *Historia*, Geoffrey turns again from romance to pseudo-chronicle. Four kings, Constantine, Aurelius Conan, Vortipore, Malgo (Maelgwn) reign successively and hold down the Saxons. These are four out of five princes whom Gildas tells of as ruling contemporaneously over the western Britain of his own day. Then comes Careticus, perhaps the king dislodged by Edwin of Deira early in the seventh century from the small British district of Elmet in Yorkshire. And to his days Geoffrey assigns the expulsion of the Britons from the eastern part of the island, which he calls Loegria, with the help of Gormund King of the Africans and his host. Geoffrey is here drawing upon the French *chanson de geste* of *Gormond et Isembard*. The Britons flee to Cornwall, Wales and Armorica, and Geoffrey will in due course translate the book of their exile. It is an unfulfilled promise. The rest of the section tells of the coming of Augustine and the massacre of the monks of Bangor, in defence of whom dies Blederic Duke of Cornwall; and of the struggle against Northumbria by three successive princes of the house of Gwynedd in North Wales, Cadvan, Cadwallo, and Cadwallader. Most of the material is from Bede, with something from the Welsh genealogies. But Bede gives Geoffrey no warrant for the temporary recovery of Britain by Cadwallo, or for the transference to Cadwallader of the death of the Saxon Ceadwalla in sanctity at Rome on 20 April 689, or for the intervention in British affairs of a Solomon of Armorica and his nephew

Alan, who belong to the dynasty of Arthur's ally or vassal Hoel. Cadwallader before his end is vouchsafed an angelic revelation of the ultimate restoration of Britain to the British, in accordance with the prophecy of Merlin, which here Geoffrey, with what looks like a singular forgetfulness of his own writing, describes as having been made, not to Vortigern, but to Arthur. And with Cadwallader Geoffrey stops, leaving, he says, the later history of the Saxons to William of Malmesbury and Henry of Huntingdon, and that of the Welsh to his contemporary Caradoc of Llancarfan.

We have seen that Geoffrey broke off the writing of the *Historia*, to take up that of the *Prophecies of Merlin*, which were published at some date between 10 February 1134 and 1 December 1135. This gives us 1134 as an initial date before which the *Historia* cannot have been completed. How much, if at all, later are we to put it? The book has come down to us with more than one form of dedication.[1] That most usually found in the manuscripts is addressed singly to Robert of Gloucester.

Do thou, therefore, O Robert Duke of Gloucester, show favour to my little book, that with thee for teacher and thee for guide it may be so corrected that it may not be thought drawn from the poor fountain of Geoffrey of Monmouth, but, being spiced with the salt of thy Minerva, may be called the output of him, whom the illustrious Henry King of the English begat, whom philosophy made learned in the liberal arts, whom a native uprightness set at the head of warriors in warfare, whence Britain now in our day hails thee with inward affection, as if she had obtained a second Henry.

[1] *Record* xiv (*a*).

Another form has long been known to exist in *Bern Stadtbibliothek MS* 568. This is a double dedication. Its first member almost exactly follows the phrasing of the single dedication. But it is addressed, not to Robert of Gloucester, but to King Stephen, 'of whom the illustrious Henry King of the English was the uncle.' Then the writer turns to Robert, 'the second column of our realm,' and devotes to him a second and longer member, the laudation of which is very like that now assigned to Stephen, and is followed by an appeal for Robert's protection of 'thy bard and the book put out for thy delight.' A recent paper by Mr Acton Griscom has called attention to the presence in not less than seven manuscripts of a third form, hitherto unknown.[1] This also is a double dedication, and its language is in close agreement with that of the *Bern MS*. But here Stephen is omitted; the first member, like the similarly worded single dedication, is addressed to Robert; and a slight difference of wording fits the second member to a third patron, Waleran de Beaumont, Count of Meulan, on whom Stephen conferred the Earldom of Worcester. The date of the Bern dedication falls within recognizable limits. There was only one short historical period during which a writer could so have coupled the names of Stephen and Robert. This was between about April 1136, when Robert swore allegiance to Stephen, and June 1138, when he renounced that allegiance, to devote himself for the rest of his life to the cause of

[1] *Speculum*, i (1926), 129.

the Empress Matilda and her son Henry of Anjou. Even by March 1137 the ill-will between Stephen and Robert was already so marked that the words of the dedication, if the writer was aware of the political situation, would have been extremely ironical. It is an ingenious suggestion of Mr Griscom's that a copy of the *Historia* was presented to Stephen at his visit to Oxford in April 1136, and that it was for this that the Bern dedication was written. But I cannot follow him in his contention that the original dedication of the work was that to Robert and Waleran jointly, and that the single dedication to Robert came last of all. Geoffrey refers to the dedicatee again at the beginning of the eleventh book as *consul auguste;* and the retention of this in manuscripts which contain the double dedication is a tell-tale of hasty revision.[1] I feel little doubt that Robert, to whom the prominence of Eldol Earl of Gloucester in the *Historia* itself seems an obvious compliment, was the original patron; that the second member of the double dedication still acknowledges the debt to him; and that the transference of this member to Waleran was only an afterthought. Mr Griscom's attempt to find a special appropriateness in its wording to the career of Waleran seems to me illusory; it is little more than a paraphrase of the single dedication. No doubt Geoffrey might have addressed Robert and Waleran jointly during 1136–38, when they were both at least nominally adherents of Stephen; but he might also have done so after Waleran had abandoned

[1] Cf. my note in *Review of English Studies*, iii. 332.

Stephen and made terms with the house of Anjou in 1141. It is possible that a clue to the date of the original dedication and with it that of the publication of the *Historia* may be found in the use of the phrase 'a second Henry.' This is very clumsy, as adapted in the Bern version to Stephen, of whose claims a real second Henry was the rival. It would have been no less tactless to apply it to Robert after 1138, when he was himself backing Henry of Anjou, or at any time in the reign of Henry I, after the birth of Henry of Anjou on 5 March 1133. Earlier we can hardly put it, as a dedication is not likely to have been written for the *Historia* before it was complete. As far as I can see, the only time at which it would have been really appropriate would have been immediately after the death of Henry I, when, as we learn from the *Gesta Stephani*, an attempt was made by Robert's friends to persuade him to claim the kingdom for himself.[1]

It is possible, then, that the *Historia* was written and dedicated to Robert of Gloucester by the end of 1135. This would fit in well enough with the date of the *Prophecies of Merlin*, which it incorporated. It is pretty certain that it was in existence a year or two later, when it was fitted with the Stephen-Robert dedication, which must have been suppressed after June 1138. And complete certainty is reached in January 1139, when the historian Henry of Huntingdon, then on a visit with Archbishop Theobald to the abbey of Bec in Normandy, was shown the 'great

[1] Howlett, *Chronicles of Stephen*, iii. 10.

44

book of Geoffrey Arthur' by Robert de Torigny, a
monk of the abbey, who in 1154 became abbot of
Mont St Michel. '*Stupens inveni*,' says Henry, and it
is a little surprising that, if the *Historia* had already
been in existence for some time, he should not have
heard of it before. It has been suggested that
Geoffrey may have written it at Bec. But even if he
did, of which there is no evidence, it is not likely that
in 1139 the copy there was unique. The dedication
to Stephen must surely imply a circulation outside
the immediate environment of Geoffrey and Robert
of Gloucester, which might have been expected to
attract the attention of Henry, who is referred to by
name in the book, and was a familiar not only of the
scholarly Theobald, but of Geoffrey's own patron,
Bishop Alexander of Lincoln. Perhaps we do not
know enough of the channels through which new
literature got distributed in the twelfth century to
pursue the speculation with profit. At any rate,
Henry did see the *Historia* for the first time at Bec
in January 1139, and in the course of the same year
he notified his discovery in a letter to his friend
Warinus Brito, giving him a short abstract of the
contents of the book. Copies of the letter are preserved in some of the manuscripts of Henry's *Historia
Anglorum* and others in those of a chronicle by
Robert de Torigny, who has added explanatory
interpolations of his own.[1] Certain details of Henry's
abstract do not quite agree with those of the *Historia*
as we have it. Thus Uther Pendragon is made the

[1] *Record* xiii (*b*).

son and not the brother of Aurelius. There is no mention of Merlin. The stories of Cordelia and of Arthur's death are more vividly and dramatically told. These discrepancies have been taken as evidence that what Henry saw was a first draft of the *Historia* and that it was afterwards revised by Geoffrey. If so, the *Prophecies of Merlin* may have been incorporated at the revision. On the other hand, the abstract is so short as to render omissions inevitable, and a writer like Henry, accustomed to treat his historical sources freely, and working after an interval, partly from notes and partly from memory, may well have modified the details of what he actually read. It is certainly to Henry himself that we must attribute the interesting comment with which he winds up the account of Arthur's end: 'Yet your relations the Britons deny his death, and regularly expect his coming.'

In itself, therefore, the abstract does not afford very strong evidence for a revision of the *Historia*. But it does not stand quite alone. There is the statement of Alfred of Beverley, an abridger of the book, that when he began his work, which must have been about 1149, the mouths of men were full of tales about British history, and anyone who did not know them was looked upon as illiterate.[1] This has been held, and again not very convincingly, to point to some fresh promulgation of the *Historia* shortly before 1149. Two new points may perhaps be added. One is that in all the versions of his dedication, Geoffrey appears to express a hope that the narrative

[1] *Record* xvii.

46

he is offering may, with the help of his patrons, be
'corrected.' But of course an intention is not an
achievement. The other is that a list of British
consules, noted by Geoffrey (ix. 12) as present at a
Whitsuntide feast held by Arthur, bears every sign
of being based upon the actual earldoms extant when
he wrote; and further that it seems to include not
only those extant at the death of Henry I, but also
the later creations of Matilda, ignoring most of
Stephen's. Now some of Matilda's creations were
probably in 1141, one certainly about June 1142, and
one at an unknown later date before April 1149. It
certainly seems difficult to resist the conclusion that
this passage at least has been revised.[1] As to whether
there was any general revision, it is perhaps best to
suspend judgment until some competent student of
mediaeval Latin has surveyed the manuscripts and
given us a critical edition of the *Historia*. And even
if there was an early draft, it may prove that no
manuscript of it has survived. Of course the present
case for a revision would be weakened, if we could
accept the suggestion of Delisle that *Leyden MS Lat.
20*, certainly at Bec before 1154, was the actual copy
which Henry of Huntingdon saw, since that MS
includes the *Prophecies of Merlin*, follows the normal
wording in describing Arthur's death, and has the
full list of *consules*. But is the suggestion based upon
anything but the fact that Henry did see a copy?
Obviously, if a new edition was issued, say a little
before the death of Robert of Gloucester on 31

[1] Cf. my paper in *Review of English Studies*, i. 431.

October 1147, so that a new dedication would not have been required, it may very well have replaced the old one at Bec before 1154.[1]

Whether Geoffrey revised the *Historia* or not, he was certainly about 1150 or 1151 still working the literary vein which he had so felicitously opened. A single thirteenth-century manuscript preserves in its full form a Latin hexameter poem of 1528 lines, under the title of *Vita Merlini*.[2] Herein is given a narrative of the later life of the prophet and magician, who dropped out of the *Historia* after the account of his shape-shifting intervention at the begetting of Arthur. In the *Vita* Merlin is a king of the Demetae in South Wales. He has a wife Guendoloena and his sister Ganieda is the wife of Rodarchus, King of Cambria. Merlin, Rodarchus, and Peredurus, King of the Venedotians in North Wales, defeat the Scots under Guennolous. But Merlin, for grief at the losses of his side, runs mad in the *nemus Calidonis*. He is brought back more than once, and uses his powers of second sight in foretelling the fortunes of those about him. Finally a house is built for him in the forest with seventy doors and seventy windows and a troop of scribes to record his sayings. Here he delivers a long prophecy to Ganieda on the future of the Britons. He is then visited by Thelgesinus, a pupil of Gildas. They hold a conversation about

[1] Waleran de Beaumont was patron of Bec, but I am informed by Dr Greg, who kindly examined the *Leyden MS* for me, that it has the single dedication.

[2] *Record* xiv (*b*).

natural philosophy, based upon the classical learning
of Pliny as filtered through Solinus and Isidore of
Seville. This is broken by further prophetic and
reminiscent utterances of Merlin, and by his return
to sanity through drinking of a spring. This good
fortune is shared by another madman Maeldinus.
Finally Ganieda in her turn breaks into prophecy,
detailing events of the reign of Stephen. A general
discussion of the relation between the presentations
of Merlin in the *Historia* and in the *Vita* I must
postpone. The events of the poem itself have nothing
to do with Arthur; they are in fact placed in the time
of Conan, who was the next but one to reign after
him. But at more than one point the dialogue recalls,
with curious variations, the themes of the *Historia*.
Merlin and Thelgesinus describe the famous islands
of the world. One of these is the *Insula Pomorum*.
This is an adaptation of the Fortunate Islands, probably the Canaries, told of by Solinus and Isidore.
It is an earthly Paradise. But the poet has added
features of his own. The island is ruled over by
Morgen and her eight sisters. And thither, says
Thelgesinus, after the battle of Camblanus, under the
guidance of Barinthus, we bore the wounded Arthur.
Morgen received us with all honour, surveyed the
wound, and gave hope of recovery after a long
healing. To her we trusted the king, and set our
sails homewards. Here is once more the alternative
version of Arthur's end, which Henry of Huntingdon
knew, and which the *Historia* passed over with its
obscure prophetic reference to an *exitus dubius*. The

prophecies of the *Vita*, again, cannot be wholly independent of the *Historia*. That of Merlin to Ganieda is declared by Merlin to be the same which he formerly delivered to Vortigern at the time of the fight of the two dragons. As a matter of fact, its details, with a few exceptions, diverge considerably, both from those of the prophecy to Vortigern and from those of the post-Arthurian narrative of the *Historia*. The prophecy of Merlin to Thelgesinus, on the other hand, like the prophecy to Vortigern, looks forward to the coming again of Conan and Cadwallader; and it is accompanied by a retrospect of Merlin's life, which with certain changes of detail is a fairly faithful summary of the reigns of Vortigern, Ambrosius, Uther, and Arthur, as recorded in the *Historia*. On the whole, the treatment in the *Vita* of such matter as it has in common with the *Historia* suggests to me, not an imitator, but a writer rehandling with considerable freedom themes upon which he has already worked. I do not therefore find anything to rebut the natural inference of Geoffrey's authorship to be drawn from the closing lines, in which that authorship seems to be explicitly claimed and the earlier treatise on the *gesta Britonum* recalled. The authorship has, however, been doubted, and the *Vita* assigned to the thirteenth century. This view, now generally abandoned, rests partly upon a failure to recognize certain historical events of the reign of Stephen in the allusions of Ganieda's prophecy and a consequent attempt to refer those allusions to the reign of John; partly upon a notion that the praises of a dedication to Robert Bishop of Lincoln would be more appropriate to the famous Robert Grosseteste than to the less distinguished Robert of Chesney, who was Geoffrey's contemporary. But a dedication is not even an affidavit.

Geoffrey's earliest patron, Alexander Bishop of Lincoln, died in February 1148, and was succeeded by Robert of Chesney on 19 December. Robert Earl of Gloucester had died on 31 October 1147. We do not know exactly what had happened to Geoffrey during the troublous years of Stephen. The *Gwentian Brut* speaks of him as chaplain to Robert's son and successor, William Earl of Gloucester, and also as having held an archdeaconry at Llandaff. It is no doubt through a confusion that modern writers sometimes call him archdeacon of Monmouth. But the *Gwentian Brut* is of little authority, and it must remain doubtful whether Geoffrey was an archdeacon at all. The evidence of charters witnessed by him suggests that he was still connected with the neighbourhood of Oxford in 1150 and 1151. Robert of Chesney, unlike Alexander, was *persona grata* at Stephen's court, and it was not unnatural that Geoffrey, after the hopes of the partisans of Henry of Anjou had vanished with Robert of Gloucester, should welcome the new bishop as *Gloria pontificum*, and express a hope that he might watch over the fortunes of his bard under better auspices than those of his predecessor. In a modest degree, his hope was fulfilled. Geoffrey signed the charters of 1151 as bishop-elect of St Asaph; and the registers of

Canterbury record his ordination as priest at Westminster on 16 February and his consecration as bishop at Lambeth on 24 February 1152. The bishopric, only recently revived after a long period of abeyance, was an unimportant one. It is improbable that Geoffrey ever took up its duties. At the time of his election St Asaph was in the hands of insurgent Welsh, and so it remained for some years. Geoffrey witnessed the accord between Stephen and Henry of Anjou, which brought peace to the realm on 6 November 1153. In 1154 he died.

CHAPTER III

THE SOURCES OF GEOFFREY

I HAVE written in the last chapter as though Geoffrey were solely responsible for his historical romances. This is not quite his own account of the matter. He has three references to his sources.[1] The most important is in a preface to the dedications. Geoffrey had been surprised, he says, to find no records, beyond the mentions in Bede and Gildas, either of the pre-Christian kings of Britain, or of Arthur and the rest, whose deeds were told abroad, as if inscribed in the jocund memories of many peoples. But at last Walter, Archdeacon of Oxford, a learned rhetorician and student of foreign history, put into his hands a very ancient book in the British tongue, which proved to hold a continuous and elegant narrative of the doings of all these kings from Brutus down to Cadwallader. And this, at Walter's suggestion, Geoffrey had taken pains to latinize in his own rustic style. He mentions this source again at the beginning of the eleventh book, saying that from it and from the stories of Walter he learnt of the battles fought by Arthur with his nephew Mordred after his return from Gaul. And finally, in his colophon, leaving the later history to William of Malmesbury, Henry of Huntingdon and Caradoc of

[1] *Record* xiv (*a*).

Llancarfan, he bids them be silent about the British kings, since they have not the *liber* in the British tongue, which Walter brought out of Britain, and from which Geoffrey has put the truth into Latin.

Walter has been noted as a fellow-witness with Geoffrey of Oxfordshire charters. He is traceable as Archdeacon of Oxford from at least 1115 and possibly 1104 to 1151, and must not be confused with Walter Map, who was also Archdeacon of Oxford at a later date. There exist Welsh translations or adaptations of the *Historia*, in widely variant forms, under such titles as *Brut Gryffydd ab Arthur*, *Brut y Brenhined*, and *Brut Tysilio*. The manuscripts range in date from the thirteenth century to the seventeenth, and some of them have colophons which make statements about Walter. One version says that he turned his book from British into Welsh; another that he turned it from Welsh into Latin and then again in his old age from Latin into Welsh. These can hardly be anything but progressive perversions of Geoffrey's own colophon. The interrelations and texts of the Welsh *Bruts* require more critical examination than they have yet received. But no case has yet been established for any independent use by them of Walter's alleged *liber*, or for any basis of written record for such additions as they may make to the *Historia*. One other possible reference to Walter's book has reached us; but the passage is extremely obscure. Geoffrey Gaimar, who wrote an *Estorie des Engles* in French verse about 1150, gives in an epilogue his sources, which also covered a lost

opening section on British history.[1] He claims to
have had from his patroness, Constance, wife of
Ralph Fitz-Gilbert, a book which Robert of Gloucester had got translated from the Welsh, and had
lent to Walter Espec of Helmsley, who lent it to
the Fitz-Gilberts. This Gaimar appears to say that
he had in his turn translated, with additions of things
omitted by the Welsh, since he had also obtained
the good book of Oxford which belonged to Walter
the archdeacon, and from this and from a book of
Winchester and an English book of 'Wassingburc'
corrected his work. Gaimar is not very likely to have
known Welsh, and the passage has also been translated as referring to a book which Walter of Oxford
'made.' In any case the book done for Robert of
Gloucester was probably the *Historia* itself, and
Gaimar regarded it as taken from the Welsh.

The *liber* has been the subject of much controversy.
A myth of its continued existence in Breton has been
exploded. It has been identified with the Welsh
Brut, which is post-Galfridian, and with the *Historia
Britonum*, which is written in Latin, does not contain
lives of the pre-Christian kings, and passed with
Geoffrey for part of the work of Gildas. Most, therefore, of those who accept the story believe the *liber*
to be lost. And many do not accept it. It was a jest,
or a literary convention or a fraud. It has been
argued that, if it was a fraud, Walter of Oxford
must have been a party to it, and that it is unlikely
'that two ecclesiastics would stoop to unqualified

[1] *Record* xviii.

mendacity in a matter not involving substantial benefit to themselves.' And it has been retorted that Geoffrey and Walter were archdeacons, and that it was a moot point in the middle ages whether an archdeacon could be saved.[1] I am not sure that Geoffrey was an archdeacon, or that he expected no substantial benefit from the *Historia*. But such psychological speculations are fruitless. There have been many literary forgeries, and the motives of them have generally been obscure. Certainly some of Geoffrey's contemporaries thought him a liar. They were probably thinking of the substance of his narrative, rather than of the specific allegation as to its source. On the other hand, Henry of Huntingdon evidently took him seriously, and if there was a jest or a convention or a fraud, failed to penetrate it. Geoffrey's manipulation of his material, where its nature is apparent to us, makes it impossible to believe that he was a completely veracious chronicler, even when due allowance is made for what he might reasonably consider as legitimate rhetorical embroidery. It does not quite follow that he had no *liber* at all, or that some of his perversions of fact may not have been due to a predecessor. But it is quite safe to say that, whatever underlies the *Historia*, it is not a mere literal rendering of ancient Celtic annals. There is too much of the twelfth century about it for that; the classical scholarship, with its drafts upon Virgil, Juvenal, Lucan, and Apuleius; the attempts at etymology; the modelling of Arthur's personality,

[1] Cf. John of Salisbury *Epist.* 166 (*P. L.* cxcix. 156).

court and conquests upon those of Charlemagne; the crusader's knowledge of siege machines and Greek fire; the interweaving of the Ursula legend, as developed in twelfth-century Cologne. The historical method is probably based upon that of William of Malmesbury, from whom there is at least one specific borrowing in an account of the Saxon days of the week. Nor is the outlook of the writer at all exclusively Celtic. He is familiar with the local legends of Amesbury and the Mont St Michel, as well as those of Snowdon and Caerleon. And to Geoffrey's own surroundings point the special interest in Gloucester and in Oxford, the detached attitude towards the archiepiscopal claims of St David's and Llandaff, the antedated prototypes of the earldoms of the anarchy. We are in the environment of a Norman ecclesiastic, rather than that of a remote Celt.

Geoffrey does not of course claim that the *liber* was his sole authority. It supplemented for him what he had already learnt from Bede and 'Gildas.' And he cites the 'jocund' popular tales, and acknowledges a debt to Archdeacon Walter for oral information as well as for the *liber*. The problem of the *liber* may therefore stand aside for a consideration of what may have been available for Geoffrey from these less formal sources. The material is of limited scope and doubtful interpretation. Celtic civilizations survived the Frankish and Saxon invasions in Wales, Cornwall and Brittany. But of early Cornish or Breton literature practically nothing is left, either in Celtic or in Latin. There is a good deal from Wales. Most of it is in documents of post-Galfridian date, and betrays the influence of the *Historia* itself. Modern scholarship, however, although still hampered by an inadequate knowledge of the early forms of Welsh, has made it possible to isolate certain notices of Arthur, which seem to represent a conception of the hero independent of Geoffrey's. These notices belong to bardic literature. The Welsh, a people to whom the occupations of pasturage and intermittent warfare left abundant leisure, had developed the arts of song and narrative at an early stage. It is an idle attempt to trace any direct continuity through the Roman period with the bards whom classic writers describe as related to the obscure institutions of Druidism. But Nennius, for what he is worth, speaks of men who were famed for song, apparently in North Britain, about the middle of the sixth century. He names Talhearn Tataguen, Neirin, Taliessin, Bluchbard and Cian of the Wheat Song; and these are called by later writers the Cynfeirdd or early singers, as distinguished from the mediaeval Gogynfeirdd or after singers. There is again a considerable gap, spanned only by slight traces of literary composition, to the middle of the tenth century, to which belongs at least the nucleus of the regional codes of law and custom preserved in later manuscripts. These codes show bardism as a well-defined and important element in the social organization. It does not differ in essentials from the minstrelsy of western Europe generally. Bards and minstrels share the double aspect of itinerant entertainers and household ap-

panages. Each chieftain had his *bardd teulu* or
domestic singer, but the bards of each kingdom were
also linked in a kind of guild with a *pencerdd* or
chaired bard at its head. The bards were freemen
and sometimes landowners, with a status and privileges analogous to those of priests. The craft ran in
families and there is evidence of an elaborate system of
apprenticeship. The musical instrument of the bards
was the stringed harp, and one of their principal
functions was the celebration of the prowess of their
chieftains and the glories of their descents. That this
would involve the preservation of ancestral legends
is obvious. The Gwentian code, probably not in its
present form earlier than the twelfth century, directs
that when the queen desires a song in her chamber,
the bard shall sing the song of Camlan, but in a low
voice for fear of creating excitement in the hall.[1] The
bardic literature was of course a recited literature.
Probably oral only gave place to scribal transmission
at a comparatively late date, and the earliest extant
manuscripts may only imperfectly represent the form
in which the compositions were actually uttered.

The only Welsh treatment of Arthur for which, in
its written form at least, an origin before the late
eleventh or early twelfth century can be seriously
claimed, consists of obscure allusions in poems
difficult to translate and ascribed to the Cynfeirdd.
They come from the great compilations known
collectively as the *Four Ancient Books*; the *Book of
Taliessin*, the *Book of Aneirin*, the *Black Book of*

[1] A. Owen, *Ancient Laws of Wales*, i. 331.

Carmarthen, and the *Red Book of Hergest*. The manuscripts of these range from the end of the twelfth century to the end of the fourteenth. Many of their poems are admittedly the productions of twelfth and thirteenth-century bards; of Meilyr, the poet of Gruffydd ap Cynan (d. 1137), who established a powerful North Welsh kingdom in Gwynedd; of Gwalchmai, the poet of Owain Gwynedd (d. 1170), who fought for independence against Stephen and Henry II; of others who followed under Rhys ap Gruffydd (d. 1197) and Llewelyn ap Iorwerth (d. 1240). Scholarly opinion differs as to whether, side by side with the poems of these Gogynfeirdd, there is also in the *Four Books* an older nucleus. It has been held that an early stratum preserves in substance the work of sixth-century Cynfeirdd; that it represents a ninth-century notion of what the Cynfeirdd would have written; that there is no early stratum at all, and that even the reference to the Cynfeirdd in Nennius is an interpolation of the days of Gruffydd ap Cynan. The controversy is pursued with some acrimony. From it one who is no Celtic scholar may find a refuge in the more detached judgment of M. Joseph Loth. M. Loth has studied the orthography and metric of the manuscripts; he finds in them traces of Old Welsh forms surviving through a later handling; and he concludes for a nucleus which may be of any date from the ninth to the eleventh century, and may echo events of still earlier date. It seems at least safe to conclude that the *Four Books* may well contain allusions to Arthur which are not derived from

Geoffrey. Unfortunately, such allusions are not numerous. The supposed Old Welsh nucleus is mainly concerned with the time of Urien of Rheged, whom Nennius puts in North Britain, and later in the sixth century than Arthur. In the *Book of Taliessin* there are only five mentions of Arthur, and of these four are trivial. A dying chief, Uther Pendragon, claims 'a ninth part in the prowess of Arthur.' A bard sings of his many incarnations, and calls on the Druids to 'prophesy to Arthur' of his antiquity. A similar piece refers to 'the steed of Arthur.' A song in praise of a chieftain alludes to a bard who is 'one of three deeply wise to bless Arthur.' It also mentions a warden of the well and a *gwledig* who arose or will arise from 'the loricated legion.' But here the chieftain praised, rather than Arthur, appears to be meant. One *Taliessin* poem only, which may be part of the nucleus, is directly on Arthur. I use the translations of Professor Rhys, with the repeated caution that Welsh scholarship has not yet reached the stage of an agreed and confident rendering of its earliest texts. Professor Rhys calls the poem *Preiddeu Annwfn* (*The Harryings of Hades*). We can dimly trace Arthur in his ship Prydwen, paying visits to the Otherworld, and finding there a magic caldron.

> I adore the noble prince and high king
> Who extended his sway over the world's strand.
> Perfect was the captivity of Gwair in Caer Sidi,
> Through the warning of Pwyll and Pryderi.
> Before him no one entered into it,
> Into the heavy dark chain a trusty youth guarded;

And at the harryings of Hades grievously did he sing,
And till doom will he remain a bard afterwards.
Three freights of Prydwen went we into it—
Seven alone did we return from Caer Sidi.

I am a seeker of praise, if my song be heard:
In Caer Pedryvan...
...from the caldron it would be spoken
By the breath of nine maidens it would be kindled.
The head of Hades' caldron—what is it like?
A rim it has, with pearls, round its border:
It boils not a coward's food: it would not be perjured.
The sword of Llwch Lleawc would be lifted to it.
And in the hand of Lleminawc was it left.
And before the door of Hell's gate lamps were burning,
And when we accompanied Arthur, a brilliant effort,
Seven alone did we return from Caer Veddwit.

I am a seeker of praise, my song being heard:
At Caer Pedryvan in Quick-door Island,
At dusk and in the blackness of night they mix
The sparkling wine, the drink before their retinue.
Three freights of Prydwen went we on sea:
Seven alone did we return from Caer Rigor.

I merit not the laurel of the ruler of letters—
Beyond the Glass Fort they had not seen Arthur's valour.
Three score hundreds stood on the wall:
Hard it was found to converse with their sentinel.
Three freights of Prydwen were they that went with Arthur,
Seven alone did they return from Caer Goludd.

I merit not the laurel of them of the long shields:
They know not which is the ruler's day or who he is,
At what hour of early day he was born or where,
Who made...went not...
They know not the Speckled Ox with the stout halter,
With seven score joints in his collar.

When we went with Arthur, anxious visit,
Seven alone did we return from Caer Vanddwy.

I merit not the laurel of those of long...
They know not which is the day of the ruler and chief,
At what hour of early day was born the owner,
Or what myriad guards the silver of the head.
When we went with Arthur, anxious contest,
Seven alone did we return from Caer Ochren.

The *Book of Aneirin* yields but little. A hero is 'an Arthur.' An allusion to the hunt of the 'porc Trwyth' does not name Arthur, but we know from Nennius, and shall see again, that he was the legendary huntsman. Rather more productive is the *Black Book of Carmarthen*. There are three poems, which may be not later than the first half of the twelfth century. The most interesting bears on the story of Arthur's end, about which Geoffrey of Monmouth was so unsatisfactory. It is an enumeration of famous graves.

> Osvran's son's grave at Camlan,
> After many a slaughter,
> Bedwyr's grave in Allt Tryvan.
> A grave for March, a grave for Gwythur,
> A grave for Gwgawn of the ruddy sword,
> Not wise (the thought) a grave for Arthur.

A fragmentary dialogue between Arthur and a porter introduces Bedwyr, who fought at Tryvryd, presumably the Tribruit of Nennius, and Kei, who slew Palug's Cat on Mona, and many other names which will meet us in the sequel. Obscure fights of Arthur's own, one with a hag, are also recorded.

Who is the porter?
Glewlwyd Gavaelvawr.
Who asks the question?
Arthur and worthy Kei.
What following hast thou?
The best of men are mine.
To my house thou shalt not come
Unless thou plead for them.
I will plead for them.
And thou shalt see them:
Wythneint of Elei,
And the wise men three—
Mabon son of Modron
(Uther Pendragon's man)
Kyscaint son of Banon,
And Gwyn Godyvrion.
Sturdy would be my men
In defence of their laws—
Manawyddan son of Llyr
Profound in counsel;
(Manawyd brought home
A pierced buckler from Tryvrwyd).
And Mabon son of Mellt
Who stained the grass with gore;
And Angwas the Winged,
And Llwch Llawynnawc,
Who were protective
Against Eidyn the gashing.
His lord would shelter him,
My nephew would amend,
Kei would plead for them,
While slaying them three at a time.
When Kelli was lost
Savagery was experienced.
Kei would plead for them
Until he might hew them down.

Though Arthur was playing
The blood was dripping.
In Awarnach's hall
A-fighting with a hag,
He slew Pen-palach
In the tasks of Dissethach.
On Eidyn's mountain
He combated with champions,
By the hundred they fell—
They fell a hundred at a time
Before Bedwyr...
On the shores of Tryvrwyd;
Combating with Garwlwyd.
Victorious was his wrath
Both with sword and shield.
It were vain to boast
Against Kei in battle.
His sword in battle was
Not to be pledged from his hand.
He was an equable lord
Of a legion for the state's good.
Bedwyr son of Bridlaw,
Nine hundred to watch,
Six hundred to attack,
Was his onslaught worth.
The young men I have—
It is well where they are.
Before the kings of Emrys
Have I seen Kei in haste.
Leader of the harryings,
Long would he be in his wrath;
Heavy was he in his vengeance;
Terrible in his fighting.
When from a horn he drank
He drank as much as four men;
When he came into battle

> He slew as would a hundred.
> Unless it should be God's act
> Kei's death would be unachieved.
> Worthy Kei and Lacheu
> Used to fight battles,
> Before the pang of livid spears,
> On the top of Ystavingun
> Kei slew nine witches.
> Worthy Kei went to Mona
> To destroy lions.
> His shield was small
> Against Palug's Cat.
> When people shall ask
> 'Who slew Palug's Cat?'
> Nine score...
> Used to fall for her food,
> Nine score leaders
> Used to...

The third early poem of the *Black Book* is headed *Gereint filius Erbin*. It celebrates the death of Gereint of Devon at a battle of Llongborth, which may be Langport in Somerset. The poet seems to regard Gereint as a follower of Arthur, for he says:

> At Llongborth saw I of Arthur's
> Brave men hewing with steel,
> (Men of the) emperor, director of toil.

A Gerontius is known to history, and may very well have fought at Langport. He was the last independent Celtic king of Dumnonia, and was conquered by Ina of Wessex in 710. This was nearly two centuries after the time of Arthur, but the Celtic historic muse cares little for chronology. Of uncertain date is a poem on a hero called Gwyn ab Nudd, who was the lover of Kreurdilad the daughter of Lludd, and fought at Caer Vanddwy, one of the Caers mentioned in the *Preiddeu Annwfn*. The poet claims to have been present at other famous battles:

> I was there where Llacheu fell,
> Arthur's son renowned (*or* skilled) in song,
> When ravens flocked on the gore.

The Gereint poem recurs in the *Red Book of Hergest*. This has no other early Arthurian verse. It contains, however, a number of prose stories, which are the most characteristic remains of early Welsh literature. They are also found in other manuscripts known collectively as the *White Book of Rhydderch*. The *White Book* is of the thirteenth century, and the *Red Book* of the fourteenth, but scribal peculiarities justify the treatment of them as transcripts of twelfth-century originals, and the substance of some of the stories, at whatever date they may have taken their present form, almost certainly antedates Geoffrey. The early elements are clearest in the group of four linked stories known as the *Mabinogi*, a term which is generally taken as meaning the stories proper to a *mabinog* or apprentice bard. The entanglement of their themes suggests that they had passed through various stages of oral transmission, before they were written down. The *Mabinogi* have personages in common with the early poems. They know nothing, however, of Arthur. Their origin appears to have been in Dyfed or South-West Wales, and, as they stand, they are legends of the ruling houses of that kingdom and the kingdom of

Gwynedd or North Wales, and of other houses which gave over-kings to the whole of pre-Saxon Britain. But their material is largely made up of marvellous *contes*, such as are familiar in classical legend and in folk-tales throughout and beyond Europe. A king marries a fairy bride. A prince is stolen at birth by fairies. There are giants and shape-shifters. A household is transformed into mice. A woman is fashioned out of flowers. A realm is put under enchantment. The head of Bran the Blessed gives magical happiness through many years. Finally it is buried in the White Hill of London, 'and it was the third ill-fated disclosure when it was disinterred, inasmuch as no invasion from across the sea came to this island while the head was in that concealment.' There are aetiological themes, explaining the names of places or the habits of a bird. There are culture-hero themes, explaining how the gifts of civilization came to men. Pwyll King of Dyfed reigns for a time in the other world, and thence came the herd of swine that belonged to Pwyll's son Pryderi, and was stolen by Gwydion. A magic caldron, with the property, like Medea's caldron, of bringing the dead to life, is taken and retaken. We have found Pwyll and Pryderi and a magic caldron with Arthur in the poem of *Preiddeu Annwfn*. Some of these folk-tale elements may have made their way long before into the pre-Christian mythology of the Celtic peoples, and have been inherited unconsciously by the tellers of the *Mabinogi*. They have their analogues in the eleventh-century literature of Ireland, where the

68

mythological element is more clearly discernible. In particular, some of the personages of the *Mabinogi* bear names which are used with no clear consciousness of a divine origin, but are in fact those of personages in Irish mythology. The children of Don, who rule in Gwynedd, are the Irish Tuatha De Danann, who were gods. One of them is Govannon, who in Ireland is the divine smith, Goibniu. Manawyddan son of Llyr is the Irish sea-god Manannan mac Lir, although in the *Mabinogi* he has become a prototype of the craftsman rather than a sea-god. The yellow-haired Llew Llaw Gyffes retains a trace of the Irish Lug, a god of light. Contact between Ireland and Wales was easy enough at all times, and the stories themselves include episodes of expeditions both hostile and friendly across the seas. Moreover, although the Brythonic variety of the Celtic language was spoken over the whole of Wales by the twelfth century, there were certainly districts in Dyfed, and probably also Gwynedd, where the Goidelic variety, to which Irish belongs, had prevailed at an earlier date. Scholars differ as to how far this was due to invasions from Ireland during more or less historic times, and how far, if at all, to survivals from a wave of Goidelic-speaking Celts who preceded the Brythonic-speaking Celts in their migration from Europe to this island. However this may be, it is generally held that it was in a Goidelic rather than a Brythonic district that the *Mabinogi* originated. On the other hand, we know even less of Brythonic than of Goidelic religion. They may have retained a common stock of cult-names and mythologic ideas. They may, either or both of them, have absorbed notions from pre-Celtic peoples. Whatever the source of the mythologic element in the *Mabinogi*, it is curiously mingled with matter from chroniclers. Side by side with the children of Don and Manawyddan son of Llyr, the rulers of Britain include Bran, his son Caradauc, and Cassivellaun, son of Beli son of Mynogan. Of these the first three can only be the historic Brennus, Caratacus, and Cassivellaunus. The name of Beli has a superficial resemblance to that of the Irish god Beli, but his patronymic reveals him as the pseudo-historic Belinus, son of Minocannus, due to scribal errors of Orosius and the *Historia Britonum*.

Arthur, so conspicuous by his absence from the *Mabinogi*, is a well-defined figure in the independent story of *Kulhwch and Olwen*, the composition of which M. Loth dates in the late eleventh or early twelfth century.[1] There is some trace of the impact of Norman upon Celtic civilization, but none of the influence of Geoffrey or of French Arthurian romance. The basis of the story is again a folk-tale, of a very familiar type. Kulhwch, the grandson of Prince Anllawdd, woos Olwen, the daughter of the giant Yspaddaden Penkawr, and to win her must accomplish a series of labours set him by the giant, who knows that the lover's success will mean his own destruction. There is a strong culture-hero element about the labours. Some of them are agricultural tasks of ploughing and sowing, for which the

[1] *Contributions* 37.

70

services of the once mythological children of Don, Amaethon and Govannon, must be requisitioned. Magic vessels must be obtained, such as a basket which will give each of thrice nine men his desired food. And for the giant's array at the wedding, two boars must be hunted down, Yskithyrwyn Benbaedd, whose tusk must be his razor, and Twrch Trwyth, the son of a prince, between whose ears are a comb and scissors. In this hunt must take part another mythological personage, Mabon son of Modron, who appears on Gallo-Romanic altars as Apollo Maponus, and in the porter poem of the *Black Book* as 'Uther Pendragon's man.' Kulhwch performs the feats; in part, as is proper to folk-tales, with the aid of helpful animals, a nest of ants, an ousel, a stag, an owl, the eagle of Gwern Abbey, the salmon of Llyn Llyw; but in part also with that of Arthur, whose cousin he is, and Arthur's companion heroes, and of Goreu son of Custennin, the giant's nephew, who proves to be also a cousin of Kulhwch. Arthur may be an accretion to the original story, and some dislocation of the incidents may have resulted. The tasks set are not all accomplished, and it is significant to be told at one point that Yskithyrwyn Benbaedd was not slain by the dogs whom the giant had named, but by Arthur's own dog Cavall. A duplication of the swine may be part of the accretion, since we know from Nennius that the hunt of the *porcus Troit* had long been assigned to Arthur and Cabal. This episode is treated with great elaboration. The hunt begins in Ireland, crosses the seas, and is pursued with geographical accuracy through South Wales, before the monster is finally driven over the Severn estuary into Cornwall and there drowned. Much aetiological explanation of place-names is involved. Professor Rhys has identified the name Twrch Trwyth, which means King's Boar, with an *Orc Treith* found in Cormac's Irish glossary, and it is possible that in this story too there are Goidelic elements. Incidentally *Kulhwch and Olwen* gives a very full description of Arthur's court, which is visited by Kulhwch to seek for help and for the initiation-rite of hair cutting which appears to have been a Celtic equivalent for knighthood. The door is kept by Glewlwyd Gavaelvawr, the porter of the poems, and here clearly Arthur's own porter. Arthur's warlike exploits have ranged far beyond Britain, for Glewlwyd has been with him in Europe and Corsica and Africa and India and when he conquered Greece in the East. Besides a porter Arthur has huntsmen, a guide, an interpreter, an architect, a champion, a magician, a priest, and Bedwini, a household bishop. His personal belongings have proper names; the hall Ehangwen, the ship Prydwen, the hound Cavall, the mare Llamrei, the sword Caledvwlch, the spear Rhongomyant, the shield Wynebgwrthucher, the dagger Carnwenhau. Caledvwlch, the Excalibur of the romances, has been equated with Calad-bolg, the fairy sword of the Irish hero Cuchulainn. One recalls that Charlemagne also had his sword Joyeuse, and Roland his Durendal.

Fortunate, too, for us was the intention of the story-teller to give a complete roll of Arthur's courtiers, which he accomplishes by making Kulhwch call upon each of them individually for succour in his enterprise. Here for the first time in a Celtic setting we meet Gwenhwyvar the queen, who has with her a sister Gwenhwyvach. Here is Gwalchmei, whose name in all Welsh documents replaces the Walwen of William of Malmesbury and the Gawain of the romances. He is the son of Arthur's sister by his cousin Gwyar, and he has a brother Gwalhavet. Here are Kei and Bedwyr, whom we found linked with Arthur in the poems. They are described in much detail. Kei appears to be the chief officer of the court, and is rebuked by Arthur for discourtesy to Kulhwch on his arrival. Before Kei's birth it was prophesied that his heart would always be cold and there would be no warmth in his hands, that he would be always stubborn, that when he carried a burden, large or small, no one would be able to see it, either before him or behind. Later we are told:

Kei had this special force, that he could breathe nine nights and nine days under water, and could exist nine nights and nine days without sleep. A blow from Kei's sword no physician could heal. A valuable man was Kei. When it pleased him, he became as tall as the loftiest tree in the forest. Another privilege—when it rained hardest, all that he bore in his hand remained dry for a palm's breadth above and below, so great was his natural heat; it would light a fire for his comrades, when they suffered most from cold.

Bedwyr was a swift runner; although he was one-handed, three warriors could not shed blood faster than he on the field of battle; his spear made one wound, but nine were made when it was drawn out. Solar mythology has been overdone, but I think that we may recognize in Kei and Bedwyr the moon and the lightning. Certainly the phases of Kei recall the nine-nights week of the Celts.[1] It appears from the romances that Gawain, whose strength waxed to midday and then waned, was once the sun. He retains no solar quality in *Kulhwch and Olwen*. Various relatives of Kei and Bedwyr are named, and there is an allusion to a subsequent slaying of Kei by Gwyddawc, and of a revenge which Arthur took for him.

The court contains other heroes of the poems; Gereint son of Erbin, who himself has a son Cadwy; Loch Lawynnyawc, a great-uncle of Arthur on the mother's side, and Annwas Adeinawc; Manawyddan son of Llyr; Gwynn son of Nudd, of whom another son is Edern. The *Black Book* allusion to Gwynn's *amours* finds explanation in an episodic narrative, of how Kreiddylat daughter of Lludd Llaw Ereint was the wife of Gwythyr son of Greidiawl, of how Gwynn took her by force, of the warfare between Gwythyr and Gwynn, of the peace imposed by Arthur, and of how Gwythyr and Gwynn were condemned to fight for Kreiddylat on every first of May to the day of judgment, when the winner shall have her. Obviously there is a reminiscence here of the seasonal contests familiar in folk-custom. And indeed we are once more on mythologic ground, for Nudd represents a Celtic divinity, traces of whose cult under the name of Nodens have been found at Lydney in Gloucester-

[1] Cf. Rhys, *Celtic Heathendom*, 360.

shire, and who may be equated with Nuada Argetlam, a king of the Irish Tuatha De Danann. And again the Welsh narrator's oblivion of the mythology he uses is illustrated. The name Lludd is itself only an orthographic variant of Nudd, and the epithet Llaw Ereint has the same meaning as Argetlam, the Silver-Handed. Lydney itself preserves this form of the name, and as it recurs in Ludgate, the divinity was probably Brythonic as well as Goidelic.

Tristan is not in the court, nor Mark; but two Iseults, Essyllt Vinwen and Essyllt Vingul, are among a group of 'island ladies who wear gold collars.' There are vassal princes. Gwillenhin, Paris and Iona are kings of France; Gwittard is son of Aedd, King of Ireland; Ysperin is son of Fergan, King of Brittany. There are other foreigners; Conchobar Mac Nessa and Curoi Mac Daere, who have strayed in under altered names from Irish legend; Maelwys son of Baeddan, who may have a similar origin; Osla Gyllellvawr, whose dagger makes a bridge for Arthur's armies, but who is probably a Saxon. There are Welsh historical or quasi-historical personages; Taliessin, chief of bards; Morvudd, daughter of Taliessin's hero, Urien Rheget; Dyvynmal Moel, the traditional legislator; Gildas the historian, one of nineteen sons of Kaw, of whom another is Hueil, who never paid homage to any lord, and with whom Arthur afterwards had a quarrel. Behind them come innumerable others. Of some of them, as of Gwynn and Hueil, the narrator may have known stories which he does not tell. But many we may suspect to be names only, perhaps introduced for the gratification of heroes who claimed them as ancestors. Some are said to be relatives of Arthur. Neither his father nor his mother is named. But there are four of his mother's brothers, sons of Loch Llawynnyawc, from the other side of the sea Terwyn. Arthur's mother must have married twice, for Gormant son of Ricca is his half-brother on that side. On the father's side Cradawc and five other sons of Kaer Dathal were akin. Kulhwch himself, Arthur's cousin, was son of Kilydd son of Kelyddon, and of Goleuddydd daughter of Prince Anllawdd. It is impossible to construct a genealogy. There is nothing of Medraut, unless, as is possible, he is to be identified with Medyr son of Methredydd, who could shoot a wren between the two legs from Kelliwic to Esgeir Oervel in Ireland. He is not said to be a kinsman of Arthur, or connected with Camlan. But there is a group so connected. Gwynhyvar, Mayor of Cornwall and Devon, was one of nine who plotted the battle. Kynnwyl Sant was one of the three who escaped from it, the last to leave Arthur on his horse Hengroen. Morvran received no blow there on account of his ugliness; all took him for an auxiliary devil; he was covered with hair like a stag. Sandde Bryd-angel, on the other hand, received no blow on account of his beauty; all took him for an auxiliary angel. These touches suggest the improvisations of a light-hearted story-teller, rather than the *débris* of an established legend. And certainly we get the *gabs* of a story-teller in the descriptions of some motley indwellers of the court whose ancestry no chieftain could be very anxious to claim. Such were Ychdryt, who spread his rough red beard over the eight and forty posts of Arthur's hall; Gwevyl, who on the day that he was sad would let one of his lips drop below his navel, while he inverted the other like a hood over his head; Kacymwri, who would beat a barn with an iron flail until the posts, the rafters and the laths were as small as oats in the mow upon the floor. We cannot envy Arthur his retainer Gwallgoyc, who, if he came to a town and he lacked anything, would let no sleep come to the eyes of a single person; or his retainer Huarwr, who asked him for such a boon as would satisfy him; it was the third great plague of Cornwall when he obtained it; none could get a smile from him, unless he was full of meat. This parodistic element can be paralleled from Irish stories, and probably the manner of the narrator has been influenced by the more early developed literature of Ireland, with which it has another common feature in the tendency to place names and incidents in triads or groups of three.

Of the other Arthurian stories in the *Red Book*, the only one with any claims to an early date is *The Dream of Rhonabwy*. The dreamer is a twelfth-century chieftain. He beholds Arthur and his host gathering at a ford on the Severn for the battle of Badon against Osla Gyllellvawr, here evidently a Saxon, but with a name borrowed from the eighth-century Offa of Mercia. Arthur is called Emperor. The warriors are of huge stature, and marvel at the little folk of later days. Men of Greece are there; men of Scandinavia under March son of Meirchiawn, Arthur's cousin; men of Denmark under Edern son of Nudd. Goreu son of Custennin is there, and others from the *Kulhwch and Olwen* list. But there are additional names. There is Arthur's son Lacheu, remembered in a *Black Book* poem. There are Drystan son of Tallwch, Cador Count of Cornwall, Hoel son of Emyr of Brittany, and Gilbert son of Katgyfro, who seems to be the twelfth-century Norman Gilbert de Clare. The dreamer's guide is Iddawc the Troubler of Britain, who brought about the battle of Camlan by bearing to Medraut a bitter instead of a conciliatory letter from Arthur. Badon is delayed by a game of chess between Arthur and Owein son of Urien, during which a troop of ravens brought by Owein harry the host; and finally a truce is made with Osla Gyllellvawr, and Arthur retires to Cornwall. The *Dream of Rhonabwy* is probably later than Geoffrey's *Historia*, and may owe to it the presence of Geoffrey's heroes Cador and Hoel, and the localization of Badon near the Severn. But in the main it seems to continue the Welsh tradition of *Kulhwch and Olwen*.

Closely related to the stories are a number of short pieces in the *Red Book of Hergest* which take the form of independent triads. These became a characteristic feature of mediaeval Welsh literature. Many of the triads in later manuscripts are based upon material from Geoffrey and the Arthurian romances. Even some of those in the *Red Book* itself show the influence of Geoffrey. Others add nothing to the indications of *Kulhwch and Olwen*. But there are a few gleanings which may serve to complete the Arthurian picture there given. There were three evil discoveries of Britain. One was that of Arthur, who took away the head of Bran the Blessed from the White Hill; he did not like the island to be guarded by another might than his own. This is an exceptional link, presumably an afterthought, between Arthur and the *Mabinogi*. A group of triads is concerned with Camlan. There were three furious blows of Britain. One was that of Gwenhwyvach to Gwenhwyvar, which brought about the battle. There were three costly pillages. One was when Medraut went to Arthur's court at Kelliwic in Cornwall; he left neither food nor drink in the court; he consumed all; he dragged Gwenhwyvar from her royal chair and struck her. Another was when Arthur went to the court of Medraut; he left neither food nor drink in the court or the district. Among the three ill resolutions was that of Arthur when he three times divided his troops with Medraut; among the three faithless households that of Alan Fergan, which deserted its lord on the march to the battle. Caradoc was one of the three favourite knights of Arthur's court, who would stand no master of household over them. Gwalchmei and Lacheu were two of the three inventors; Kei and Drystan two of the three crown-bearers. Arthur himself appears, oddly enough, among the three frivolous bards. He had three mistresses, Indec, Garwen and Gwyl. The

79

three chief ladies of his court were Gwenhwyvar daughter of Gwryt Gwent, Gwenhwyvar daughter of Gwythyr ab Greidiawl, and Gwenhwyvar daughter of Ocvran the giant. Unfortunately we are not told which was the queen. In later Welsh literature she is generally the daughter of Ocvran. The three great swineherds of Britain were Pryderi, Drystan and Koll. Drystan kept the pigs of March son of Meirchyon, while the swineherd went on a message to Essyllt. Arthur, March, Kei and Bedwyr came all four, but could not get a single pigling out of him, by ruse, force or theft. One of Koll's sows was with pig. It was prophesied that Britain would suffer from her litter. Arthur pursued it with an army to the sea at Penryn Austin in Cornwall. Here again we get a note of the culture-myth, for the pig dropped grains and a bee at spots which were afterwards productive of corn and honey. Sometimes Arthur seems to have been superimposed upon a pre-existing triad. There were three red fighters of Britain. But a greater was Arthur. For a year no herb or plant grew where one of the three marched, but for seven where Arthur marched. There were three eminent prisoners. But a greater was Arthur, who was three nights in prison at Caer Oeth and Anoeth, three by the act of Gwen Pendragon, three in an enchanted prison under Llech Echymeint. It was Goreu son of Custennin, his cousin, who delivered him on all three occasions.

A divergent and less glorified conception of Arthur is found in some Latin *Vitae* of South Welsh saints, roughly contemporary with him or with Maelgwn, who ruled in North Wales a little after his time. Herein he appears less as an emperor than as a local *tyrannus*, with an undisciplined character which occasionally calls for saintly correction. Naturally the ecclesiastical point of view is not quite that of the bard. The composition of the *Vitae* is put by scholars, not with complete unanimity, in the late eleventh or the early twelfth century. The manuscript is a hundred years younger, and there may be added touches. The *Vita* of St Cadoc is ascribed to Lifric, a schoolmaster at Llancarfan about 1075.[1] Cadoc's father Gwynnlyw, a king in Glamorganshire, was in flight from Brychan, a king in Brecknock, whose wife Gwladys he had taken. He fell in with three mighty heroes, who were gambling on a hill. They were Arthur and his 'equites' Kei and Bedwyr. Arthur was smitten with desire for Gwladys. But Kei and Bedwyr reminded him that it was their wont to succour the helpless and distressed, and he gave protection to Gwynnlyw. It is a little difficult to believe that this passage, with its apparent echo of the romantic reputation of the Round Table, dates from 1075. Many years later, Cadoc was Abbot of Llancarfan. Arthur was in search of Ligessauc son of Eliman, who had slain three of his knights. Cadoc concealed the aggressor for seven years, and ultimately persuaded Arthur to accept his arbitration, with that of St David, St Teilo and others, on the banks of the Usk. They awarded Arthur a hundred

[1] *Record* vii.

cows for the knights. Arthur insisted that every cow must be red before and white behind. The resourceful saint enchanted a herd of ordinary cows to this colouring, but, when Kei and Bedwyr led them over the ford, they were all turned into bundles of fern. Arthur was humbled, and dedicated the spot as a sanctuary under the name of Trefredinauc or Ferntown. More harmonious were Arthur's relations with St Carannog.[1] He was a missionary from Cardigan to South Britain. God gave him an altar, whose colour no man could tell. As was the wont of missionary saints, he set it adrift on the Severn, for a divine guide to his landing. It floated to the realm of Cato and Arthur, who dwelt in Dindraithov. He met Arthur, seeking for a serpent which had devastated the district of Carrum. Arthur received his blessing, and the saint asked for news of his altar. Arthur promised to tell him where it had landed, if he would secure the serpent for him. So Carannog prayed, and straightway with a great noise came the serpent, like a calf running to its mother, and bowed its head before the servant of God. Carannog put his stole round its neck, and it followed him like a lamb, lifting neither wings nor talons. It was taken to Cato in the citadel, and fed before the people in the hall. They would have killed it, but Carannog said that it had been divinely sent to destroy sinners in Carrum, and bade it leave the country for ever. Then Arthur produced the altar. He had meant to make a table of it, but had found that everything placed upon it

[1] *Record* viii.

82

was flung off. He gave Carrum to the saint in perpetuity, and afterwards built a church there. Carannog floated his altar again, and it landed at the port of Guellit. Here too a church was built and the town called Carrov. Carrum has been identified with Charmouth in Dorset, but that is not on the shores of the Severn. Carannog is the patron of St Crantock's in Cornwall. But obviously the locality of the serpent story is the district between the Quantocks and the spurs of Exmoor. Here are Carhampton and Williton, and the great citadel of Dunster, which is probably meant by Dindraithov, although Dundry, on the north of the Quantocks, affords a closer etymological equivalent. There is said to have been a chapel of St Carannog at Marsh Farm near Carhampton. Cato is less likely to be Kei than Cadwy son of Gereint. And Cadwy may be the King Cathovius, whose worldly fame is recorded in Urdisten's life of the sixth-century Breton St Guenolé. The life of St Illtud only records that he was a son of Bicanus and Rieingulid daughter of King Anllawdd, and that he travelled from his father's home in Brittany to the court of his cousin Arthur, where he saw a great abundance of knights.[1] But we find a conflict of saint and king again in that of St Padarn.[2] The *tyrannus* Arthur, who wandered the country-side, came to the cell of Padarn, and coveted his tunic. Thereupon the saint made the earth open, and swallow up Arthur, who was not released until he craved pardon.

[1] *Record* ix.   [2] *Record* x.

A *Vita Gildae* does not belong to the same group, and is of later date.[1] But it is of similar type. It is ascribed in a Durham manuscript, probably written by 1166, to that Caradoc of Llancarfan, who figures in the colophon to Geoffrey's *Historia*, and the part played by Llancarfan in the narrative makes the ascription plausible. There is no obvious sign of influence by the *Historia* itself. The writer gives a version of the story of a quarrel between Arthur and Hueil the brother of Gildas, which is mentioned in *Kulhwch and Olwen*. Arthur, he says, was king of all Greater Britain, and much loved by Gildas. But the twenty-three brothers of Gildas, who would obey no lord, resisted the *rex rebellis*; and in particular Hueil, the eldest, a warrior of renown, who was constantly conducting raids from Scotland. At last, however, Arthur made war upon him, and slew him in the Isle of Man. Gildas, then in Ireland, was deeply grieved, and joined Arthur and Hueil in his prayers. Presently he visited Britain, on his way to Rome, and hosted with St Cadoc at Llancarfan. There was a gathering of the chiefs and ecclesiastics of Britain, to bring about an atonement with Arthur for the homicide. Gildas gave Arthur the kiss of peace, and Arthur underwent penance and made such amends as he could to his life's end. A later episode in the *Vita* once more brings Gildas into contact with Arthur. The saint was at Glastonbury, preaching and writing his histories of the kings of Britain. Melvas, who was then king *in aestiva regione*, by

[1] *Record* xx.

which we must clearly understand Somerset, had carried off Guennuvar, the wife of the *tyrannus* Arthur, and brought her for security to the marsh-engirt sanctuary. The *rex rebellis* sought his wife for a whole year, before he learnt her whereabouts. Then he gathered the forces of Cornwall and Devon and made war on Melvas. But Gildas and the Abbot of Glastonbury made peace between the kings. Guennuvar was restored, and the kings recompensed the abbey with lands and privileges. Maelwys, son of Baeddan, is also named, although without any detail, in *Kulhwch and Olwen*. But the story of the rape of Guinevere and the problem of the relation of Glastonbury to the Arthur legend must be reserved for later treatment.

We have now to consider how far Geoffrey, in search of material to help the play of his fancy in supplementing the chronicles, may be supposed to have drawn, through the alleged *liber* or otherwise, upon a Welsh tradition about Arthur resembling those just described. I think it is obvious that he did not use the *Vitae*. His Arthur lives and dies in the odour of sanctity, and he had no use for a *rex rebellis* or *tyrannus* recalcitrant against the proper authority of God and his saints. Moreover the ecclesiastics with whom he brings Arthur into contact are those, not of Glastonbury or Llancarfan, but of Gloucester, St David's and Llandaff, whose *Vitae* he probably knew, although he deliberately transfers some of them to his imaginary see of Caerleon. And even when we compare the *Historia* with the vernacular

Welsh literature, the analogies are not so close or numerous as we might expect. I do not lay much stress on the difference of tone. It is true that, if chronology permitted, one might be tempted to regard the court of Arthur in *Kulhwch and Olwen* as a literary burlesque of the court of Arthur in the *Historia*. Apparently it does not permit, and it must be acknowledged that, if Geoffrey had any such model as *Kulhwch and Olwen* before him, he would naturally eliminate its more fantastic elements, and replace the Celtic by a Norman atmosphere. He was professing to write dignified history, and would not treat Arthur as the harrier of Hades or as the huntsman of a magic pig. The miraculous, for him, was concentrated in Merlin. Chronology, again, makes it necessary to admit that, before Geoffrey, the Welsh had arrived at the conception of Arthur as a world-conqueror. This conception is coloured in Geoffrey by a conscious analogy with Charlemagne, but the Arthur of *Kulhwch and Olwen* has already ranged beyond Britain and even Europe, and subdued the Greeks of the East.

On the other hand, it is difficult to trace much direct filiation between the details of Arthur's family, *comitatus*, equipment, and final disaster, as given in the *Historia* and in the Welsh documents respectively, and there are some obvious discrepancies. Geoffrey's Arthur is the son of Uther Pendragon and Igerna. His sister Anna, wife of Lot, is the mother of his nephews Gawain and Mordred. He has another nephew, Hoel of Brittany, and an uncle, David the archbishop. He is succeeded by his kinsman Constantine son of Cador of Cornwall. Little of this could be gleaned from the Welsh documents. Naturally their writers would assume a knowledge of Arthur's parents, but in fact there is no evidence that anyone before Geoffrey made him the son of Uther Pendragon. Uther is in the poems, but his claim of 'a ninth part in the prowess of Arthur' does not suggest parentage. The Welsh documents do not name Igerna or Anna. Geoffrey would in any case know of Gawain as Arthur's nephew from William of Malmesbury. He is probably the same as Gwalchmei, although the philological equivalence of the two names is doubtful. *Kulhwch and Olwen* makes Gwalchmei Arthur's nephew by an unnamed sister, and his father is not Loth, but Gwyar. If Loth is Loch Lawynnyawc, he was Arthur's great-uncle. The Welsh documents, no more than the *Annales Cambriae*, say that Medraut was Arthur's nephew. They do not relate Arthur to David. Constantine might be Custennin, but he seems to be of the wrong generation. Hoel of Brittany and Cador of Cornwall first appear in the post-Galfridian *Rhonabwy*. Both Geoffrey and the Welsh give Arthur a wife Guanhumara or Gwenhwyvar, but for the Welsh she is the daughter of Ocvran the giant, for Geoffrey a noble Roman lady brought up in the chamber of Cador. Geoffrey in his turn has nothing of Arthur's Welsh son Lacheu, or his kinsmen Anllawdd and Kulhwch, Goreu son of Custennin, Gwalhavet brother of Gwalchmei, March son of Meirchiawn, Gormant son of Ricca.

87

So, too, with Arthur's retinue. Both the *Historia* and the Welsh have Kei and Bedwyr; they are in the *Vita* of Cadoc too, and were probably an established tradition. Geoffrey of course strips them of mythological trappings and conceives of them as Norman household officers. Both have Ider son of Nut and Taliessin's Urien. Geoffrey gives Urien a son Eventus, who recurs in *Rhonabwy* as Owein. A few other Welsh names may be traced, sometimes in odd connections, in the *Historia*. Annwas Adeinawc, who is found with Loch Lawynnyawc in the poems, may underlie Geoffrey's Auguselus, whom he makes, like Loth, a king of Scotland. Gwittard of Ireland may be his Guitardus of Poitou. Maelwys he seems to have fitted with a doublet Gwynvas, and to have used the pair twice, firstly as Melga the King of Picts and Guanius the King of Huns in the story of Ursula, and secondly as Malvasius King of Iceland and Gunvasius King of the Orkneys among Arthur's vassals. That is very like him. On the other hand, he makes no use of Geraint, or of Tristan and Iseult, or of Kreiddylat's lovers Gwynn and Gwythyr, although Kreiddylat herself figures, with the wrong father, in the earlier story of Lear. And it is noteworthy that, when Geoffrey wants to make up a full court for Arthur at Caerleon, he goes, not to the crowd of *Kulhwch and Olwen*, but to the tenth-century Welsh genealogies. Arthur's sword Caliburnus and spear Ron may be equated with the Welsh Caledvwlch and Rhongomyant, but the ship Prydwen has been turned into a name for the shield of the Latin chronicles. Finally there is the battle of Camlan. This was certainly, as the reference in the *Gwentian Code* shows, a topic familiar to the Welsh writers. The stories and the early triads are full of allusions to the events which led to the battle, and to heroes whose participation in it is claimed. They do not in fact assert a rape of Guinevere by Mordred or a usurpation of the kingdom. And they have no direct echoes in the *Historia*. This is not perhaps surprising. Geoffrey was not likely to represent the disaster of his hero as arising out of court brawls in which rival chieftains eat up one another's household, and ladies exchange blows and are dragged from their thrones. It is more important that the Welsh documents say nothing of the survival of Arthur, which, although only obscurely referred to by Geoffrey, was clearly part of the tradition from which he started.

One must conclude then that, apart from the use of certain common names, there is no obvious draft by the *Historia* upon the body of pre-Galfridian Welsh tradition about Arthur, so far as that has been preserved to us. It is, of course, probable that much has not been preserved, and some of it may well have been more serious in tone than either *Kulhwch and Olwen* or the triads. But there is no ground for assuming that its analogies to the *Historia* were any closer. And certainly, in view of the way in which Geoffrey habitually handles his materials, it is idle to attempt to reconstruct vanished traditions on the basis of anything which he gives; to treat, for example, with Professor Rhys, a Melvas and a Gwynvas as contrasted figures of Celtic mythology, or to argue, with a later writer, that Geoffrey was painfully conflating two established versions of Arthur's parentage, one of which made him the son of Uther and the other of a Cador-Cadwy. Geoffrey did nothing painfully, and whatever he was, he was no respecter of tradition.

There is the alternative that any Celtic material used by Geoffrey may have come to him from Cornwall, or from Brittany, which, as a result of the influx of its Celtic population from the south-west of this island, may have developed an Arthurian tradition more in harmony with that of Cornwall than with that of Wales. The absence of early Cornish or Breton romantic documents naturally makes speculation very unsure. We have seen that Geoffrey himself is on the whole more likely to have been of Breton than of Welsh parentage. Two other things are noticeable. One is the very considerable part which personages both from Brittany and from Cornwall play in the annals of Arthur and his house as represented in the *Historia*. Armorica is settled from Britain by Conan Meriadoc, a comrade of Maximian. In return it provides a founder for the Arthurian dynasty in Constantine, a brother of Conan's descendant Aldroenus. Budecius of Armorica protects Aurelius and Uther in the time of Vortigern. Hoel of Armorica, the son of Dubricius, perhaps a scribal slip for Budecius, is the faithful ally of Arthur. After Arthur's death come more Hoels and Alans and a Solomon, who bring the story to the end of the seventh century.

These names can hardly be strung on any historical thread. Most of them are traceable in Breton records, but, with the exception of Budecius, at dates long after those assigned to them by Geoffrey. Nor does he appear to know of the few real early names which history preserves; unless indeed the fifth-century Rhiotimus is to be found, curiously transmogrified, in the giant Ritho of Snowdon. Historical or not, however, the constant intervention of these Armorican personages gives a marked Breton colouring to Geoffrey's story. Hardly less prominent is Cornwall. Conan Meriadoc seeks a wife in Ursula daughter of Dionotus, the brother and successor of Caradoc. Gorlois of Cornwall supports Aurelius against the Saxons, and Uther takes his wife. Apparently a daughter of Uther marries Cador of Cornwall, who becomes a mainstay of the realm, and brings up Guinevere. Arthur himself is called *aper Cornubiae* in Merlin's *Prophecies*. His successor is Cador's son Constantine.

The second point is that, even in the Welsh stories, Arthur seems to be located in Cornwall, rather than in Wales itself. His capital is Kelliwic. *Celli* means a wood in Cornish, and Kelliwic has been variously identified with Gweek wood on the Helford river, with Kelly Rounds near Damelioc, and with Calliwith near Bodmin, which was the seat of a bishopric from the eighth to the tenth century, and of an abbey from the tenth. Here Bedwini, whose name is not otherwise traceable, may be supposed to have been a bishop. The battle of Camlan is not located in the early documents, but no Welsh alternative to the river Camel in Cornwall has been suggested. If we turn to the *Vitae*, these also, so far as they are precise, seem to put Arthur in the southwest of Britain, although rather in the east of Dumnonia than in Cornwall. It would of course be natural that as Somerset and Devon became Anglicized, traditions once common to the whole of Dumnonia should tend to concentrate themselves in Cornwall, which remained predominantly Celtic.

It is therefore quite a plausible view that, so far as the *Historia* incorporates Celtic traditions, these had developed in Dumnonia, and, while they had certainly spread to Wales, had reached Geoffrey through Breton channels. And now we come back to Geoffrey's alleged *liber*. It was *Britannici sermonis* and was brought by Walter of Oxford *ex Britannia*. I am not going to lay undue stress upon this terminology. In the ordinary Latin of the twelfth century *Britannia* means Brittany, unless it is used historically of the undivided pre-Saxon island. Wales is *Cambria* or *Gualia*. But it has been sufficiently demonstrated that the practice was not uniformly followed by writers of Welsh affinities. It is possible, therefore, so far as language goes, that Geoffrey may have meant to refer to a Welsh book. It is obvious, however, that he may also have meant to refer to a Breton book. A learned historian of Brittany, M. Arthur de la Borderie, thinks that he has found traces of such a book, or at least of a document derived from it. The late fourteenth-century *Chronique de Saint Brieuc* cites upon the conquest of Albion by Brutus and Corineus *nonnullae authenticae historiae*, doubtless those of Geoffrey or his followers. It also cites a *legenda sancti Goeznovii*. Such a *legenda* was seen by Albert Le Grand in the seventeenth century. He describes it as written by William chaplain of Bishop Eudo of Léon in 1019, and composed of nine lessons in prose, interspersed with passages of accentual Latin verse. It was evidently one of the *historiae rhythmicae* or festal offices for saints' days, familiar in mediaeval liturgy. It is not very likely that Le Grand saw an actual manuscript of the eleventh century, in which the name would have been written Guuohednovius. At any rate, no early copy is now known. But there are substantial extracts in a fifteenth-century manuscript once belonging to the cathedral of Nantes, which answer to the description.[1] They include a dedication by William *presbiter* to Bishop Eudo in 1019. No see is, however, named, and no Bishop Eudo of Léon has in fact been traced. The dedication is followed by the notice of Brutus and Corineus, cited as from an *Ystoria Britannica*, and this by an account of the settlement of Armorica by Conan Meriadoc, which differs in several respects from Geoffrey's. There is no mention of Maximian. Various Breton place-names are introduced. And there is a tale of how the invaders cut out the tongues of native women, 'lest through them the British language should be changed,' and took them to wife. The Bretons and the insular British are said to have

[1] *Record* vi.

lived long on friendly terms. The next section tells
of the usurpation of Vortigern, the coming of the
Saxons, the victories of Arthur both in Britain and
in Gaul, and 'when Arthur was called from human
activity' the final Saxon conquest, which led to a
further emigration from Britain to Brittany. Here
the history ends and the life of St Goeznovius begins.
Obviously a Latin *historia rhythmica* does not answer
to the specification of a book in the Breton tongue.
But if any reliance can be placed on the date 1019,
it follows that Breton writers, long before Geoffrey,
had glossed the narratives of Gildas and Nennius
both by making Arthur a conqueror of Gaul and by
introducing the episode of Conan Meriadoc. This is
not likely to have been earlier than about 880 when
Urdisten in his life of St Guenolé only uses Gildas
and not Nennius for his account of the emigration
to Armorica. There was of course plenty of time
between 1019 and 1134 for much further elaboration
and for translation of Latin into Breton. The
ultimate source of Conan Meriadoc is unknown. The
name Meriadoc appears in romance, possibly of
Breton origin. But the invasion story is no part of
that romance.

I need not say that, if anything like the story of
the *Legenda Goeznovii* lay before Geoffrey, he treated
it as arbitrarily as he did the rest of his sources. The
tongueless wives disappear, and to replace them
Geoffrey interweaves a version of the legend of St
Ursula and the eleven thousand virgins, which had
become exceedingly popular in the twelfth century,

owing to 'discoveries' of relics of the saint from 1106 onwards. He probably used a *Passio* of about 1100, in which the name of Ursula's British father first appears as Deonotus. Of course the legend really belongs to Cologne and the fourth-century persecutions of Diocletian. Geoffrey has perhaps been led to divert it to Armorica through his confusion of Diocletian's associate Maximian with the British tyrant Maximus. He has made Dionotus a Cornishman, added Picts to the Huns of the legend, and supplied names for their leaders.

Something must be added as to the origin of Merlin. It can be brief, since Merlin seems to have been wholly a creation of Geoffrey's active brain. This is a hard saying for many Celticists, who cling to a pre-Galfridian Welsh tradition of Merlin. Professor Rhys goes so far as to construct for him an elaborate mythological personality as a Brythonic representative of a Celtic Zeus or Heaven God. But in fact the name of Merlin is untraceable in any assured pre-Galfridian document. He is not with Taliessin and Aneirin in the Nennian list of sixth-century bards. Nor can he, except by an illegitimate transference backwards from the *Historia*, be read into the main narrative of Nennius as the prophetic boy who expounds to Vortigern the omen of the dragons. This was clearly meant to be Vortigern's dreaded rival, the young Ambrosius. He is not in the *Mabinogi* or in *Kulhwch and Olwen*, or in the earliest Welsh poems. There is, indeed, a group of fairly early poems which contain prophecies ascribed to Myrrdin, for so the Welsh wrote the name, and mention in their obscure and allusive way personages and events associated with him in the *Vita Merlini*. Some are in the *Black Book of Carmarthen*; others in the *Red Book of Hergest*. But the balance of opinion among competent scholars regards the majority of these, on grounds both of metre and of historical allusions, as post-Galfridian. It does not, of course, absolutely follow that they were based solely upon Geoffrey, but this seems, in view of the general trend of Welsh twelfth-century literature, the most natural interpretation of them. They are the first examples of an outburst of vernacular prophecies, to which he gave the stimulus, and, like the Latin variations of John of Cornwall, they had many successors throughout the middle ages. The greatest doubt attaches to a dialogue of Myrrdin and Taliessin in the *Black Book*, since this occurs in the first part of the manuscript, which was probably written between 1148 and 1160. It is thought to be more archaic in manner than its fellows, and it has a reference to the battle of Tribruit, which is in Nennius but not in Geoffrey. But it is not demonstrably earlier than the *Vita Merlini* of 1150 or 1151, and there does not seem to be much reason for treating it as of different inspiration from that of the rest of the group. Nor can much stress be laid upon a fairly early triad in which Clas Myrddin is said to have been a name of Britain, since even the earliest triads may not be altogether free from Galfridian influence. I think, then, that Geoffrey, casting about for a mouthpiece of the

Prophecies, in which he proposed to give literary form to the vague rumours of a British hope, invented Merlin, and deliberately identified him with the prophet of Nennius. It seems an audacious proceeding, but Geoffrey had no conscience about prophecies. In the second book of the *Historia* he mentions a prophecy of an eagle which spoke while the wall of Sefovia was building, but declines to give it because he does not think it true. But he reverts to an eagle of Sehstonia in the twelfth book and treats it as prognosticating the return of Cadwallader. The place intended is doubtless Shaston, which is Shaftesbury, and a prophecy of the Eagle of Shaftesbury duly made its appearance in the reign of Henry II. It has been left to modern scholarship to discover that Geoffrey's eagle was lifted from the pages of Pliny, and that it was really an eagle, not of Shaston, but of Sestos on the Hellespont. One can but guess as to where Geoffrey may have got a hint for Merlin's name. It does not seem to carry any suggestion of a hawk, which would be the natural meaning of the Latin word. The Irish St Molingus was a prophet, but he does not seem ever to have been confused with Merlin. Possibly Geoffrey knew of Melinus, introduced in Jocelyn's *Vita Patricii* as a worker of evil, who claims, like Simon Magus, to be God, and is brought low from a flight in the heavens by the prayers of the saint. If so, he has altered the spelling in accordance with his usual love of false etymologies. Merlin is found in the *Historia* at the gates of Carmarthen, which in Welsh is

Caermyrddin, and Geoffrey evidently intends him to be an eponym of the town. But Caermyrddin is really Ptolemy's Maridunum, the *dun* or fort on the sea.

When Geoffrey took up the *Vita Merlini*, he expanded the story of Merlin, as we find it in the *Historia*. There Merlin is a contemporary of Vortigern and Aurelius, and disappears after operating the marvellous conception of Arthur through the shapeshifting of Uther. It is just possible that this was not so in the original issue of the *Prophecies*, and that a trace of an earlier version may survive in the reference under the reign of Cadwallader to a prophecy of Merlin to Arthur. But this may be merely a slip by Geoffrey or a scribe. At any rate, in the *Vita*, Merlin survives Arthur, takes him to the Isle of Apples, and lives to fight in a battle which must be that of Arderydd, placed by the *Annales Cambriae* in 575. Geoffrey is still thinking of his Carmarthen etymology. Historically, the combatants of Arderydd seem to have been all chieftains of the north. But Geoffrey turns one party into princes of Wales, and calls Merlin himself a king of Dyvet, in which Carmarthen lies. In other respects he draws for the *Vita* upon northern stories, and makes a wholesale transfer to Merlin of adventures which really belong to one Lailocen, a madman who figures in various lives and fragments of lives of the Scottish St Kentigern. It is, no doubt, a Celtic tale and has an Irish analogue; but the episodes of divination are of ultimate oriental origin. It is quite clear that

Geoffrey meant the Merlin of the *Vita*, who in fact reviews his relations with Vortigern, to be the same personage as the Merlin of the *Historia*. But the inconsistencies of treatment led to an early confusion by which there were supposed to be two Merlins. The responsibility probably lies with Giraldus Cambrensis, who distinguishes in the *Itinerarium Kambriae* between Merlin Ambrosius and Merlin Calidonius or Sylvester, whom he thinks the older prophet of the two, and claims to have found *Merlinum Silvestrem, diu quaesitum desideratumque* at Nevin in 1188.[1] Presumably he is speaking of some early collection of Welsh imitations of the *Prophecies*.

[1] *Itinerarium Kambriae*, ii. 6 (*Op.* vi. 124).

CHAPTER IV

THE ACCEPTANCE OF ARTHUR

WHATEVER the origin and whatever the good faith of Geoffrey's *Historia*, it had the fortune to win early and enduring acceptance as a credible narrative. We have seen that so serious a historian as Henry of Huntingdon, while greeting his discovery of 1139 with some amazement, did not hesitate to use it as material for the revision of his own work; and that Alfred of Beverley a few years later wrote a summary of its contents and noted the stir it was causing. These are only the precursors of innumerable chroniclers, Latin, English, and French, throughout the middle ages, who treat Geoffrey as the primary authority for their accounts of Celtic Britain. They may question his individual statements or weigh them against those of other writers. They may add details from romance or perhaps here and there from oral tradition. They may exercise their own imaginations in interpretation or expansion. None the less, Geoffrey remains the fundamental source.

Translations and paraphrases soon brought the material of the *Historia* into literature, and a series of vernacular *Bruts* links chronicle to romance. Of Latin adaptations it is only necessary to mention a *Gesta Regum Britanniae* in hexameter verse dedicated about the middle of the thirteenth century to Cadioc, Bishop of Vannes in Brittany, by an anonymous writer, who has been somewhat arbitrarily called Pseudo-Gildas. The Welsh *Bruts* have already been referred to, and all Welsh Arthurian literature, from the *Dream of Rhonabwy* onwards, is much affected by borrowings from Geoffrey. The French *Bruts* probably began with that lost one which preceded the *Lestorie des Engles* of Geoffrey Gaimar. A fragment, not dealing with Arthur, may be preserved in a Munich *MS*. Another version, from Picardy, is also only known in a fragment. And the earliest which has come down to us in full is the *Geste des Bretons* of Maistre Wace, which was completed in 1155 and dedicated to Eleanor, the wife of Henry II. Wace, to whom has been given without authority the baptismal name of Robert, was a Jersey man by birth. He dwelt long at Caen, where he was *cler lisant* under the two Henries and under a third, the 'young king' who died in 1183. Ultimately he became a canon of Bayeux. His *Brut* is a poem of some 15,000 lines in octosyllabic couplets. In structure Wace follows the *Historia* pretty closely, but with a poet's freedom of phrasing, and with much rhetorical embroidery in speeches and descriptive passages. He emphasizes the elements of chivalry and *amour courtois*, laying stress on the character of Gawain and elaborating the relations of Mordred and Guinevere. All this was to be expected of a Norman *trouvère*. He omits the *Prophecies*, of which he could make nothing. Probably he had a better text of Geoffrey than any which has reached us, or at least any which has been printed. A good example of the *trouvère* manner is to be found in the considerable elaboration which Wace gives to the account of Arthur's twelve years of peace between his coronation and the Roman wars. Of Arthur himself he says:

> Jovenciax estoit de quinze ans,
> De son aage fors et grans.
> Chevalier fu mult vertuos,
> Mult proisans et mult glorios,
> Contre orgilleus fu orgillos,
> Et contre humle dols et pitos.
> Mult ama pais, mult ama glore,
> Mult valt son fait metre en memore.
> Servir se fit cortoisement
> Et mult se maintint noblement,
> Tant com il vesqui et raina,
> Fors et hardis et conquerans,
> Et se besoigols le requist,
> S'aider li pot, ne l'escondist.
> Tos autres princes sormonta
> De cortoisie et de proesce
> Et de valor et de largece.

As was Arthur, such was his court:

> Por les nobles barons qu'il ot
> Dont cascuns mieldre estre quidot;
> Cascuns s'en tenoit al millor,
> Ne nus n'en savoit le pior,
> Fist Artus la Roonde Table
> Dont Breton dient mainte fable:
> Iloc seoient li vassal
> Tot chievalment et tot ingal;
> A la table ingalment seoient
> Et ingalment servi estoient.

> Nus d'als ne se pooient vanter
> Qu'il seist plus halt de son per;
> Tuit estoient assis moiain,
> Ne n'i avoit nul de forain.

Thus arose a great fellowship.

> En cele grant pais que jo di,
> Ne sai se vos l'aves oi,
> Furent les mervelles provees
> Et les aventures trovees
> Qui d'Artu sont tant racontees,
> Que a fable sunt atornees:
> Ne tot mençonge ne tot voir
> Tot folie, ne tot savoir;
> Tant ont li conteor conte
> Et li fableor tant fable
> Pour lor contes ambeleter,
> Que tout ont feit fables sanbler.

Arthur's court is thus already in Wace, more definitely than in Geoffrey, reaching its mediaeval status as the mirror of knighthood and centre of romantic *aventures*. Geoffrey's hint as to the relation of *amour courtois* to military prowess is emphasized in the mouth of Gawain.

> Bone est la pais apres la guerre,
> Plus rice et mildre en est li terre.
> Mult sunt bones les gaberies,
> Li deduit et les drueries.
> Por la noblesce de sa mie
> Fait jouenes hom cevalerie.

It is clear from these extracts that, besides the *Historia*, Wace knew of stories which many a *conteor* and *fableor* had already attached to Arthur. But if

he himself drew upon such sources, his borrowings
are insignificant. A possible exception is to be made
for the famous Round Table, which here makes its
first appearance. A discussion of its origin must be
deferred. Wace has other references to it, notably
in his account of Camlan and the death of Arthur,
an account which is more explicit in its mention of
the hope of Arthur's return than is the *Historia* as
we have it.

> La peri la bele jovante
> Que rois Artus avoit norie
> Et de plusieurs teres coillie;
> Et cil de la Table Roonde
> Dont tex los fu par tot le monde.
> Artus, se l'estore ne ment,
> Fu navres el cors mortelement;
> En Avalon se fit porter
> Por ses plaies mediciner.
> Encor i est, Breton l'atandent,
> Si com il dient et entandent;
> De la vandra, encor puet vivre.
> Maistre Gasse qui fit cest livre,
> N'en valt plus dire de sa fin
> Qu'en dist li profetes Merlin.
> Merlins dist d'Artus, si ot droit,
> Que sa fin dotose seroit.
> Li profete dit verite:
> Tostans en a l'on puis dote
> Et dotera, ce crois, tos dis,
> Ou il soit mors, ou il soit vis.
> Porter se fist en Avalon,
> Per voir, puis l'incarnation,
> Sis cens et quarante deus ans;
> Damage fu qu'il not enfans.

> Al fil Cador de Costentin
> De Cornuaille, un sien cosin,
> Livra son raine, si li dist
> Qu'il fut rois, tant qu'il revenist.

It is perhaps a *glossator* who adds in one manuscript:

> Chil prist la terre, si la tint,
> Mais ainc puis Artus ne revint.

Recent research has made it probable that Wace's *Brut* underwent a considerable expansion into a form which has not been preserved, but which seems to have left its traces upon several later works. It may be the *Brut* ascribed in a French romance to a certain Martin of Rochester, who is otherwise unknown. Possibly it arose from a conflation of Wace and Gaimar; possibly it drew upon an oral or written tradition, distinct from that of Geoffrey. The hypothesis has it that this expanded *Brut*, rather than Wace's, was the immediate source of the first English *Brut*, written between 1189 and 1205 in about 32,000 irregular alliterative lines by Layamon, a priest of Arley in Worcestershire. This has many divergences from Wace, some of which recur in French writings, and they are more likely to have been due to a predecessor than to Layamon himself, who shows no signs of Celtic knowledge and whose literary manner is that of the Teutonic epic. If so, the expander of Wace had probably drawn upon Geoffrey's *Vita Merlini*, since Layamon's picturesque account of Arthur's departure for Avalon gives him a companion there in Argante, whose name is best explained as a corruption of Geoffrey's Morgen. The wounded Arthur himself prophesies to Constantine:

'I will to Avalun, to the fairest of maidens, Argante the queen, an elf most fair. And she shall make whole my wounds, and restore me with healing draughts. And after I will come again to my kingdom, and dwell among the Britons in great joy.' Even with the words came a little boat from the sea hard by, floating on the waves, and therein two women, wondrous to look upon. Anon they took Arthur, bearing him swiftly, and laid him gently down, and fared away. Then was it fulfilled what Merlin once spake how great sorrow should be of Arthur's passing. The Britons believe that yet he lives and dwells in Avalun with the fairest of elves, and ever they await his return. Was never man born, or chosen by a woman, who knows the truth, to say more of Arthur. But once was a sage called Merlin; he said with words—and his sayings were truth—that an Arthur should yet come to make an end of the English.

One other touch in Layamon is noteworthy. At the birth of Arthur come elves, and bless the child with the gifts of valour and riches and long life and virtue. If Layamon is writing of his own, these beneficent godmothers are perhaps a borrowing from Teutonic rather than Celtic folklore.

Thus Geoffrey imposed himself upon the mediaeval imagination through the double channel of historic and romantic chronicle. But, before leaving him, it must be pointed out that contemporary learning was not without its notes of dissent. William of Newburgh, composing his *Historia Rerum Anglicarum* in Yorkshire between 1196 and 1198, is explicit enough.[1]

---

[1] *Record* xxviii.

For his *proemium* he still relies upon Bede and Gildas. Gildas was honest. In our own day, on the other hand, has emerged a writer, who attempts to clear the reputation of the Britons by weaving together ridiculous figments and exalting their valour beyond that of Rome and Macedon. This is Geoffrey, surnamed Arthur, from the fables of Arthur which he took from the ancient figments of the Britons and added to on his own account, clothing them in Latin speech to give the colour of an honest history. More audacious still, he has translated and expanded the deceitful divinations of a certain Merlin and sent them abroad as authentic prophecy. The happenings in England since Geoffrey's death reveal these deceits, and no one with any knowledge of ancient history could have a doubt as to his wilful and impudent lying. In particular, William falls foul of Geoffrey's 'Britannic fable' of the transference of Arthur to the island of Avalon, and does not know whether to ascribe it to an unbridled lust for mendacity, or to fear of the Britons, many of whom are said to be so *bruti* that they expect Arthur to come again and cannot endure to hear of his death. The invective of William of Newburgh finds a more humorous parallel in the references of the Welsh ecclesiastic and antiquarian, Giraldus Cambrensis. Giraldus was interested in the metropolitan claims of the see of St David's, of which he hoped to become bishop, and had to meet opponents who probably relied upon Geoffrey's preference for the unhistorical Caerleon in stigmatizing these claims as 'Arthurian

fables.'[1] In his *Itinerarium Kambriae* of 1191 he tells
a story of one Meilerius of Caerleon who claimed the
power of telling truth from falsehood by the help of
daemonic familiars. The devils were exorcised by
placing the Gospel of St John on his bosom, whereat
they flew away like birds and vanished. But when,
adds Giraldus, by way of experiment, the gospel
was removed and Geoffrey Arthur's history of the
Britons put in its place, then the devils all came back
far thicker than before. Some ten years later, in his
Descriptio Kambriae, Giraldus refers more seriously
to a bit of false etymology, *sicut fabulosa Galfridi
Arthuri mentitur historia*. It must be added that
Giraldus does not hesitate on occasion to use the
fabulosa historia as a quotable authority.

But between the days of the *Historia* and those of
its critics there had been some independent development of the Arthurian legend. It has been apparent
throughout the course of this survey that behind the
quasi-historical narrative of Geoffrey lay the persistent Celtic belief in the second coming of Arthur.
This was not apparent in the Welsh literature,
although it might very well have developed in the
national movement of the early twelfth century to
which that literature is related. But Hermann of
Tournai records it as active at Bodmin in 1113, and
apparently also in Brittany about 1146. It is dismissed as *nugae Britonum* and *antiquitas naeniarum* by
William of Malmesbury. Geoffrey himself is obscure
about it in his prophecy of the *exitus dubius*, but

[1] *Record* xxvi (*a*) and (*c*); cf. *Opera*, iii. 78, 328; iv. 149.

adorns it with fancy in the *Vita Merlini*. It was known to Henry of Huntingdon and his friend Warinus Brito in 1139, and is well established in the *Bruts*. The balance of evidence is in favour of treating it as in origin a Breton rather than a Welsh belief. Certainly, however, like other Arthurian notions, it spread to Wales. A *continuator* of Gaimar's *Lestorie des Engles* writes about 1150 of the border fights of Normans and Welsh after the Conquest:[1]

> Apertement le vont disant,
> Forment nus vunt manaçant,
> K'a la parfin tute l'avrunt;
> Par Artur la recoveront,
> E cest païs tut ensement
> Toldrunt a la romeine gent,
> A la terre sun num rendrunt:
> Bretaine la repelerunt.

This may be an anachronism for the date in question. But Giraldus, in the *Descriptio Kambriae* already cited, ascribes precisely the same boast to the Welsh of his own day, and represents them as relying upon the vaticinations of Merlin for its justification. Nevertheless, it is still in Brittany that during the latter part of the twelfth century the belief appears to have been most vivid and to have assumed a political aspect. An important testimony is that of Alain de Lille, commenting in his *Prophetia Anglicana* between 1167 and 1183 on the prophecy of the *exitus dubius*.[2]

---

[1] Gaimar (ed. Rolls Series), i. 278.
[2] *Record* xxii.

That it was most true is proved to-day by the varying opinions of men on Arthur's death and life. If you do not believe me, go to the realm of Armorica, which is lesser Britain, and preach about the market-places and villages that Arthur the Briton is dead as other men are dead, and facts themselves will show you how true is Merlin's prophecy, which says that the ending of Arthur shall be doubtful. Hardly will you escape unscathed, without being whelmed by the curses or crushed by the stones of your hearers.

Beside this account may be set a very curious episode in the Latin poem *Draco Normannicus*, apparently written in 1168 and plausibly ascribed to Etienne de Rouen, a monk of Bec.[1] The subject of the poem is an expedition of Henry II into Brittany during 1167. A little historical retrospective is desirable. After suffering from Norman invasions during the tenth century, the Bretons secured their independence and were long ruled by a succession of native dukes, Conans and Alains and Hoels. In spite of any differences of opinion as to the death of Arthur, they dwelt on fairly good terms with their powerful neighbours. Many of them took part in the Norman invasion of England, and received English lands. Troubles began in 1148 when the heir Conan IV was a minor. He had difficulty in securing his dukedom, and Nantes expelled his supporter Count Hoel in favour of Geoffrey of Anjou, a brother of Henry II. On Geoffrey's death in 1158 both Conan and Henry claimed Nantes. Conan gave way, and when Henry put forward a further demand in 1166 for the tutelage of Brittany and the hand of

[1] *Record* xxi.

its heiress Constance for his own son Geoffrey, was weak enough to abdicate. Then began a long struggle between the despotic Angevin and the patriotic leaders of a rebellious Brittany, among whom was conspicuous one Roland of Dinan. It is to the early years of this struggle that *Draco Normannicus* relates, and Roland figures in its Arthurian episode. As *dapifer* of Arthur he writes a letter to the hero, who was then dwelling *apud antipodes*, and calls upon him for help in person or by deputy against the tyrant. In response Arthur himself writes a letter to Henry, in which he describes at some length his own conflicts with the Romans and with Mordred, his quest of the healing herbs of his sister Morganis in the *insula Avallonis*, and his present domination over the *antipodes*. If any one wants to know more of his deeds let him study them as told by *Monumetensis*. It is noteworthy that the Arthurian details of the poem do not appear to be drawn from any source other than the *Historia* and the *Vita Merlini*. The *antipodes* are presumably due to the poet's own learning. Arthur's epistle concludes with a warning to Henry to leave the Bretons alone, since he has now returned, and is making ready his legions in the woods of Cornwall. Finally we are told how Henry, *subridens sociis*, *nil pavefactus*, reads out the letter, and, lest Arthur should think himself contemned, indites a reply, in which he asserts his claims to Brittany and his intention of completing its conquest. But he will rule as Arthur's vassal.

Hanc sub iure tuo, sub pace tua teneamus.

I I I

This particular writer is of course not quite serious, but it is obvious that the patriotic struggle was likely to lead to an exploitation of the old legend. It lasted to 1181. Then Geoffrey married Constance, warred in his turn with his father, and ruled as Duke of Brittany to his death in 1186. A posthumous son was born on 29 March 1187, and a register records:[1]

Natus est Arturus filius Gauffridi ducis Britanniae, desideratus gentibus.

It is at this time that Glastonbury comes into the story. Here the resting-place of Arthur, unknown to the Welsh poets, unknown to William of Malmesbury, was at last 'discovered.' There are two independent contemporary notices of this event. The fullest is that in the *De Principis Instructione* of Giraldus Cambrensis.[2] This treatise was not published as a whole before 1217, but the first book, in which the narrative occurs, was probably composed between 1193 and 1199. Arthur, according to Giraldus, had been a patron and benefactor of the abbey. And in our days, he says, the body of the king, which fables had made into something fantastic in its ending, as if it had been carried far away by spiritual agency and was not liable to death, was found between two stone pyramids in the churchyard at Glastonbury, and taken honourably to the church for decent burial in a marble tomb. It lay deep in the ground in a hollowed oak, and was marked with wonderful and, as it seemed, miraculous tokens. One

[1] A. de la Borderie, *Hist. de Bretagne*, iii. 286.
[2] *Record* xxvi.

of these was a leaden cross attached to a stone beneath the coffin, with an incised inscription on its inner face towards the stone. This Giraldus had himself seen and traced the lettering, which read *Hic jacet sepultus inclitus rex Arthurus cum Wenneveria vxore sua secunda in insula Avallonia*. He notes the evidence that Arthur had two wives, and says that two-thirds of the coffin held the bones of a man and the other third those of a woman. Here too there was a lock of golden woman's hair, still fresh and full of colour, which was snatched up by a hasty monk, and fell into dust. The search had been motived, partly by indications in abbey records, partly by imperfectly legible inscriptions on the pyramids, partly by visions and revelations of religious men, but mainly by the advice of Henry II, who told the monks on the authority of an old British singer that they would find the body sixteen feet deep and not in stone but in a hollowed oak. This depth of burial and the concealment of the inscription was intended to preserve the remains from disturbance in the event of the Saxons occupying the island after Arthur's death. The thigh-bone and skull, which the abbot showed to Giraldus, were of gigantic size, and on the latter were ten wounds, all of which had healed except one great one, which was evidently the cause of death. A quarter of a century later, in his *Speculum Ecclesiae*, Giraldus gave a very similar account, with some moralizings on *mundana pulchritudo*, as illustrated by the incident of the monk and the tress. But here he introduces confusion into the chronology, by dating the discovery at once in the reign of Henry II, who died on 6 July 1189, and in the time of Abbot Henry, who was appointed later in 1189, and became Bishop of Worcester in 1193. The date is given as 1191 in the *Chronicon Anglicanum*, compiled for the years 1187 to 1224 by Ralph of Coggeshall.[1] This was followed by several later chronicles, such as the *Chronica Majora* of the St Albans historians. Ralph has much less wealth of detail than Giraldus. He ascribes the discovery to the desire of a monk to be buried between the pyramids, the letters on which were illegible. He mentions the leaden cross, gives the inscription, differently from Giraldus, as *Hic jacet inclitus rex Arturius in insula Avallonis sepultus*, and adds that Glastonbury, once surrounded by marshes, was called the island of Avallon, which meant the island of apples. Ralph's version of the inscription is nearly that given by Leland from a cross which he saw on the tomb of Arthur in the sixteenth century. The version of Giraldus, with its quite exceptional record of Guinevere as a second wife of Arthur, remains a puzzle.

These contemporary records do not come from Glastonbury itself. Adam of Domerham, who was a monk of the abbey and wrote its history about 1291, cannot have been an eye-witness. But he would have had abbey tradition to draw upon. Adam calls the abbot Henri of Sully (*de Soliaco*). He says that Arthur had been buried for 648 years, and as he probably reckoned from Geoffrey's date of 542 for

[1] *Record* xxv.

Camlan, the discovery may have been in 1190, not 1191. Perhaps he adds a significant detail, when he tells us that, on the day when he gave the order to dig, the abbot had the spot surrounded with curtains.[1]

We have now, however, to consider, not so much the good faith of Abbot Henry, as the purposes which the 'discovery' may have been intended to serve, and the relations, if any, between Glastonbury and the Arthurian legend before 1190. Had there, in fact, been any earlier identification of Glastonbury and Avalon? The answer would be easier if we could rely upon the *De Antiquitate Glastoniensis Ecclesiae* of William of Malmesbury, as it is preserved in the Trinity College, Cambridge, manuscript of the middle of the thirteenth century, which seems once to have belonged to Adam of Domerham. But two recent and independent investigations have made it quite clear that only a nucleus of this can be the authentic work of William.[2] These appear to be the facts. When William completed the original version of his *Gesta Regum* about 1125, he regarded Glastonbury as a foundation of Ina, King of Wessex, in the eighth century. Later he made a careful study of the abbey records and came to the conclusion that Ina's was only a refoundation, and that there had been a long prehistory. On one of the pyramids in the church-yard and in a painting in the church itself he found the names of certain British abbots, and he accepted

[1] *Record* xxxiv.
[2] Cf. the treatises of W. W. Newell and J. Armitage Robinson cited in *Bibliographical Note*.

as genuine a donation by a king of Dumnonia in 601, in which one of these, Bregored, appeared as a witness. This king, he thought, must have been a Briton, since he called the land donated Ineswitrin. He believed that St Patrick had been one of the abbots, that Gildas and Bridget and other Celtic saints had been sojourners, and that the relics of Aidan and Bede had been translated from Northumbria. On the main issue of the Celtic antiquity of the religious settlement, there is no reason to differ from William's view. That part of Somerset in which Glastonbury is situated did not come under the domination of the Saxons until a date at which they were no longer likely to destroy a Christian shrine. No doubt the historian was on less sound ground when he credited the belief that the church had been built by missionaries from Pope Eleutherius in the second century, since the story of this mission is now known to rest upon an error in the Roman *Liber Pontificalis*. A variant account which would ascribe it to disciples of St Philip the Apostle he politely waves aside as probably *opinionum naenias*. William put his researches into a treatise on the antiquity of the church, which he dedicated to Henry of Blois, who was abbot from 1126 to 1171, and he also incorporated them in passages which he added to a new edition of the *Gesta Regum* between 1135 and 1140. These passages appear, so far as the British period is concerned, to contain all the substance of the original *De Antiquitate*; and nothing of importance in the Trinity College manuscript is likely to proceed from William unless it receives support from the *Gesta Regum*. The alterations and interpolations are numerous and extensive. They replace William's cautious and scholarly conclusions by confident assertions. They add many unverifiable details about the Celtic saints. They adopt both the evangelization legends, and attempt to combine them with the aid of a fictitious narrative in a *Carta* ascribed to St Patrick. This professes to provide indulgences for pilgrims, of a kind quite impossible before the latter part of the twelfth century. Other evidences of late date are to be found in borrowings from Geoffrey of Monmouth, and in allusions to the death of Henry of Blois and to a fire which destroyed the church in 1184.

All the references to Arthur in the *De Antiquitate* belong to the interpolated matter.[1] Glastonbury, for which the only British name given in the *Gesta Regum* is Ineswitrin, is in three places called the isle of Avallon. Two sections are specially devoted to the hero, whom William never connects with Glastonbury. After describing several burials, the writer says:

I pass over Arthur, the famous King of the Britons, entombed with his wife in the graveyard of the monks between two pyramids, and over many other British princes. This Arthur, in the year of the incarnation 542, was mortally wounded by Mordred near the river Camba in Cornwall, and thence was born to the island of Avallon for the healing of his wounds, and died there in the summer about Pentecost, being nearly a hundred years old or thereabouts.

[1] *Record* xxiii.

The date 542 is presumably from Geoffrey of Monmouth; the basis for making Arthur a centenarian is unknown. Considerably later in the manuscript comes a section headed *De illustri Arturo*. This is a story from the *gesta* of the king. Arthur was keeping Christmas at Caerleon, and had given knightly decoration to a brave youth, Ider, the son of King Nuth. By way of trial, he took him to the Hill of Frogs, now called Brentecnol, to fight against three wicked giants who were known to harbour there. Ider outstripped Arthur and his company and slew the giants alone. When Arthur came up he found Ider overcome with toil and unconscious, took him for dead, and mourned over him. He then returned home, leaving the body until a vehicle could be sent for it. And deeming his own slowness the cause of the youth's death, he established twenty-four monks for his soul, with possessions and lands, and liberal gifts of gold and silver, chalices and other ornaments of the church. A forged charter of Henry II, apart from the *De Antiquitate*, professes to confirm donations to Glastonbury by Arthur among others, and a marginal note to the Trinity College manuscript names Brentemareys as given by him.

It is probable that the process of interpolating the *De Antiquitate* was a gradual one, and extended well into the thirteenth century. The *marginalia* in the manuscript may be due to Adam of Domerham himself. An isolated appearance of the name of Joseph of Arimathea among those of the first evangelizers looks like a late gloss. There is no further reference to him in the document, such as would be expected if his cult at Glastonbury had reached its full proportions before the compilation was complete. This is a topic which belongs to a discussion of the Grail legend, rather than of Arthur. The first half of the thirteenth century is also a likely date to which to ascribe the *Carta* of St Patrick with its indulgences. This is recorded in a list of the abbey muniments in 1247, but not in a list of privileges confirmed by Pope Innocent III between 1198 and 1216. On the other hand, a starting-point for the whole business may very plausibly be found in the disastrous fire of 1184 by which both the churches and most of the abbey buildings were consumed. The abbey was then vacant, and Henry II, who held the temporalities, assigned them in full to his Chamberlain, Ralph Fitz-Stephen, for the purposes of rebuilding. The church of St Mary on the site of the original *vetusta ecclesia* was already complete before the death of Henry II and the appointment of Abbot Henry in 1189 cut off this source of revenue. A beginning had also been made with the greater church to the east. But there was still much to do, and the financial stringency was increased in 1193, when the pretension of Bishop Savaric to hold the abbacy as a dependency of Wells led to a quarter of a century of costly litigation at Rome. There was an obvious temptation to exalt the claims of Glastonbury to antiquity and the possession of relics, and thereby to attract the offerings of pilgrims. And if Arthur was only a hero of romance and not a saint, his fame too might help the good work. The researches of M. Joseph Bédier upon the Charlemagne romances have shown how much of their development was due to the enterprise of those responsible for the maintenance of shrines upon the haunted way from France to Spain. The discovery of Arthur's tomb in 1190 came, therefore, at a very fortunate time for the abbey. There is no very obvious reason why the Arthur and Avallon passages in the *De Antiquitate* should not all belong to about this same period. It is true that the passage in his burial does not in terms refer to the discovery, as might have been expected if it had already taken place. But it shows a more precise knowledge of the exact spot than either Giraldus or Ralph of Coggeshall give us any reason to suppose that the abbey had previously claimed to possess. On the other hand, I do not feel clear that the Ider story may not be of earlier date. It is in a quite distinct section of the *De Antiquitate* from that which deals with the burial; and it will be observed that the two propositions—'Arthur was buried in Glastonbury, which is Avallon' and 'Arthur gave Brent to Glastonbury'—are in no way mutually dependent, and may well have been evolved at different times. And in fact the conception of Arthur as a benefactor of Glastonbury is certainly much earlier than 1190. It comes, although with no specific mention of Brent, in the *Vita Gildae* ascribed to Caradoc of Llancarfan, which has already been considered.[1] The date of Caradoc's death is uncertain. A Welsh notice, not

[1] *Record* xx; cf. ch. iii.

earlier than the fifteenth century and of uncertain authority, puts it in 1156. Evidently he was alive, when Geoffrey of Monmouth referred to him at the end of the *Historia* about 1135. Ider is one of the older figures in the Arthurian *comitatus*, and the manner of his story so closely resembles that of Melvas in the *Vita Gildae*, that it might very well be by the same hand. Nor is a twelfth-century motive lacking, which might fit in with the date of Caradoc, in certain disputes between Glastonbury and Wells as to the church of South Brent, which ended with its cession as a prebend of Wells in 1173.

Avallon as a name for Glastonbury must, I think, go with the burial story. The only British name is Ineswitrin in the *Gesta Regum* and Ynisgutrin in the *Vita Gildae*, which adds that it was still so called by the native Britons, that *ynis* meant island and *gutrin* glassy (*vitrea*), and that the English translated it into Glastigberi, with the same sense of *Vitrea Civitas*. Glastonbury is first Avallon in Ralph of Coggeshall and Giraldus Cambrensis. Ralph calls it *insula Avallonis*, glosses this as *insula pomorum*, and explains that it was an island surrounded by marshes. Giraldus in the *De Principis Instructione* uses the form *insula Avallonia*, and says that Glastonbury was so called *antiquitus* in Celtic and that Inis Avallon meant *insula pomifera*. The reason was that it abounded with apples, for which the British is *aval*. And he adds, rather oddly,

Therefore Morganis, a noble matron who was ruler and patron of those parts and akin to King Arthur by blood, took him after the battle of Kemelen to the island which is now called Glastonbury for the healing of his wounds.

Some connection seems to have been present in the mind of Giraldus between apples and healing. He knows that the island was also called Inis gutrin and gives the same explanation as the *Vita Gildae* of the equivalence of this with Glastingeburi. The account in the *Speculum Ecclesiae* is substantially the same, but here Giraldus gives an alternative etymology. The name may be from *aval*, or it may be from one Vallo (apparently a scribal error for Avallo), once a ruler of that territory. The Ider story in the interpolated *De Antiquitate* only speaks of Glastonia, and the passage on Arthur's burial names the *insula Avallonis* without comment. But a separate section has a curious story which elaborates the apple theme. The eponym of the island was Glasteing of the race of Cunedda, who was in pursuit of a pig from Wells, and found it under an apple tree, whence it had come down that the fruits of that tree were traditionally called the Old Church apples and the way to Wells the Sow Way. And the interpolator or another adds an excursus *De diversis nominibus eiusdem insulae*. It was called Ynswytrin which the Saxons interpreted as Glastinbiry; or perhaps this was from the Glasteing already told of. It is also notoriously (*celebriter*) called the *insula Avalloniae*, and this name means the island of apples and was given to it by Glasteing who found apples there, a rare fruit in those parts. Or it may be called after one Avalloc, who is said to have dwelt there with his daughters, for the secrecy of the spot. Most of this twelfth-century etymologizing we may of course dismiss. It is probable that Witrin is really a personal name, and pretty certain that Glastonbury, of which an eighth-century form is Glestingaburg, is really the 'burh' or fortified place of the Glestings. That Iniswitrin was the proper Celtic name of the island and Avallon an afterthought of about 1190 seems beyond question. The duplication of terminology remains unconcealed in the documents. To Avallon as a Celtic name for the Otherworld I shall return. Here it is only necessary to note that the Otherworld was also represented as an isle of glass, and that a poet's use of this conception for the realm of Melvas may perhaps have given a hint for the identification of Avallon with Glastonbury.[1]

Arthur, *desideratus gentibus*, was born in 1189, and the grave of Arthur, *inclytus rex*, was found a year later. Whatever the motive of the abbey officials, it is possible that Henry II, if he was really concerned in the matter, may have had another in the desire to put an end to the 'British hope' by a demonstration that the long-expected hero was veritably dead. If so, he was imperfectly successful. Giraldus, repeating his euhemerism about the noble matron Morganis in the *Speculum Ecclesiae* of 1216, is still contending against the *fabulosi Britones* and their *cantores*, who have made her into a *dea quaedam phantastica*, and believe that, when she has healed Arthur's wounds:

The King will return in strength and power, to rule over the Britons, as they think, according to his wont; wherefore

[1] Cf. p. 212.

they still await his coming, even as the Jews their Messiah, deceived by an even greater folly and unhappiness, and infidelity to boot.

Even a century later, the 'hope' was still capable of recrudescence, now in Wales, as a political creed. After the fall of Llywelyn ap Gruffyd in 1282, the crown of Arthur was one of the *jocalia* ceded to the victorious Edward I at Carnarvon.[1] 'And thus,' says the chronicler, the glory of the Welsh, although against their will, was transferred to the English.' But still a biographer of Edward II can record the confidence of sporadic rebels, based upon the sayings of Merlin, in an ultimate recovery of the whole island.[2] 'They are often deceived,' he adds, 'and labour in vain, because they do not know the appointed time.' In the main, however, even before the *Speculum Ecclesiae* was issued, the notion of Arthur's survival was beginning to pass, with such writers as Gervase of Tilbury, into the realm of sheer folk-lore, which is not for this chapter. If the later chroniclers sometimes profess not to know whether Arthur is alive or dead, that is obviously a mere convention. Meanwhile, Arthur himself was becoming an English rather than a Celtic hero. The kings of chivalry revere him. Richard I, crusading to the Holy Land, gave Arthur's sword Caliburnus to Tancred of Sicily on 6 March 1191.[3] It is not said that he professed to have found it with the bones. Perhaps it is a reasonable inference that he did; and if so, as the

1 *Record* xxxiii.   2 *Record* xxxvi.
3 *Record* xxvii.

124

chroniclers began their years with 25 March, Adam of Domerham's 1190 and not Ralph of Coggeshall's 1191 is the right date for the 'discovery.' On 19 April 1278 Edward I, who was keeping Easter at Glastonbury with Queen Eleanor, ordered the opening of Arthur's tomb.[1] The bones were found in two coffers, adorned with images and arms. The queen's image was crowned, but the king's crown had come away. His left ear had been cut off, and there were marks of his death-wound. Apparently the tomb had stood up to 1278 in a chapel near the south door of the greater church leading to the treasury. The exact locality of this is not identified in Mr Bond's reconstruction of the ruins. The head-bones were removed as relics, and the tomb replaced for a time, 'until it could be more decently disposed of elsewhere,' and ultimately transferred to the middle of the presbytery before the high altar. Here it was in 1428.[2]

> At Glastynbury on the queer,
> They made Artourez toumbe there,
> And wrote with latyn vers thus
> Hic jacet Arthurus, rex quondam, rexque futurus.

And here Leland saw it, when he visited Abbot Whiting between 1534 and 1539.[3] It was of black marble. There were two lions at each end, and an image of the king at the foot; and there were epitaphs bearing the name of Abbot Henry, which is here

[1] *Records* xxxiii, xxxiv; cf. Leland, *Assertio Arturii* (1544), 137.
[2] *Liber Rubeus Bathoniae* (*E.E.T.S.*).
[3] *Itinerarium*, i. 288.

given as Henricus Swansey. They did not include the words of the 1428 poem, but ran:

> Hic jacet Arturus flos regum, gloria regni,
> Quem mores, probitas commendant laude perenni

and

> Arturi jacet hic conjux tumulata secunda
> Quae meruit coelos virtutum prole fecunda.

So too Adam of Domerham records them. Leland saw and handled the leaden cross which lay upon the tomb. This is said to have remained in the possession of a Hughes family of Wells, to the eighteenth century.[1] John of Glastonbury, at the beginning of the fifteenth century, tells us that a *crux cristallina, quam beata virgo contulit inclito regi Arthuro* was then also among the relics of the insatiable monks. One other sixteenth-century reminiscence is worth quoting. Sir John Harington, among other discursive notes in his translation of the *Orlando Furioso* (1591), put this upon Arthur:

He was himselfe of stature very tall, as appeares by the proportion of him left (as they say here in our countrey of Somerset) in a doore of a Church by the famous Abbey of Glassenbury, in which Abbey his wife Queene Guenever was buried, and within our memory taken up in a coffin, with her body and face in shew plainly to be discerned, save the very tip of her nose, as divers dwelling thereabout have reported. But what manner of death King Arthur himselfe died, it is doubtfull, and that which they report seems meerly fabulous, namely that he was carried away in a barge from a bridge called Pomperles, neare the said Glassenbury, and so conveyed by unknown persons (or by the Ladie of the

[1] Robinson (1926), 58.

Lake) with promise to bring him back againe one day: upon which it seemes the foolish people grounded their vaine saying (King Arthur comes againe).

I do not know any other record of this third exhumation, presumably after the monastery was dissolved. The great king in the north doorway of St Mary's chapel is Herod. But are we to infer that the persistent folk of the sixteenth century had come to believe that only Guinevere was found in 1190 and not Arthur? Leland saw the 'bridge called *Pontperlus*, wher men fable that *Arture* cast in his swerd,' so that evidently the battle as well as the burial had been localized. The bridge, rebuilt, still stands over the Brue, and a 'pont perilous' at Glastonbury was known to the author of the English *Libeaus Desconus* before 1350.[1]

I return to the Anglicizing of Arthur. In the middle of the thirteenth century he begins to figure in the *ludi* of the English court, where the Round Table gave its name to a form of joust. It is not quite clear how this differed from the ordinary tournament. It was fought on horseback with blunted lances, in the presence of ladies, and it may be presumed that it had a mimetic element, with champions figuring as Arthur's knights. The earliest *mensa rotunda* upon record was at Wallingford in 1252; the next at Kenilworth in 1279; a third at Nevin in Carnarvon-shire in 1284 formed part of the triumph over Wales.[2] The exercise was used on the Continent as well as in

---

[1] Robinson (1926) 28.   [2] *Records* xxxii, xxxiii, xxxv.

England, and its primary inspiration may be due to romance rather than to politics. But an intention to treat Arthur as a patron of England was clearly manifest, when Edward III, after a three days' hastilude at Windsor in 1344, took a solemn vow to re-establish the company of the Round Table as Arthur had left it, to the number of at least three hundred knights, and gave orders for a *domus* two hundred feet in diameter to be built for its sessions.[1] Probably this was never finished. The preparations for war with France delayed its progress. Moreover, it came to Edward's knowledge that Philip of Valois was busied on a Round Table of his own, in order to deter the chivalry of Italy and Germany from resort to England. There was a feast in 1345 and then no more, and when the English order of knighthood came to be set up in 1348, it was an Order of the Garter and not the Round Table, and St George, not Arthur, was its patron. On the other hand, Cambridge, a century later, chose to claim Arthur as its founder, in reply to the Oxford tradition of Alfred.

Nor was the affiliation of the English dynasty to Arthur of service for sportive purposes alone. When Edward I, in 1301, laid his case for dominion over Scotland before Pope Boniface VIII, he supported it with many arguments drawn from the veridical pages of Geoffrey of Monmouth, including the tenure of the realm by Auguselus as a vassal of Arthur.[2] It is not, therefore, surprising that, as Scottish national

[1] *Record* xxxviii. [2] Rymer, *Foedera*, i. 932.

feeling developed, chroniclers on the other side of the Tweed adopted an attitude towards the *Historia* somewhat different from that prevalent in England. They do not reject the narrative, but they give it a new balance, and colour it with their own judgment of the personalities involved. There is a trans-valuation of all values. This tendency is first apparent in the *Chronica Gentis Scotorum* of John Fordun about 1385, and reaches its full proportions in Hector Boece's *Scotorum Historia* of 1527. The Scots and even the Picts are treated as allies of the Britons against the Saxons. There is an exaltation of Loth and his house. Loth is King of Pictland, and, since Arthur is illegitimate, Loth's marriage with Anna makes Mordred the rightful heir to Britain. Arthur's character is depreciated throughout. He is allowed no foreign conquests. His courtly gatherings are wanton revels. And he is fundamentally treacherous. The war in which he dies is due to the breach of his promise to recognize Mordred as his heir. The final battle in which the kings fall is on the Humber, and thereafter Guinevere is carried away to life-long captivity in Pictland. Here she dies, and here is her tomb. The Scottish view of Arthur is summed up in the closing words of one of Boece's translators:

> Considdering all his infelicitie,
> Haif e to richt and lat affectioun be,
> I hald him for the maist vnhappie king
> Off all the Britis that did in Britane ring.
> For-quhy he wes so faithles and wntrew
> To king Modred, befoir as I 30w schew,

And manesworn als, the hand of God thairfore,
As ressone wald, it tuechit him full soir.
Britis before quhilk wes of sic renoun,
Sensyne tha tynt baith thair kinrik and croun;
As plesis God, till all men weill is kend,
Falsheid come neuir till ane better end.[1]

We are far here from the native judgment of
Caxton, in the preface to his print of Malory's
Morte Arthur in 1485. For Caxton Arthur is the
head of the Nine Worthies, 'the most renowmed
Christian king, first and chief of the three best
Christian and worthy, which ought most to be remembered among us Englishmen tofore all other
Christian kings,' and his court a mirror of 'joyous
and pleasant histories, and noble and renowmed acts
of humanity, gentleness and chivalries.' Caxton
knows, indeed, that there are those who 'hold opinion
that there was no such Arthur, and that all such
books as been made of him been feigned and
fables, because that some chronicles make of him no
mention, ne remember him nothing, ne of his
knights.' Perhaps Caxton is thinking of Ranulph
Higden, a translation of whose *Polychronicon* (1327–
42) he had already printed.[2] Higden had asked
ironically how it was that, if Arthur, as Geoffrey
claims, had conquered thirty kingdoms, and subdued
the King of France, and slain a Roman governor in
Italy, none of the Roman and French and Saxon
historians, who told so many lesser things of lesser

[1] W. Stewart, *Chronicles of Scotland*, 27977.
[2] *Record* xxxvii.

men, had taken any notice of his deeds. But Higden in the fourteenth century, like William of Newburgh in the twelfth, is only a solitary voice against the general acceptance of the Galfridian legend around him. And even in the sixteenth, a similar criticism by Polydore Virgil was to arouse a storm of protest from Leland and others. But for Caxton himself, although he puts the words in the mouth of an imaginary disputant, 'in him that should say or think that there was never such a king called Arthur, might well be aretted great folly and blindness.' And he can cite material evidences to the contrary, the Glastonbury sepulchre and other remembrances of Arthur and his knights in divers places of England.

First in the abbey of Westminster, at St Edward's shrine, remaineth the print of his seal in red wax closed in beryl, in which is written, *Patricius Arthurus Britannie, Gallie, Germanie, Dacie Imperator*. Item in the castle of Dover ye may see Gawaine's scull, and Cradok's mantle: at Winchester the Round Table: in other places Launcelot's sword and many other things. Then all these things considered, there can no man reasonably gainsay but there was a king of this land named Arthur.

The seal at Westminster is described also in John Rastell's *Pastime of the People* (1529), and in Leland's *Assertio Inclytissimi Arturii* (1544). I do not know what became of this; it does not appear in any of the published inventories taken at the dissolution of the abbey. The Winchester Round Table still hangs in the old castle hall. Probably it is a relic of some joust or pageant. It is first mentioned in the *Chronicle* of John Hardyng (1457–64). It is known to have been repaired in 1517, and its present decoration, in the Tudor white and green and with the Tudor double rose, can hardly be older. Most but not all of the names of knights inscribed upon it are to be found in Malory.

CHAPTER V

ARTHUR AND THE ROUND TABLE

IT does not fall within the scope of this essay to give any full account of the *matière de Bretagne* as one of the three great divisions of French romance. But something must be said of the origin of that *matière*, and of its relation to the quasi-historical presentment of Arthur left by Geoffrey. This presentment, passing through the *Bruts*, had an authority to which the romance writers constantly defer. It fixed the central conception of the adventurous British court and its tragic ending. But it was by no means the only channel for the infiltration of Celtic motives into French literature. There are indications that Arthurian names and even Arthurian stories may have spread over the Continent before Geoffrey wrote. Too much stress must not be laid on the names. Men were called Tristanus and Yvanus near Lake Constance in the eighth and ninth centuries, and Artusius, Walwanus and Merlinus in late eleventh-century or early twelfth-century Italy. Merlinus, no doubt, may well have had some other derivation. The forms Artusius and Walwanus look as if they had passed through the French. The names do not by themselves testify to more than the presence on the Continent of Bretons or other Celts who bore them. More significant is a sculpture on the archivolt of the *Porta della Pescheria* of the Duomo at Modena. It represents a tower besieged by armed knights, and most of the figures bear names. In the tower stand Mardoc and a woman, Winlogee. From one door issues a horseman Carrado, meeting three others, Galvaginus, Galvariun and Che; from the other an axeman on foot, Burmaltus or Durmaltus, also meeting three horsemen, of whom two are Artus de Bretania and Isdernus. Some of the personages are obscure, but we can recognize Arthur, Meriadoc, Caradoc, Gawain, Kay and Ider. The Duomo was begun by one Wiligelmo in 1099 and finished in 1184. Some writers think that the sculpture belongs to a late stage of the work, but the balance of expert opinion, based partly on the style of the armour, puts it in the first half of the century, and perhaps quite early in that period. There is similar work at Bari and Bobbio, and the most recent investigator is confident that he can prove an origin in a *conte* told at a visit of Alain Fergent, Duke of Brittany, to Bari in 1096.[1] The proof has, however, not yet appeared.

We know from Wace that *li conteor* and *li fableor* were embroidering the history of Arthur before 1155. He does not say whether they were French or Celtic. Nor does he furnish any distinction between the two terms which he uses; they may be synonymous. To such tales we perhaps owe the Round Table, as well as later accretions to Wace, which are reflected in Layamon. The earliest extant French handling of

[1] R. S. Loomis (*J.E.G.P.* xxiii. 484).

the *matière de Bretagne*, outside the *Bruts*, is to be found in the *lais* of Marie de France. We know little with certainty of Marie. She tells us herself that she was *de France* and dedicates her *lais* to a *nobles reis*, who was probably Henry II of England. A contemporary calls her *dame*. She has been conjecturally identified with an illegitimate sister of Henry, who became Abbess of Shaftesbury; and also with Marie Countess of Champagne, the daughter of Henry's wife Eleanor of Poitou by her first husband Louis VII of France. She writes in French, with dialectic touches which suggest the Norman border of the Île de France. Twelve of her *lais* are preserved in a thirteenth-century manuscript. They may date from about 1165–67. In most cases she claims to take them from *contes*, on which *li Bretun* had made *lais*. To the precise meaning of this I will recur. They are all short narrative poems, of less than a thousand lines, in octosyllabic couplets. There are tales of licit or more often illicit love, of battles and tournaments, of children lost and found again, of tasks to be achieved and tests to be undergone. Many of the themes are common to the popular literature of all countries; they draw on folk-superstitions; on werewolves and speaking animals; on magic ships, food and drink and tokens; on shape-shifting and fairy lovers. Most of the personages are Bretons, and most of the action takes place in Brittany. Once it is in Normandy, once in Cornwall, and thrice, wholly or in part, in Loengre, which is insular Britain. The Cornish story (*Chievrefeuil*) is of Tristan and Iseult. Marie's only definitely Arthurian story is *Lanval*. Arthur is keeping his Pentecost at Kardoil. This is Carlisle, which the romance writers make a chief seat of Arthur. He is engaged in preserving Loengre from the Picts and Scots. Lanval is a friend of Walwain and Yvain, but a poor knight, who has had no gift from Arthur. He obtains a fairy mistress, under a taboo of secrecy, and by her is made rich. Then the queen, who is not named, falls in love with him, is rejected, and adopts the methods of Potiphar's wife. Lanval breaks his taboo, by declaring that he has a mistress of far greater beauty than the queen. He is to die unless he can prove it. At the critical moment the fairy appears to be the proof, and carries Lanval away to Avallon, *en un isle qui mult est beals*.

But, if Arthur's court was not essential to the Celtic borrowings of Marie de France, it is otherwise in the more fully developed romances of Chrétien de Troyes. And it is Chrétien who really fixes the *genre* of the *matière de Bretagne* for French poetry, as it has been preserved to us. He was a man of some classical learning and made translations of Ovid. It has been thought that he visited England, and it has been thought that he was a herald; but both points are uncertain. However this may be, his days were spent in the atmosphere of courts; firstly that of Marie de Champagne herself at Troyes, and afterwards that of Philip of Alsace Count of Flanders, either at Paris, where Philip was for some time Regent of France, or at Bruges. An early romance on Tristan is lost, and of six that survive, one of *Guillaume d'Angleterre* is not certainly his. The other five have all an Arthurian setting. Their dates are variously ascribed between 1160 and 1180, or even later, but their order is fairly certain. Probably the *Erec*, *Cliges*, *Conte de la Charrete* and *Yvain* followed each other during Chrétien's service of Marie, whose wedding was in 1164; the *Conte del Graal* was certainly begun for Philip of Flanders. In *Cliges* the Arthurian element is only slight. The personages are princes of Constantinople, and here the main action takes place. Alexander, the father of Cliges, visits Britain for knighthood, and helps Arthur to recover Windsor from a Mordred-like rebel, Engres. Dying, he enjoins Cliges to follow his example. This Cliges does, and wins distinction against Arthur's knights in a tourney. It does not affect his real story, of a love-affair with Fenice the wife of the emperor, whom he wins through the device of a magic potion, which throws her into a trance mistaken for death. When the fraud is discovered, the lovers sojourn with Arthur, until the death of the emperor enables them to return and live happily at Constantinople. Obviously the connection with Britain is here external and artificial. It is more fundamental in *Erec* and *Yvain*, since the heroes of these are themselves British. *Erec* begins with the chase of a white hart, the prize for which is to be a kiss from the fairest damsel at court. Erec leaves the chase, to chastise a strange knight, who has been insolent to Guinevere. This is Ider, son of Nut. Erec defeats him at a tourney for a sparrow-hawk, and sends him to Arthur, whose retinue he joins. Erec marries Enid, the daughter of a poor vavasour, who has lent him a horse and arms for the tourney. She is declared the fairest damsel, and Erec shines in a tourney at court. He then falls into sloth, and Enid incurs his anger by observing it. There follows a story of the Patient Griselda type. Enid accompanies Erec through a series of loosely-knit adventures, during which he will not speak to her, until her submission and helpfulness bring about a reconciliation. In one of these episodes, Erec, already wounded, unhorses Kay, and is brought by Gawain to court, where his wounds are healed with an ointment of Morgain la Fée, the sister of Arthur. The final adventure is that of the Joie de la Cour, in which Erec, by defeating a knight, releases a damsel from spell-bound sleep in an orchard ringed round with a magic wall of air. He now succeeds to his father's kingdom, and is crowned by Arthur at Nantes. In *Yvain* the hero leaves Arthur's court to attempt the adventure of the Fountain of Broceliande in Brittany, where water thrown on a stone evokes a storm. He slays the defender of the fountain, enters his castle, is made invisible with a magic ring by the damsel Lunete, marries Laudine, the widowed lady of the castle, and becomes himself the defender of the fountain. Arthur in turn tries the adventure, but Yvain avoids a fight with him. He obtains permission from Laudine to follow Arthur for a year, but over-stays his time, becomes mad as a result, and is cured by Morgain's ointment. There is again a loose sequel of adventures. Yvain acquires a helpful lion by rescuing him from a serpent. He frees Lunete from a false accusation. He slays a giant. He fights with Gawain. He destroys an evil custom of the Isle of Maidens, by which girls are annually offered to monsters. Finally he returns to the fountain, and is reconciled by Lunete to Laudine. In the *Conte de la Charrete*, Chrétien handles a more central Arthurian theme. It is in essentials the story of the abduction of Guinevere by Melvas which we found in the *Vita Gildae*. Meleagant, son of Baudemagus King of Gorre, whose capital is Bade, comes to court. He has many of Arthur's subjects captive in his father's realm. It is a land *don nus estranges ne retorne*, reached only by two bridges, of which one is a sword-edge and the other under water. Meleagant offers to restore the prisoners, if he may take Guinevere, and if a knight can recover her from him in single combat. Kay claims the adventure, and is defeated. But Gawain and Lancelot have also set out. Lancelot loses his horse and reluctantly accepts unknightly transport in a cart. He crosses the sword-bridge, and rescues Guinevere. She is cold to him, on account of his hesitation at the cart; but relents when he attempts suicide, and a love affair begins. Lancelot, entering the queen's window by night, cuts his hand on the bars, and the traces of blood bring suspicion on Guinevere of relations with the wounded Kay. Lancelot undertakes to fight Meleagant again in her defence, but Meleagant decoys him into prison. Meanwhile Gawain leads Guinevere back to Arthur.

Here Chrétien resigned the pen to Godefroi de Leigni, who wrote a conclusion in which Lancelot escapes and slays Meleagant. Unfinished also, and an enigma for ever, was Chrétien's *Conte del Graal*. It is of Perceval li Galois. He is brought up unchivalrously by a widow mother in a Welsh forest. He rides to Arthur's castle of Carduel, and a fool prophesies that he will be the best knight in the world. He is knighted and slays a red knight, who has taken a golden cup from Arthur. After divers adventures, in the course of which an old knight warns him not to talk too much, he reaches a castle to which he is directed by a man fishing in a river. He finds the lord of the castle lying on a couch, and is given a sword, which will break in one peril, known only to its forger. Then enters a procession; a lad with a bleeding lance, two more with lighted candles, a maiden bearing a Grail which outshines the candles, another maiden with a silver carving dish. Perceval, remembering the counsel of the old knight, does not ask what these things mean. In the morning he finds the castle deserted and his horse and armour waiting. In a forest he meets a damsel who tells him that his host was the Fisher King, who had been lamed by a wound through his thighs. He ought to have asked for whom was the service of the Grail, for if he had, the king would have been healed. Further adventures, in which, like Yvain, he unhorses Kay and is courteously entreated by Gawain, bring Perceval back to court. Then arrives a loathly damsel, who reproaches Perceval with his failure at the Grail Castle, and announces adventures of the Chastel Orguellous and of Mont Esclaire. These are taken up by Giflet fis Do and Gawain respectively; Perceval will ride until he learns of the lance and the Grail. He does ride for five years, until he comes across a hermit, who proves to be his uncle, and tells him that the Fisher King was also his uncle, and that a father of them both still lives, nourished by a host borne in the Grail. But now the story is mainly concerned with Gawain, who is diverted from the quest of Mont Esclaire by a challenge from Guigambrésil to single combat before the King of Escavalon. When Gawain, somewhat deviously, reaches Escavalon, the combat is put off for a year, that he may seek the bleeding lance. He gets entangled in other affairs, enters an enchanted palace with a marvellous bed which shoots arrows upon its occupant, breaks the enchantment by slaying a lion, learns that the dwellers in the palace are Arthur's mother and his sister the wife of Loth, and becomes committed to a fight with a new adversary, one Guiromelans. Chrétien wrote no more. *Explycyt Percevax le viel*, says a scribe. The *Conte* is followed in some manuscripts by the work of one or more unknown writers, who bring in adventures, perhaps originally independent, of Gawain, and others, certainly independent, of Caradoc. It was more directly continued, from the point at which Chrétien left Perceval, by Wauchier de Denain about the end of the twelfth century; and Wauchier's instalment had itself two distinct continuations, a decade or so later, by a Manessier and by a Gerbert, who may be Gerbert de Montreuil. Attempts are also made to complete Chrétien's work in the German *Parzival* of Wolfram von Eschenbach, who claims as his source a somewhat mysterious Provençal Kyot, and in prose romances, of which something will be said later. It is doubtful whether any of Chrétien's successors knew how he meant to finish his poem, or what the significance of the Grail was. It would take me too far from my theme to discuss the conflicting theories of modern scholarship on the topic.

Marie de France and Chrétien de Troyes belong to the class of *trouvères*. They are persons of good birth or at least of assured position in courtly households, for whom poetry is an occupation not inconsistent with gentlehood. If they have a reward, it is something more permanent than the mantle flung to the minstrel. And they do not write for hasty recitation, to the notes of the harp, before a crowded throng in hall or market-place. Their compositions are to be copied in delicate manuscripts, and read, silently or aloud, by the after-supper fire, or in the quietude of the bower or the midday hush of the garden close. A tradition of conscious literature has begun. It makes its appeal to a society largely dominated by women, which has found leisure to cultivate the arts of peace, and has learnt to take a pleasure in the decoration of verse, as well as in its subject-matter. This society claims novelty. It is a little weary of the heroisms of its native Charlemagne and Roland. It already knows the romances of Thebes and Troy and Alexander, in their mediaeval forms. The *matière de Bretagne* brings this novelty, with its exotic names, its distant and fabulous Arthur, its atmosphere of transformations and cities caught in magic. And even more than novelty, the society claims sentiment, above all the sentiment that gathers round the relations of sex, which get such free play in the artificial life of courts, where the women have little to do, and the men come and go from their wars. Of the two writers, Marie is less sophisticated than Chrétien. She does not wholly lose the simplicity and freshness of the folk-tales which she incorporates. But even her imagination plays much upon the amorous side of life. And the romances of Chrétien are drenched in mediaeval sentiment, quite alien from anything that we find in *Kulhwch and Olwen* or Geoffrey of Monmouth. It is not for nothing that he translated Ovid, and belonged to the *entourage* of those Poitevin ladies who brought the antinomian *amour courtois* of the south to the capitals of northern France. It is no more than sentiment, stopping short of the passion which a modern reader looks for in romance. So far as that got into the *matière de Bretagne*, it was through Tristan. Chrétien's Tristan poem is lost, and we are at liberty to believe that he would not have made much of it. He is no high or deep poet, and has no feeling for unity of motive. But there is a good deal of charm in the rapid and varied movement of his octosyllabic couplets, in his gift for picturesque description, in his skilful interweaving of love and adventure, even in his handling of love itself, when this is not too much clogged with the amorous casuistry of Provence. Far more than Marie, he was the founder of a poetic school. There are only a few *lais* of Marie's type, outside her own manuscript, and of some of these she may herself be the author. But there are many Arthurian romances in verse, which begin soon after Chrétien's own, and extend right through the thirteenth century and even into the fourteenth. For good or bad, they are much in Chrétien's vein, with an even greater entanglement of inconsequent adventures and with many borrowings, alike from him and his continuators and from each other, and from the prose romances, which overlap them and to which any substantial development of the Arthurian theme now passes. In inferior hands, they easily become tedious. The sparrow-hawk tournament and the chase of the white hart, even if it is an enchanted Celtic hart, are not slow to pall. There are also adaptations in other tongues, chiefly German and Dutch, some of which seem to preserve stories of which no French versions exist.

If we ask what, if anything, in the way of French Arthurian romance lies behind Marie and Chrétien, we enter a region of controversies, most of which have been inconclusive, while some have been embittered. Marie acknowledges a debt, direct or indirect, to Celtic *contes*. Once only she refers, rather obscurely, to *la lettre et l'escriture*. Chrétien tells us that he took *Cliges* from a book belonging to the church of St Pierre at Beauvais, and the *Conte del Graal* from a book given him by Count Philip of

Flanders. For the *Conte de la Charrete*, it was Marie de Champagne to whom he owed the *matière et san*; the Melvas theme, one supposes, and the sentiment so characteristic of the *amour courtois*, which transferred the rescue of Guinevere from Arthur the husband to Lancelot the lover. It is not necessary to assume that he took the whole of any story from a single source, and indeed the episodic method of construction suggests a piecing together of originally independent motives. In the case of *Cliges* this is fairly demonstrable. There is no obvious reason why Chrétien should not have carried out the process of combination for himself, and one view regards him as the creator of his *genre* without any help from predecessors. It is probably exaggerated, although less so than the contrary view, which holds that all the best Arthurian romances antedated Chrétien and are lost, and that he only represents a decadence. At any rate there is some reason for inferring the existence, side by side with and even before the *trouvère* romances, of others due to wandering French minstrels. These would have been for oral recitation, and if they were written down, it would be to help the memories of the owners, or for instruction at the schools of minstrelsy, rather than for publication. The evidence of Wace is inconclusive, since his *conteor* and *fableor* may have been Celts. But Chrétien himself contrasts his *Erec* with the perversions of those who live by telling stories, and Peter of Blois about 1190 records the fables of *histriones* on Arthur and Gawain and Tristan, which moved the hearers to compassion and even to tears.[1] Possibly some of the Gawain and Caradoc stories in the earlier continuations of the *Conte del Graal* may belong to romances of this type; they show traces of the catchwords and appeals to the audience which helped the minstrels along. But the only pre-Chrétien romance of which we can be fairly certain was on Tristan. It does not exist. There are fragments of a version by an Anglo-Norman Thomas, which was probably written between 1155 and 1170, and may therefore itself be earlier than Marie or Chrétien. Thomas knows of other tellers of the *conte*, and of an *estoire* on which he relies. There is a longer fragment from a later twelfth-century version, of which part at least is by Beroul, a minstrel of continental Normandy. There is a fragment of a thirteenth-century prose version buried under accretions. There are several *lais* dealing with individual episodes of the story. And there are several adaptations in German, Norse, English and Italian. The ingenuity of M. Joseph Bédier and others, working through an analysis of the agreements and disagreements of these, has successfully reconstructed the outlines of an archetype, which may be the *estoire* of Thomas. It is perhaps a conjecture that this was itself a French poem. It can hardly have been written before 1155. Any earlier French romances on the *matière de Bretagne* can only be arrived at by guess-work.

We have still to consider the relation of the French poets to their Celtic sources. Perhaps we get nearest

[1] *Record* xxiv.

to this in the case of Marie. She professes to base her *lais* upon *contes* which she has heard, and *contes* upon which *li Bretun* have made *lais*.

> Que hum dist en harpe e en rote,
> Bone en est a oïr la note.

Originals partly narrative and partly lyric are suggested. The word *lai* seems to be Celtic; in Irish *laid* or *loid* is a song. The lyric *lais* of *li Bretun* must be distinguished from Marie's own *lais*, which are narrative and not for singing.

> Rimé en ai e fait ditié.

M. Loth thinks it possible that the early epic of the Welsh bards may have had a mixed form, consisting partly of lyric sung to a musical accompaniment, and partly of explanatory prose narrative, variable at the will of the reciter. The poems and at least the drift of the prose stories would at first have been orally transmitted from bard to bard. The process of writing them down, as we find them in the *Four Books*, may have begun in the twelfth century. He conjectures that parts of *Kulhwch and Olwen* may once have been in verse. Such an explanation would help to account for the obscure and allusive character of the extant Welsh poems; the incidents chanted in them may be lost with the prose settings. And a similar combination of narrative and lyric may also lie at the back of Marie's references. Later French literature preserves an analogy in the *cantefable* of *Aucassin and Nicolette*. Obviously at some stage there must have been bilingual intermediaries. Chrétien shows no sign of knowing any Celtic tongue, and

Marie only knew enough to blunder over Breton words. Probably the bilingualism was on the side of the Celts. If their harpers undertook to make an entertainment for non-Celtic neighbours, they would have to turn their narrative *contes* into intelligible language. A rather unnecessary controversy has flamed about the issue, whether the transmission took place wholly on continental, or partly on continental and partly on insular ground. Marie's *Bretun*, more certainly than Geoffrey's *Britannia*, must in accordance with contemporary usage mean 'of Brittany.' Probably Brittany was the main channel. The carvers of Modena seem to have come thence. Most, but not all, of Marie's stories are located there. The romancers, other than Thomas, are French or Norman, not Anglo-Norman, and therefore neighbours of Brittany, not of Wales. The evidence of name-forms is somewhat ambiguous, especially as names do not always pass orally in accordance with strict phonetic laws. But there is no reason to exclude the possibility of transmission also on the borders of South Wales, where there was much Norman penetration from the eleventh century, or in Cornwall, which was completely occupied at the Conquest. There is still less to exclude the passage of tales to Brittany from other Celtic-speaking countries. Bretons followed the Norman invasion and settled both in Cornwall and on the Welsh marches. Communication by sea between Cornwall and Brittany and across the Severn between Cornwall and Wales was easy. Irish stories, too, could come either direct by sea or through Wales. A spirited attempt has been made to identify an individual who may possibly have been an intermediary. Thomas cites the authority of a certain Breri—

> Ky solt les gestes e les cuntes
> De toz les reis, de toz les cuntes
> Ki orent esté en Bretainge.

A Bleheris is similarly appealed to in one manuscript of the anonymous additions to the *Conte del Graal*. There are variants; one is Bleobleheris, and Blioberis appears as a knight in several romances, of which the earliest appears to be Renaud de Beaujeu's *Li Biaus Descouneus* (1185–90). Wauchier de Denain also cites *le conte Bleheris*—

> Qui fu nés e engenüis
> En Gales dont je cont le conte
> E qui si le contoit au conte
> De Poitiers qui amoit l'estoire
> E le tenoit en grant memoire
> Plus que nul autre ne faisoit.

Finally a late interpolation at the beginning of the *Conte* mentions not only Blihos Bliheris as a knight, but also Maistre Blihis, who knew, fortunate man that he was, all about the Grail. Now such an allusion in any one romance may be a mere literary convention. But the convergence of allusions does seem to indicate some personality, real or imaginary, behind them. It may be that we have only to do with an echo of Geoffrey of Monmouth's pre-Roman king Blegabredus, who was so musical *ut deus ioculatorum videretur*. But on the other hand the romancers seem

149

to be confirmed by Giraldus Cambrensis, who refers in the *Descriptio Kambriae* to *famosus ille fabulator Bledhericus, qui tempora nostra paulo praevenit.* No similar name has been traced in Brittany, but Domesday Book has a Tre-Bleri in Cornwall, where Geoffrey puts a *Bledericus dux Cornubiae* after Arthur's day. And more than one Welshman bore the name Bledri. In particular, there was a Bledri son of Cydifor who had charge of a Norman castle near Carmarthen in 1116, and is probably identical with a Bleheric the Welshman, who was a knight of the honour of Carmarthen in 1130, with a Bleheri whose neighbours had to pay seven marks for carrying off his daughter in the same year, and with a Bledericus Latemeni or Latemeri who gave land at Newchurch to the priory of Carmarthen about 1129-34. Latimer may mean 'interpreter,' and it is this Bledri who has been suggested as a go-between for the romances. His date would fit in well enough with the reference of Giraldus. Wauchier's Comte de Poitiers may be William VIII (1127-37), the father of Queen Eleanor and grandfather of Marie de Champagne. One does not know how Bledri got to Poitiers, but the Provençal troubadours show an early knowledge of Tristan, on whom Thomas cites Breri.

One must beware of exaggerating the Celtic element in the *matière de Bretagne*. It is an affair partly of nomenclature and partly of incidents. There is always, of course, the dominating presence of Arthur. The early romances do not make use of Bedwyr. But they do of Gawain, Kay, Ider and

150

Yvain, who are companions of Arthur both in the *Historia* and in the Welsh documents, although without much in the way of independent adventures. Geoffrey naturally reduces such heroes to an historical level. But it is probable that they were the subjects of Celtic stories. William of Malmesbury is already familiar with the fame of Gawain. He is by far the most prominent hero in the early romances. Philology seems content to derive his name from the Welsh Gwalchmei, although it is not quite certain how the transmutation into French was effected. His characteristic in the romances is his great courtesy, and he has a foil in the churlish and unlucky Kay.[1] This antithesis is perhaps foreshadowed in *Kulhwch and Olwen*, where Gwalchmei is the best of knights and Kei is rebuked for discourtesy. In the romances, from Raoul de Houdenic's *Meraugis de Portlesguez* (c. 1200) onwards, Gawain's strength of battle grows greater at midday. It appears to be a touch of Celtic solar mythology, and recalls the analogous qualities attributed to Kei and Bedwyr, although not to Gwalchmei, in *Kulhwch and Olwen*. Guinglain, the son of Gawain, is also well known to the romancers, and to him belongs the adventure of the *fier baiser*, which transforms a loathly serpent into a fair maiden. Another early hero is Ider, whom we have found in a Glastonbury legend. He is in the carving at Modena, with Arthur and Gawain and Kay, and also with Caradoc and Meriadoc, whom Geoffrey

[1] Cf. Chaucer, *Squier's Tale*, 87, 'Gawayn, with his olde curteisye.'

makes contemporaries of an earlier date than Arthur. Presumably the carving rests upon some Breton story of a rape of Guenloie by Meriadoc. There is something like it in Marie de France's *Guigemar*, where Meriadoc is besieged in a castle to which he has carried an unnamed lady. Ider is the lover of Guenloie in the thirteenth-century romance which bears his name. But here Meriadoc does not recur, although Gawain and Kay do. Most of the names in Marie's *lais* did not get into the romances. But there are others which are doubtless Breton. Thus Erec, unknown to Geoffrey, is probably the Breton Weroc, and when the Welsh took over his story, they replaced the name by that of Gereint. Tristan and Iseult and Iseult's husband Mark are not in Geoffrey, but they are in the Welsh documents, and a triad connects Tristan and Mark with Arthur in an episode which forms no part of the extant romance. Tristan's name is probably Cornish. On the other hand Perceval is French, and although he is very definitely *li Galois* in the romances, the Welsh themselves substituted the name Peredur, which properly belonged to a northern warrior of the sixth century. Lancelot is also French, and indeed his whole personality seems to have been a development of the French romancers, although there may have been some nucleus in a Breton tale of a water fairy and a changeling. And of course there are other names of purely French origin, such as the Count Oringle de Limors of *Erec*, or of palpable invention, such as the Orgillos de la Lande of the *Conte del Graal*. These descriptive names are indefinitely multiplied in the later romances.

It is rarely possible to trace with certainty the origin of specific incidents. Parallels have been readily collected from Welsh and still more from Irish stories independent of Arthur. The process is rather illusory, since we do not know how far there may have been similar parallels in lost Cornish or Breton or even French sources, and many of the fundamental *motifs* are common form in the folk-lore of all peoples. Even what looks to modern eyes like the glamour of the Celtic imagination is not conclusive, for poets bring their own imagination, and the materials of fairydom and magic are widespread. In any case the parallels are generally only for isolated features, and do not extend to the linking together of these in complete stories. Much must be allowed for the conscious literary activity of the Arthurian romancers. They are not like tellers of folk-tales, tied to traditional narratives, or only gradually elaborating them from mouth to mouth. They exercise the arts of selection and combination and deliberate invention. They borrow freely from each other and from earlier cycles of romance. And they certainly bring in elements which are not of Celtic, but of oriental, or even of classical origin. Nothing is more dangerous than an uncritical application of the methods and canons of storyology to a fully developed literature. The *Tristan* is probably an exceptional case of a more or less wholesale transference of a story from Celtic to French. Even here there may be classical echoes in the Midas-like horse ears of Mark, and in the white and black sails which, for Tristan as for Theseus, are to herald a successful or unsuccessful voyage. There are Breton and French elements as well as Cornish. But in the main the narrative may well have taken shape in Cornwall, much as it appeared in the early French *estoire*. Its setting is Cornish and its insular geography more precise than is usual in the romances. The personages may even have had a real existence on Cornish ground. A monument bears the inscription *Drustagni hic jacet Cunomori filius*. Drustagnos may properly become Tristan, and a ninth-century *Vita* of the sixth-century saint Paulus Aurelianus preserves the memory of a King Marcus, *quem alio nomine Quonomorium vocant*. The tragic burden, primitive manners and closely knit texture of the story give it a place apart in Arthurian romance. Tristan, with his agility of hand and foot, his woodcraft, and his making of *lais*, is never quite the typical knight of the Round Table. Perhaps another exception may be found in a favourite theme of a stranger who offers himself for decapitation, on condition that the man who accepts his challenge will afterwards incur the same risk at his hands. It is, of course, magic. The adventure is for Caradoc and others in French romances, and for Gawain in a later English one. But it is already an articulated story in the Irish *Bricriu's Feast*, which may date from the eleventh century. Here also the transference seems to be more than merely episodic. On the other hand it does not seem possible to claim that the *Gereint*, *Owein* and *Peredur*, which are attached to the *Mabinogi* in the *Red Book of Hergest*, represent original Welsh compositions. It has been claimed in the course of a controversy which is not yet closed. But the tone of these stories is entirely different from that of the *Mabinogi* proper, and betrays the influence of continental chivalry. And their outlines are based on those of Chrétien's *Erec*, *Yvain*, and *Conte del Graal*, although with considerable modifications, especially in the *Peredur*. The only real issue is as to whether they are adapted from Chrétien's poems, or derive with these from common sources in earlier French romances now lost. But, as has been said, it is unlikely that Chrétien had any such comprehensive sources.

Arthur himself is a rather passive figure in his cycle, just as Charlemagne is in his. The Round Table becomes a framework, within which the poets place their gathering of adventures, originally independent or of their own devising. The hint is taken from Geoffrey's twelve-year period of peace between the Saxon and Roman wars, in which Arthur's court was a model for the knights of all the world, and was filled with feats of valour crowned by the loves of chaste ladies. To facilitate the romances, Arthur acquired the convenient habits of always granting a boon before he knew what it was, and of declining to eat at high feasts until an adventure had presented itself. His own story, however, and with it that of Merlin, received some development in the vast body of prose romances, to which I must now turn. I cannot attempt any discussion of the widely disparate views which are held as to the dates, authorships and inter-relations of these. French prose literature began in the latter half of the twelfth century with lives of saints. It is possible that the first prose romances followed very quickly. But it is at least safe to say that the earliest group with which we are concerned came into existence not later than the second decade of the thirteenth century. It is connected with the name of a certain Robert de Boron. He has been conjecturally identified with a man of this name, who appears to have dwelt in England, and gave land at Cockenhatch in Hertfordshire to the monastery of Montreuil-sur-Mer in Picardy. However this may be, he probably took his name from Boron near Delle, where he was a neighbour of Gautier de Montbéliard, Count of Montfaucon. And for Gautier, probably inspired by Chrétien's *Conte del Graal*, he wrote a poem in which he claimed to trace a history of the Grail before the days of Perceval in apocryphal adventures of Joseph of Arimathea after the death of Christ. His original intention was apparently to carry the history onwards to Perceval through descendants of Joseph. All that we have, however, in verse beyond the *Joseph*, is a fragment, perhaps a good deal later, of a *Merlin*, in which the mage becomes a link in the Grail story. But we have also a prose version of the poems, not necessarily by Boron's own hand, which goes on to complete the *Merlin* and to add a

Perceval, largely based on Chrétien and Wauchier de Denain, and a short *Mort Artu*. Some think that the *Perceval* and the *Mort Artu* are the work of yet another hand. At any rate the four sections taken together contribute a fairly complete Grail romance. I am, of course, only directly concerned with Arthur and Merlin. The *Mort Artu* adds little of importance about Arthur to the *Bruts* upon which it was founded. The Britons awaited his return for more than forty years, and a folk-lore touch records that often he was seen hunting in the forest with his dogs. The *Merlin* gives the sage a marvellous origin in a plot of the devils to defeat the Redemption through a son begotten by one of their number upon a pure virgin. By the grace of God, the offspring inherits his father's supernatural power, without his sin. He performs many feats of divination, and appoints a scribe Blaise, who sits in Northumberland and records both the Grail story and Merlin's own adventures. Is Blaise 'Master Blihis' again? No doubt the writer, directly or indirectly, knew the *Vita Merlini* as well as the *Historia*. He gives the Vortigern episode, the building of Stonehenge, and the shape-shifting at Arthur's conception. And he ascribes to Merlin's advice the foundation by Uther, not Arthur, of the Round Table. It is on the model of a Grail Table established in the *Joseph*. There is a vacant seat, to be filled only by the knight who achieves the Grail. This links up with an incident in the *Perceval*. Merlin, who disappears from the *Historia* after Arthur's birth, lives on in the prose romance.

He takes the boy and has him brought up in retirement by one Entor. When Uther dies the nobles are in doubt for a king. Merlin bids them await the choice of God. An anvil makes its appearance, with a sword fixed in it and an inscription that he who can draw out the sword shall be king. After a false claim by Kay to have performed the feat, it is accomplished by Arthur, and he is crowned. Here the *Merlin* closes. But the sage continues to direct the Grail adventure of the *Perceval*. He watches over the hero, and at the end of the *Mort Artu* brings him the news of the tragedy, and makes himself an *abitacle*, which he calls his *esplumeor* or 'mew,' at the gates of the Grail castle. To this he retires and is seen in the world no more.

The comparatively short 'Boron' cycle of prose romances gave the inspiration for a much longer one, which may be roughly assigned to the third decade of the thirteenth century. In fact the *Merlin* was taken in as an integral part of this, although it gets an elaborate continuation or *suite*. For the rest, the longer cycle is also a Grail romance. But much more it is a *Lancelot* romance, drawing upon Chrétien's *Conte de la Charrete* and probably also upon a lost Lancelot poem, which is thought to have been the basis of an extant German *Lanzelet* by Ulrich von Zatzikhoven. It has been maintained that the prose cycle, apart from the *Merlin*, was the work of a single hand; but the majority of scholars think that it grew up by a process of accretions and expansions. In its completed form it has acquired a certain epic unity, in spite of an intolerable tangle of detailed adventures; and the large number of manuscripts shows that it had a wide circulation. It is generally known as the 'Vulgate' cycle. There are five 'branches,' an *Early History of the Grail*, a *Merlin*, a *Lancelot*, a *Quest of the Grail*, a *Mort Artu*. The manuscripts ascribe the last three branches to Walter Map, a well-known figure at the court of Henry II. Chronological and other difficulties make it almost impossible that he should have written them; it is conceivable that he might have had something to do with the underlying Lancelot poem. The Vulgate continuation of the original *Merlin*, sometimes called the *Livre d'Artus*, takes up the story where the 'Boron' *Merlin* left it. The vassal kings revolt from Arthur, and are not appeased when Merlin reveals his parentage. He defeats them with the aid of Ban King of Benoic. They rebel again, and most of the *Livre d'Artus* is occupied with Arthur's wars against them, and against the Saxons, and against the Romans. Gawain is the chief hero, and Merlin's advice is invaluable throughout. Much of this is mere elaboration of the *Bruts*, but Ban is important, because he is the father of Lancelot. I will disentangle the more romantic themes. Arthur fights for Leodegan of Carmelide against the giant Rion, Geoffrey's Ritho. He falls in love, as Merlin intended, with Leodegan's daughter Guinevere, but unfortunately he has already begotten Mordred on his sister, the wife of Loth, in ignorance of her identity. He marries Guinevere, in spite of a plot, frustrated by Merlin, to substitute her half-sister,

a false Guinevere. Loth makes war on Arthur to
recover his wife, but they are reconciled by Gawain.
The Round Table knights take a vow to aid all
damsels in distress. After the conquest of Rome
Arthur fights with the monstrous cat of Lausanne.
And now Merlin announces his passing. He has had
his independent adventures. He has visited Julius
Caesar at Rome and divined his wife's adultery for
him, in the guise now of a stag, now of a wild man.
It is another echo of the *Vita Merlini*. He has also
visited Jerusalem. He has taught his crafts to
Morgain la Fée. And he has himself fallen in love
with Niniane, and given her the secret of magic.
This is his undoing. She puts him under a spell, and
keeps him in bed in a tower in the Forest of Broceliande, which replaces the *esplumeor* of Robert de
Boron. Gawain rides by and Merlin tells him that
no man will hear his voice again. Now we pass to
the *Lancelot*. The essential theme is an elusive
trackway through a jungle of intricate and generally
irrelevant episodes. The boy Lancelot, after the
death of Ban, is carried off by the Lady of the Lake.
She is identified with Merlin's Niniane, and the lake
is mere enchantment. She brings him up well, and
in due course sends him for knighting by Arthur.
At Camelot, which is Arthur's chief seat in this
romance, Lancelot sees Guinevere, and is smitten
with love. He undertakes adventures, and acquires
the castle of Dolorous Gard. Here Arthur and
Guinevere visit him. He frees the castle from en-
chantments which at first hold the inmates captive,

and renames it Joyous Gard. The sight of the queen throws him into love-trances. Further adventures give him a friend Galehaut, and Galehaut is the go-between for Guinevere's first kiss.[1] The Lady of the Lake sends a cleft shield which will not join until Lancelot and Guinevere come together. This takes place on a night on which Arthur himself is unfaithful with a Saxon Camille. The false Guinevere reappears, and claims to be the true one. Lancelot fights for the queen, but Arthur is infatuated with her rival, and for a time Guinevere leaves him. Now intervenes Morgain la Fée, who hates Guinevere. She entraps Lancelot, takes from him a ring of Guinevere's, and sends it to court, with news that he is mortally wounded and repents his sin against Arthur. Guinevere protests her innocence, and Arthur believes her. A quest for Lancelot begins. Morgain releases him, but he runs mad, and is cured by the Lady of the Lake. Then is incorporated a version of the Meleagant story from the *Conte de la Charrete*. Many other adventures follow. Lancelot comes and goes from court, and other knights come and go in quest of him. He is again thought dead, but sends messages and tokens to Guinevere. A new motive is now introduced. Lancelot visits the Grail Castle and under the influence of a magic draught takes the daughter of its king for Guinevere. The result is the birth of the Grail hero, Galahad. Lancelot returns to court, to fight unknown at a tournament, but the sight of

[1] Cf. Dante, *Inferno*, v. 137, 'Galeotto fu il libro e chi lo scritte.'

Guinevere unnerves him. His identity is revealed, and in an interview with Guinevere, she laments that their sin will prevent him from achieving the Grail quest. He leaves the court again, is again captured by Morgain, and before escaping paints pictures of himself and Guinevere on the walls of his prison. More adventures, largely repetitive, follow, but the story makes no advance. Then begins the *Quest of the Grail*. It is heralded by the young Galahad, who comes to court and takes his seat in the Siege Perilous left vacant at the Round Table. Galahad achieves the quest, and beholds the vision of the Grail. But Lancelot may not, and falls to bitter repentance. Nevertheless, at the beginning of the *Mort Artu*, he is again Guinevere's lover. His enemy Agravain warns Arthur, but the king will not believe the warning. There is an episode in which Guinevere becomes jealous of a maid of Escalot, who dies for love of Lancelot. He therefore quits the court once more; and thus the suspicions of Arthur, to whom Morgain has shown the paintings at her house, are lulled. A knight gives Guinevere some poisoned apples, in the hope that she will hand them to his enemy Gawain. She hands them to another knight, who dies. She is accused of murder, and has forty days to find a champion. None will come forward, until at the last moment Lancelot hears of her peril and returns. Then the relations between the lovers become an open scandal in the court. Agravain at last succeeds in convincing Arthur, who sanctions a plot. Gawain will have no part in it. The lovers are

taken in Guinevere's chamber. She is condemned to
the stake, but Lancelot rescues her and carries her
to Joyous Gard. In the fray he unwittingly slays
Gawain's brother Gaheriet. Grief turns Gawain
against his old fellow in arms. There is a siege of
Joyous Gard. Arthur is unhorsed, but Lancelot will
not slay him. The Pope intervenes and Lancelot
restores Guinevere to Arthur. But Gawain still
presses for revenge. Arthur makes an overseas expedition against Lancelot in Benoic. The kingdom
is committed to Mordred. Gawain challenges
Lancelot to single combat, and receives a wound
which proves mortal. The Romans now attack
Arthur. He defeats them. But meanwhile Mordred
has spread a false report of Arthur's death, and has
seized the kingdom. Guinevere resists him in a
castle, and sends a message to Arthur. Gawain,
before dying, entreats the king to seek aid from
Lancelot, but Arthur refrains. He fights Mordred,
and both are mortally wounded. Arthur bids Gifflet
throw Excalibur into a lake. A hand rises from the
lake, and grasps the weapon. Morgan comes in a boat
full of ladies and bears Arthur away. Guinevere ends
her days in a convent and Lancelot in a hermitage.
They never meet again. The *Mort Artu* is the best
knit and the most human branch of the romance.

The Vulgate cycle was not the last word of the
prose writers. It was conflated with a long prose
Tristan in a fresh compilation to which the scribes
attached the name of Robert de Boron. It is not
preserved as a whole, but there are substantial

fragments, and the outlines of the rest are traceable in foreign adaptations. One of these is the *Morte d'Arthur* of Sir Thomas Malory, for part of which it was the source. It has an episode, evidently inspired by the Vulgate conclusion, in which Arthur receives Excalibur from a hand in a lake. And it elaborates the account of Mordred's birth with a Herodian story, in which Arthur sets all the children born on the same day in a pilotless vessel, but Mordred escapes. There were also independent revisions of individual sections of the Vulgate. One of these, now lost, must have been the source of the *Mort Artu*, as we find it both in Malory and in a fourteenth-century English metrical *Morte Arthur* of considerable charm. It improves upon the Vulgate narrative, and in it Bedwyr, insignificant in most of the romances, makes a reappearance as Sir Bedivere, to whom, instead of Gifflet, is confided the disposal of Excalibur. There is a farewell between Lancelot and Guinevere before their retirement, and finally Lancelot visits Amesbury and sees Guinevere dead. The last French compilation which I need name is the *Perlesvaus*, known in translation to English readers as the *High History of the Holy Grail*. It is a distinct romance, although probably inspired by the Vulgate, and has been thought to have a connection with Glastonbury. Essentially it is a Grail quest. But it introduces Arthur's son Lohot, the Lacheu of the Welsh documents, of whom Geoffrey made nothing, and who rarely figures in the romances. He is here slain by Kay. And it has a rather interesting introduction, in which the repute of the Round Table is in decline through Arthur's lack of spirit, and Guinevere, like the faithful wife in *Erec*, is distressed. Arthur bids a squire accompany him to the chapel of St Austin to pray for recovery. The night before, the squire has a dream, in which he is parted from Arthur on the way, and enters another chapel, where is a dead knight with candles in golden sticks burning round him. He takes a stick, and is challenged by a black giant. In his flight he is stabbed. He awakes from his dream, and there is the golden candlestick, and a knife is in his side. He dies and the candlestick is presented to St Paul's. Arthur then rides alone to St Austin's, and sees a vision of the physical Christ in the Mass. He is healed of his spiritual listlessness, holds a great festival at Pannenoisance, which is Penzance, and here begins the Grail quest. The story of the candlestick recurs in the fifteenth-century abbey chronicle of John of Glastonbury, and is here located at the hermitage of Beckery near Glastonbury. Probably John took it from the *Perlesvaus*.

Is there, in all this long development of prose romance, any new draft upon Celtic tradition? Probably very little, except perhaps Lohot and whatever may have come through the lost Lancelot poem. This may well be no more than the initial folk-tale of a fairy changeling. We are in the full tide, not only of literary, but of ecclesiastical invention. The new stories of Merlin, in so far as they are not inspired by the *Vita* itself, seem to be of oriental origin, and his retreat is placed in Broceliande, because Wace and Chrétien de Troyes had made the fountain of that forest famous. The romance is probably responsible for late Welsh stories in which the mage retires by sea to a glass house, which is ultimately located in Bardsey, although Celtic notions of the Otherworld as a translucent abode have doubtless affected these versions. The tragic loves of Lancelot and Guinevere have clearly been modelled upon those of Tristan and Iseult. They have been linked up with the Grail quest through Lancelot's son Galahad, and the Galfridian account of Arthur's *débâcle* has been profoundly modified, to enable them to bring about the catastrophe. Arthur's infidelities are obviously invented to palliate Guinevere's; his parenthood of Mordred to sharpen the tragedy. The hostile Morgain and the helpful Lady of the Lake are ingenious machinery, and the former is a flagrant departure from tradition. The prose writers are not likely to have been themselves in continued touch with Breton *conteurs*. But they may have had sources unknown to us, and through these Celtic episodes may have been incorporated. If so, it is probably no longer feasible to distinguish such episodes from those which are due to literary borrowing or fabrication. Irish parallels have been cited for the anvil test at Arthur's coronation, but others may be found in the stories of Theseus and of Sigmund. A Celtic glamour has been claimed for the incident of Excalibur and the lake, but I am afraid that Celtic glamour is often subjective.

William of Malmesbury or an interpolator appears to connect Gawain with Galloway, and it is conceivable that legends of the hero may have lingered in the north, and contributed to a group of northern or north midland poems which belong to the alliterative revival of the fourteenth century. They are *Sir Gawayne and the Grene Knight*, *The Awntyrs of Arthure at the Terne Wathelyne*, and *The Avownge of King Arthur*. But in the main all the English Arthurian literature is based upon French works, although not always works which have survived. And there is little of it before the fourteenth century. An alliterative *Morte Arthure* (14 c.) and a fragmentary *Arthur* (15 c.) among the Marquis of Bath's manuscripts are, like Layamon's poem, chronicle *Bruts*. French poems are responsible for a *Sir Tristrem* (13 c.), a *Libeaus Desconus* (14 c.), a *Sir Perceval* (14 c.), Thomas Chestre's *Lanval* (14 c.), an *Ywain and Gawain* (15 c.), a *Golagors and Gawane* (15 c.); French prose originals for an *Arthour and Merlin* (13 c.), a *Joseph of Arimathie* (14 c.), a stanzaic *Morte d'Arthur* (14 c.), a *Lancelot of the Laik* (15 c.), and Henry Lovelich's *Merlin* and *Holy Grail* (15 c.), and for a prose *Merlin* (15 c.). There are a few other short poems and ballads, mostly on Gawain themes. There is not much poetic merit, except in *Sir Gawayne and the Grene Knight*, the *Awntyrs of Arthure* and the alliterative and stanzaic *Mortes*. Malory has his own temper and his own incomparable English. The materials for his *Morte d'Arthur* (15 c.) were disparate. He may have gathered them for himself, from elements partly belonging to the Vulgate cycle and its variants, and partly to the derivative 'Boron' cycle.

CHAPTER VI

THE HISTORICITY OF ARTHUR

HISTORY, asked to determine how much of veritable fact may underlie the imposing structure of the Arthurian legend, can only give a cold response. Most of that legend, whether it comes to us in the pseudo-historic form of Geoffrey's chronicle, or in the romantic form of the Welsh stories, or in the hagiographic form of the *Vitae Sanctorum*, can be no more than the play of imagination about the meagre details furnished by *Harleian MS* 3859. The documents contained in that manuscript, whatever their origins, are of uncertain and divided authorship. The earliest of them cannot be relied upon as taking us beyond the ninth century. And already they contain legendary elements in the shield of Guinnion and the *mirabilia* of Buelt and Ercing. Stripped of these, they tell us that Arthur fought against the Saxons, that he won the battle of Badon, which Gildas records without mention of him, that he won eleven other battles at named places, that he fell with Medraut at Camlan, that Badon was in 518 and Camlan in 539, and that he had a son Anir, whom legend has forgotten or perhaps confused with his own burial-place *Licat Anir* into Lacheu. There is nothing of Guinevere, of Kei and Bedwyr, or of Gawain, whom William of

Malmesbury accepted as Arthur's nephew. Beyond the bare notice of Badon, the reports lack confirmation. The most that history can say is that they are not inconsistent with what we do know of the period to which they relate. I hope to show that it can say that. But it amounts to little, in view of the obscurity which envelopes the fortunes of the island during the greater part of the fifth and sixth centuries.

Modern writers construct confident pedigrees for Arthur; they are quite valueless, being based mainly upon Geoffrey, or upon mediaeval Welsh attempts to reconcile Geoffrey with native genealogies. We do not even know what were his relations to Ambrosius Aurelianus, who is so important in Gildas, and about whom Nennius is so far from explicit. I have sometimes thought that they might be doublets of the same personality, reaching Nennius through two name-forms of which one had undergone scribal corruption from Aurelianus into Arthur. But on the whole, this does not seem very probable. Arthur is not a common name in early Celtic records. But it does occur, from a date not long after that ascribed to the hero.[1] Oddly enough, the first example is from a Goidelic source. Arturius is given in Adamnan's *Vita Columbae* as the name of a prince of the Scoto-Irish kingdom of Dalriada, who fell in battle in 596. Irish, too, was Artur the grandfather of one Faradach who appears in a list of ecclesiastics compiled in 697. And it is an Irish record which

[1] Zimmer, *Nennius Vindicatus*, 284; Meyer and Nutt, *Voyage of Bran*, i. 137.

assigns to an Arthur the death of the Ulster chief Mongan in Scotland in 620. This Arthur, however, is said to have been the son of a British prince Bicuir. And a fairly historical Arthur is traceable in south-west Wales about the beginning of the seventh century.[1] He belonged to the house of Dyvet, and had a father Petr and a son Nougoy. His great-grandfather was Vortiporius, whose monument exists, and whom Gildas notes as ruling in his time. The derivation of the name has been the subject of much discussion. It has been connected with Celtic words meaning respectively 'god,' 'bear,' 'plough-land,' 'stone' and 'hammer,' with the Cornish *aruthr* 'cruel,' with the Sanscrit *ṛta* 'exactly,' and with the Latin Arcturus. Some of these suggestions are related to mythological speculations, which will require consideration in due course. There is, however, a fairly general agreement that it might have an origin in the Roman *gens*-name Artorius, which would normally undergo aspiration on passing into Welsh. There was a Lucius Artorius Castus, who played a conspicuous military part in Britain during the second century.[2] It is a rather fantastic notion that an expedition of this Artorius to Armorica was the germ of Arthur's fabulous continental empire. But Professor Oman points out that he may well have left relatives or freedmen in the island.

An attempt to fit Arthur into history must take account both of his chronology and of his locality.

[1] Loth, *Mabinogion*, ii. 330, from *Harl. MS* 3859.
[2] *Corp. Inscr. Lat.* iii. 303, 2131.

The *Annales Cambriae*, subject to the slight uncertainty as to their exact *annus i*, put Badon in 518 and Camlan in 539. Their general dating gets a good deal of support from Irish annals, but it has been suggested that its earlier years may have suffered through the conflation of documents starting from different eras. Even scholars who do not accept this conjecture are often inclined to think any such date as 518 impossibly late for Badon. The scepticism rests mainly upon an interpretation of the forty-four year period mentioned by Gildas as running from Badon to the writing of the *De Excidio*. I have taken it, with a minority, as the span of the warfare between Britons and Saxons ended by Badon. Gildas has only one other precise time-reference to help us. The letter written to Agitius, who must be Aetius, was during his third consulate, which fell in 446. Thereafter Gildas describes two periods of indefinite duration. In the first there are a famine, a hill-warfare *per multos annos*, a final defeat of the Picts and Scots. They retire, *post non longum reversuri*. Meanwhile the country becomes rich. *Luxuria crescit*. Cruel kings are chosen and slain. Obviously this interval, although not 'long,' must also be thought of in terms of years, rather than months. It ends with a rumour of a new invasion from the north, a plague, and a council at which the Saxons are called in. In the second period the Saxons turn on their allies and blaze from sea to sea, touching even the western ocean. The cities fall. The Britons are slain, become serfs, emigrate, or flee to the hills. Then, *tempore interveniente aliquanto*, the Saxons return home. Ambrosius Aurelianus arises, challenges the conquerors, and is victorious. Again we cannot tell just what lapse of time these events may have covered. But *ex eo tempore* began the forty-four years fighting up to Badon; that is, most naturally, from the victory of Ambrosius, rather than from his rise or from any earlier stage of the invasion.[1]

By the ninth century the *Adventus Saxonum*, by which must be meant the calling in of Hengist and Horsa, has become a chronological era. Bede places it, rather vaguely with a *tunc*, in the seven years' reign of the Emperors Marcian and Valentinian.[2] This, by a one-year error, of which there are other examples in his datings, he begins with 449 instead of 450. Nennius, or the documents incorporated by Nennius, give several conflicting dates. Some of these can be disregarded as scribal slips, such as are easily made in copying Roman numerals. Others seem to be traceable to historical confusions. Thus a date of 375 in the consulate of Gratian and Equantius, who should be Equitius, is plainly absurd. It looks as if the date of the letter to Agitius had been taken to be that also of the *Adventus*, and Agitius identified with Equitius instead of Aetius. More important perhaps is a statement that, after the tyrant Maximus was slain and the Roman dominion ended, the Britons lived in fear for forty years until the reign of Vortigern. The Roman dominion is generally regarded as terminating in 409. Nennius shows some sign of

[1] *Record* ii.   [2] *Record* iii.

knowing this date. An addition of forty years would give 449 for the *Adventus*, which is compatible with Bede. It is possible that Bede, and also Nennius, if he did not use Bede, may have had some lost annals which justified the forty-year calculation. On the other hand, if the forty years are reckoned rrom the death of the well-known western tyrant Maximus Magnus in 388, they would end with 428; and this date, correctly placed in the consulate of Felix and Taurus, is in fact assigned to the *Adventus* in the introductory *computus* of the *Annales Cambriae*.[1] Again there may have been some historical blundering. Nennius evidently knew something of Maximus Magnus. But he duplicates him with a Maximianus. Can he also have heard of a much more obscure Maximus, who was set up by a British general as an emperor in Spain, somewhere about the year 409? If so, and if he meant to begin his forty years with this Maximus, the computist may easily have supposed him to refer to Maximus Magnus. Alternatively the relations between Vortigern and Germanus taken by Nennius from the *liber Germani* may have been ascribed to the first visit of the saint in 429, instead of to his later visit shortly before his death in 444–50.

I have already described the *computus*, and conjectured that its final term was meant to be the consulate of Aetius in 446.[2] Even if we do not accept its 428 in place of 449 for the *Adventus*, it is interesting here, for some rather precise details, not found elsewhere and conceivably resting upon some

[1] *Record* v.   [2] Cf. p. 14.

authority independent of Gildas, about the reign of
Vortigern. It makes his first year that of the consulate (425) of Theodorius (for Theodosius) and
Valentinian, and puts the *Adventus* in his fourth year.
And by what looks like an interpolation, since the
statement is not needed for the purposes of the
computation, it tells that from the reign of Vortigern
to the *discordia* of Guitolinus and Ambrosius there
were twelve years. Then the interpolator, or perhaps
at least one other, adds *quod est Guoloppum, id est,
Catguoloph*. We are not, unfortunately, told what was
the nature of the *discordia*, or how long Vortigern's
reign lasted, but it is not unreasonable to find in the
battle (*cat*) of Guoloph the name of the victory
won by Ambrosius Aurelianus over the Saxons. The
place may be Wallop in Hampshire. Nor is it
necessarily illogical to reject the computist's 428 for
the *Adventus* and at the same time to accept the
interpolator's twelve years between the reign of
Vortigern and the battle of Guoloph. If we put the
beginning of Vortigern's reign in 446, the *Adventus*
in 449, the end of Vortigern's reign in 462, the
battle of Guoloph in 474 and the battle of Badon
in 518, we should be doing no violence either to the
narrative of Gildas or to the dating of Badon in the
Annales Cambriae.

It is not, of course, enough to reconcile Gildas
with documents which after all were themselves
based in part on Gildas. The result must be checked
by such other evidence as is available. There is little
of it. The continental chronicles have almost for-

gotten Britain. But a few scattered notices may be
collected. The earliest of these tell of a sequel to the
great invasion of Vandals across the Rhine on the
first day of 406. This for a time cut Rome off from
the western provinces. The troops in Britain set up
a series of tyrant emperors, of whom the last, Constantine by name, crossed with the greater part of the
insular army to Gaul and established himself there.
This proved the signal for a Saxon raid, and an entry
for 409–10 in a brief set of annals of Gallic origin
records that Britain was devastated.[1] From Zosimus
we learn that the provincials took matters into their
own hands, raised forces against the invaders, and
expelled the Roman officials, presumably those
appointed by Constantine. The legitimate emperor,
Honorius, confirmed their action, and bade them see
to their own protection.[2] These events are generally
regarded as the end of the Roman domination. It is
true that a military *cadre* for Britain still appears in
the western division of the survey of imperial administration known as the *Notitia Dignitatum*, which
seems to have been drawn up in 428 and possibly
revised later. Professor Bury has argued from this
that Britain was included in the reorganization of the
west by Honorius after the repulse of the Vandals,
and that the domination may have lasted to the middle
of the century. This view, however, has not met
with much acceptance, largely because of the absence
from archaeological discoveries of any Roman coins
or other datable evidence of occupation later than

[1] *Record* i.   [2] Zosimus, vi. 5.

409. It need not, however, be assumed that the patriots of 409 regarded themselves as definitively cut adrift from the empire, or as ceasing to be *cives Romani*. The appeal to Aetius, a powerful general who had done much to hold back the barbarians on the Rhine, would of itself negative this. Probably the control of Britain passed in the first instance to the *civitates*, which were Roman cantonal units of civil administration, and from these to the heads of leading families, some of native, some of Roman extraction, who gradually became *tyranni* or *reges*. Some opposition between the racial elements and some revival of a Celtic civilization may be assumed. Certainly this country was not wholly defenceless during the forty years' *metus*. Troops left by Constantine and veterans settled on the land would provide a military nucleus. And we may suppose some federation of *reges* under shifting hegemonies. It is perhaps to the military leader of such a hegemony that properly belongs the designation *guleticus* or *wledig* which is applied to Ambrosius by Nennius and to several outstanding personages in Welsh writings. Professor Rhys has suggested that the *wledig* may have been the later representative of some Roman official, *dux* or *comes*, whose functions he assumed. One may tentatively venture the alternative explanation that the term is the equivalent of the honorific title *protector*, which was given by the emperors to notable provincials and in fact appears upon the monument of Vortiporius. However this may be, Vortigern, if more than a legend, was

probably at the head of a hegemony. The centre of his power must be uncertain. It is not likely to have been Kent, since Nennius names one Guyocyranon as King of Kent, when it was ceded by Vortigern to Hengist. The Nennius stories rather point to central Wales, where Gwerthrynion was a district in Radnorshire. If so, Vortigern no doubt represented the Celtic element, and Ambrosius the Roman.

The next continental references are again in Gallic chronicles.[1] That already cited places about 441, and another, which is a little later, about 439, a statement that Britain had fallen *in dicionem Saxonum*. This has led some scholars to suppose that 428 rather than 449 must be the right date for the *Adventus Saxonum*, and that the letter to Aetius, if it was historical, must have been for help against the Saxons, and not, as Gildas says, against the Picts and Scots. But such statements must not be pressed too hard. Taken at their face value they defeat themselves. Certainly a great part of the island, in the south and west and north, was still outside any permanent Saxon *dicio* for more than a century after the chroniclers wrote. They may well have known that communications between Gaul and Britain were interrupted by a Saxon settlement on the coasts of Kent, but this interruption would of itself make them bad authorities as to what was going on in the interior. Moreover, even the interruption may only have been temporary. Communications were in fact open for St Germanus about 449 as well as about 428, and a

[1] *Record* i.

passage of Sidonius Apollinarius suggests that they were still open in 475.[1] This is just about the date which I have been led to assign to the victory of Ambrosius. The accounts of the *Adventus Saxonum* may reasonably be read as implying a calling in of Hengist from an existing settlement in Kent rather than direct from the continent. But in any case the *Adventus* is only a conventional era. It was certainly not the first appearance of Saxons in the island. They were enemies of long standing. Already at the beginning of the fourth century the Romans had built a chain of forts against them and provided a *comes littoris Saxonici*. Ammianus mentions them in 364, and Claudian celebrates Stilicho's triumph over them about 395. We have seen that they took the opportunities of 409. It was against a combined force of Saxons and Picts that the old warrior St Germanus helped the Britons to win the Hallelujah victory about 429. We have to distinguish between the sporadic raids of pirates, or even temporary coastal settlements, and a deliberate attempt to colonize the island as a whole. And it was the latter that the *Adventus* initiated. I do not think that the continental references forbid us to place it about 449.

And now we come to the *Saxon Chronicle*. This is not an authority upon which much reliance can be placed for the first invasions. It can hardly have been written down, even in a lost early form, before the middle of the ninth century. Its dates may be a late addition and some of them suggest an artificial

[1] *Epist.* ix. 9, 6.

symmetry. Several of its personal names look like explanations of place-names, and that of its first Wessex hero, Cerdic, is regarded, with some dissent, as Celtic rather than Teutonic. The *Adventus* is placed in 449, but here the compiler probably followed Bede. Then come, in 455, 457 and 465, three battles, of which the first is said to have been against Wyrtgeorn. They might correspond roughly in period to the battles ascribed by Nennius to Vortigern's son Vortimer. The names are different, but each reporter would naturally dwell on the victories of his own side. The death of Horsa in one of the battles is a common feature. There is one more unnamed Saxon victory in 473, just a year before the date suggested above for Guoloph; then a notice of the reign of Hengist's son Aesc over Kent for twenty-four years from 488, and then no more about Kent for a century and a half. There is nothing here which conflicts with the British chronology. The *Chronicle* is, however, primarily a Wessex document, and its Wessex entries are the more interesting in their relation to Gildas. They put the first invasion by Cerdic unexpectedly late, in 495; and this may be connected with a fairly evident attempt to ignore an earlier occupation of Hampshire by the Jutes, whom the West Saxons dispossessed. The earlier entries represent Cerdic as gradually mastering that district. There is nothing which relates itself to our chronological problem before a battle against the Britons in 519 at Cerdicesford. This may be Charford in the Avon valley, near the borders of Hampshire and

Wilts. Then comes another battle against the Britons at an unidentified Cerdicesleag in 527, and then a conquest of the Isle of Wight, presumably from the Jutes. Thereafter the record of battles stops for many years. It is reopened, long after Cerdic's death, with victories by his son Cynric in 552 at Salisbury and in 556 at Beranburg, probably Barbury Down between Marlborough and Swindon. After another interval of internecine warfare with Kent and perhaps Mercia, the onward progress is resumed by Ceawlin, whose victory at Dyrham in 577 gives him possession of Gloucester, Cirencester and Bath. All this does not square badly with Gildas. Cerdic is still fighting the Britons for some years after the date ascribed to Badon. But he then turns to the consolidation of what he has already conquered and the completion of his mastery over the Jutes. There is no western advance during a period of many years, which corresponds with the long peace described by Gildas as still prevailing when he wrote the *De Excidio*. This was before the death of Maelgwn in 549, and therefore before the renewed conquests of Cynric.

It is of course odd that Gildas should make no mention of Arthur. He is, however, primarily a preacher rather than an historian, and is chiefly concerned to flagellate the vices of the kings of his own day. These were Maelgwn of Gwynedd, Vortiporius of Dyvet, Constantine of Dumnonia, Aurelius Caninus, perhaps of Wilts, Cuneglassus, perhaps of Powys. There must also still have been British rulers in the north of the country, but they did not come within the purview of Gildas. It has been suggested that Arthur may still have been alive when Gildas wrote, and even that he may have been Cuneglassus, who is somewhat cryptically described both as a bear and the charioteer of a bear. But the bear etymology for Arthur is very doubtful, and, if Camlan was in 539, Gildas, born in 518, cannot have already written the *De Excidio*, over which he had meditated *spatio bilustri temporis*. No doubt Caradoc's *Vita Gildae* makes him a contemporary of Arthur, just as earlier *Vitae* bring Arthur into the lives of other saints of the latter part of the sixth century. This is hardly evidence. Nor is it safe to identify Maelgwn with Medraut, merely because he is said to have supplanted his uncle. For what it is worth, we must admit that there is no echo of Arthur in Gildas.

And now it is necessary to consider how far the literary records are confirmed by the findings of archaeology. Many Saxon graveyards of the pagan period have been unearthed, and the utensils and ornaments found in them can often be approximately dated by comparison with continental types. They lie mainly along the river basins, and their distribution supports the inference from the texts that the first invaders were Jutes, who occupied the Kentish districts south of the Thames estuary. A second wave consisted of Anglo-Saxons, who pushed further up the Thames valley. They too may have come up the estuary. But it is also possible that they landed in the Wash, and reached the Thames valley by the line of the Icknield Way along the inner face of the Chilterns. They may, indeed, have used both routes. It was probably from the Thames valley and not from the southern ports that they entered Hampshire, and here they may well have displaced earlier Jutish settlers. The main difficulties are of chronology. Some of the gear found is believed to have been manufactured not later than the first quarter of the fifth century. There were specimens in the grave of a warrior and his wife as far up the Thames as Dorchester. No doubt such articles might remain in use for a considerable time. And sporadic raiders, or Saxon legionaries brought by the Romans, although for these there is not much evidence, might have died in Britain. Whatever the solution of the Dorchester puzzle, a regular Saxon settlement is indicated by the discovery of not less than a hundred and thirty burials of men, women and children, still further up the valley, at Fairford. Here the gear belonged to the end of the fifth century. It is difficult to reconcile this with the date of 577 in the *Saxon Chronicle* for the occupation of Cirencester, only a few miles from Fairford. Further, there is no archaeological evidence of any British use of Cirencester, Gloucester and Bath after the Roman period, and in the case of Bath fairly definite evidence to the contrary. Even if these cities were sacked in raids of 409, it is difficult to understand why the Britons should have left them deserted up to 577. The suggestion of archaeology, then, is that, especially in the *Saxon Chronicle*, the invasions may have been post-dated. I doubt whether this is strong enough to outweigh the literary evidence. But at any rate we have to assume that, during the years of peace between Badon and the conquests of Ceawlin, Britons and Saxons were able to inhabit the upper Thames valley in close proximity and comparative peace.

We have, therefore, to think of any stand made by Ambrosius and Arthur as directed against enemies moving slowly from a base in the Thames valley, colonizing level ground to the south and north of it, and only gradually adapting themselves to hill warfare. The strength of the Britons lay in their hill fortresses, and in such relics as they had preserved of Roman discipline and military skill. It is in this light that we must now consider the localities traditionally associated with Arthur's name. What may be roughly called a folk-memory of Arthur is somewhat wide-spread. Occasionally there is a story; more often only the attachment of the hero's name to one of those *mirabilia*—caverns, fantastically shaped or marked rocks, forts and other relics of forgotten civilizations—upon which the fancy of the folk always delights to linger. Here Arthur, as a god-father, has to take his turn with the giants, the devil, and Robin Hood. The records are not as a rule very early. The boundary indications of mediaeval charters yield a few, and possibly a systematic investigation of such sources might add to their number. Leland and other early antiquarians collected some. The majority date from the nineteenth-century interest in folk-lore. The earliest of all are the *mirabilia* of Nennius, already described, in Buelt and Ercing. Then come the Arthur's Chair and Arthur's Oven, seen by the monks of Laon in what they were told was *terra Arturi* on their journey from Exeter to Bodmin during 1113; and from these, in the very centre of the ancient Dumnonia, a topographical survey may well start. The spot is, I think, still identifiable. Arthur's name has dropped out. But modern maps show a King's Oven near the Warren House Inn, about a mile from where the Exeter and Bodmin road climbs to its highest point on Dartmoor at Merripit. Further east in Dumnonia are Glastonbury, already sufficiently dealt with, and Cadbury Castle, a camp on one of the southern outliers of the Somersetshire Mendips, not far from Salisbury. This both Leland and Camden call Camalat, no doubt identifying it with the Camelot which Chrétien de Troyes and other French romancers treat as a residence of Arthur. The actual origin of this name is unknown; one philological guess finds it in Camuludunum, now Colchester. In fact the camp is in South Cadbury; but two or three miles away are villages of Queen's Camel and West Camel, on a stream called the Cam. The camp shows traces of late Celtic and Roman occupation, and huddled burials at its foot may indicate a battle. Leland tells us that it was believed locally to be Arthur's, and that many Roman coins, and within the memory of man a silver horse-shoe, had been dug up there; and Camden that the natives called it Arthur's Palace. The silver horse-shoe still survives in local tradition, and has been related to Arthur.

Folks do say that on the night of the full moon King Arthur and his men ride round the hill, and their horses are shod with silver, and a silver shoe has been found in the track where they do ride, and when they have ridden round the hill, they stop to water their horses at the Wishing Well.

This is King Arthur's Well in the lowest rampart of the camp; his Palace is a natural elevation on its crest; and his Lane or Causeway an ancient trackway passing from the camp in the direction of Glastonbury. Here a labourer 'sometimes, on rough winter's nights, heard King Arthur and his hounds go by along the track.' Another tale makes Arthur and his knights come down on Christmas Eve to drink from a second well by the village church of Sutton Montis. The hill is believed to be hollow, and there are iron gates which a native saw as a boy, but which cannot be exactly located. A local poem calls them golden gates, and if you look through them on St John's Eve, there is a king sitting in the middle of his court. But in tradition the event of St John's Eve is 'something strange' which no one has put to the proof. Arthur shares the spot with the fairies. They carry up corn from the arable 'fore-side' below the camp. When bells were put into the church, they went away and left gold behind them. Most of the local stories were collected about 1890; it may have been a little later that a party of antiquaries were asked by an old man whether they had come to take the king away.[1]

The memories of western Dumnonia, which is Cornwall, are thickest in the north-east of the county.

[1] Robinson (1926), 53.

Here Slaughter or Bloody Bridge, on the Camel, hard by Camelford, is the traditional site of Camlan. The original bridge was a stone slab, nearly ten feet long, which still exists, but has been displaced, and is now called Arthur's Tomb. It is in fact sepulchral, and bears the incised inscription *Latini ic jacit filius Magari*. To earlier antiquarians it was illegible, and Richard Carew in his *Survey of Cornwall* (1602) says that 'the old folk hereabouts will shew you a stone, bearing Arthur's name, though now depraved to Atry.' To the south-east of Camelford are the fort of Arthur's Hall, Dozmary Pool on Bodmin Moor, where Bedivere is said to have thrown away Excalibur, and Arthur's Bed, a group of rocky tors. Still further in this direction is North Hill, near Callington, with another Arthur's Hall and Arthur's Troughs, rocky basins where he fed his dogs. To the north-east of Camelford is Arthur's Grave or the Giant's Grave in the camp of Warbstowe Bury. To the north-west is Tintagel, where Geoffrey of Monmouth placed the episode of Uther and Igerna. It has the ruins of a mediaeval castle, which may have replaced some earlier fortification. Here you may see Merlin's Cave under the headland, rock-hollows called Arthur's Chair and Arthur's Cups and Saucers, and Arthur's Quoit, which is the capstone of a cromlech. Further to the west along the coast are Cadon Barrow, the traditional tomb of Cador, and the camp of Damelioc, which Geoffrey also brings into the Uther story. An outlying locality of this group is Arthur's Hunting Seat in Castle an Dinas near St Columb, whence

Arthur rode on Tregoss Moors. A stone in St Columb bears four footprints of his horse. Along the greater part of the south coast there is little of Arthur. Carew declines to derive the name of Bodrugan, near Mevagissey, from Sir Bors de Ganis, 'though the neighbours so say.' An eighteenth-century visitor is said to have been rebuked for shooting a raven on Marazion Green, because Arthur still lived in the form of that bird. Probably it was not a raven but a Cornish chough, to which later writers say that the legend attaches. Off Mousehole harbour is a Merlin's Rock. Carew says that the Spaniards landed here when they burnt Paul and Penzance and Newlyn in 1595, and thus fulfilled one of Merlin's prophecies. In the churchyard of St Levan is a cleft stone to which Arthur and Merlin once paid a visit. Trereen Dinas claims to have been a castle of Arthur, and at Pendeen, on the north side of the Land's End promontory, an enquirer was told that the land 'swarmed with giants, until Arthur, the good king, vanished them all with his cross-sword.' The high moors in this region have an independent Arthur legend of their own. Red-headed Danes landed on Gwenvor Sands in Whitesand Bay near Sennen; and at the junction of the townships of Zennor, Gulval and Madron is a flat stone, on which Arthur and four Cornish kings dined, when they gathered the British forces to meet the invaders at the battle of Vellan Drucher. Two of the Scilly Isles, finally, are known as the Great and Little Arthur.

Arthurian localities occur throughout Wales, but most frequently in the south-eastern and the northern counties. Monmouth has its Round Table near Caerleon, and here or at the neighbouring Caerwent, which he probably confused with Caerleon, Caxton seems to have placed Camelot. To Caerleon also belongs one of many stories of Arthur's watchful slumber in a cave, until the day shall arrive for the freeing of Britain. These are folk-versions of the 'survival' myth, and will be analysed in the next chapter. Glamorgan has its Arthur's Stone on Cefn Bryn, its Guinevere's Monument at Llaniltern, and its cave legend at Craig y Dinas. Carmarthen, too, has its cave legends at Ogo'r Dinas and at Pumsaint, as well as a Grove and Hill and a Cave of Merlin. The *mirabilia* of Nennius in Ercing and Buelt belong respectively to Herefordshire and to Brecon. Here the Carn Gafallt is still known. It is odd that both Nennius and *Kulhwch and Olwen* give the name Cabal or Cavall to Arthur's dog, since the folk-stories always ascribe the footprints on stones to his horse, and *cafall* is in fact a Welsh loan-word from the vulgar Latin *caballus*, a horse. It looks as if here the folk-stories had preserved the more primitive notion, and as if Nennius had slipped, and misled the author of *Kulhwch and Olwen*. But there is no such folk-story now at Carn Gafallt. Brecon has also its Arthur's Table at Mocras, an Arthur's Hill-top, of which a mention is preserved from 1592, and Arthur's Chair between two peaks of the Beacons, which was known still earlier to Giraldus Cambrensis.

In Herefordshire a cromlech near Dorston is Arthur's Stone; the philologists will not allow it to have ever been Thor's Stone. In Merioneth Arthur slew an *afanc* or lake monster at Llyn Barfog and his horse's print is on a stone. There is also an unlocated legend of a Cave of Arthur. But, according to Professor Rhys, it is only by the English that Cader Idris has been made into an Arthur's Chair. Caergai, near Bala Lake, is the traditional home of Kay. Anglesea has a Round Table and an Arthur's Quoit, and a cave where Arthur sheltered in a war with the Goidels. Carnarvon has a River of Arthur's Kitchen and a cave legend at the Great Horse Lake, both in Llandegai near Bangor. Nant Gwythern claims the grave of Vortigern, and Dinas Emrys on the Snowdon range is the traditional scene of his meeting with Ambrosius. But here too are a Cairn of Tristan, and a Cairn of the Giant, said to be the Ritho whom Arthur slew, and a Cairn of Arthur, with another cave legend. In Denbigh Leland found a Round Table at Llansannan. Flint has an Arthur's Hill and an Arthur's Stone, with a hoof print.

Cumbria, long a Celtic district, has but scanty Arthurian reminiscences. At Tarn Wadling, the scene of one of the English romances, was garnered a set of ribald verses from the mouth of an inn-keeper.

> When as King Arthur ruled this land,
>   He ruled it like a swine;
> He bought three pecks of barleymeal
>   To make a pudding fine.

His pudding it was nodden well,
    And stuffed right full of plums;
And lumps of suet he put in
    As big as my two thumbs.

There is no trace of Gawain, whom more than one poem connects with this region. Arthuret in Liddesdale is not Arthur's Head, but the Celtic Arderydd, with which Arthur was not concerned. There is, however, an Arthur's Seat in Liddesdale. Carlisle, which the romances make a court of Arthur, knows him not. Maryborough has a Round Table, and Brougham Castle tells of a giant killed in a cave by Lancelot. Both are near Penrith. Pendragon Castle, near Kirkby Stephen, claims an Arthurian foundation, but perhaps only from the sixteenth century. At Manchester, much further south, a story of Lancelot and Turguin appears in the seventeenth.

On the other hand, there is a rather surprising wealth of Arthurian associations in Scotland. Most of these were collected, and others, I fear, vainly imagined by Mr Stuart Glennie in 1869. They fall into three groups. One belongs to the western Lowlands, which with Cumbria formed in Arthur's time the British kingdom of Strathclyde. Drummelzeier in Peebles disputes two spots for Merlin's grave, one of which claims in virtue of a thorn, the other of a cairn. Lanark has an Arthur's Fountain at Crawford, which was already a boundary in 1339. Renfrew has the place-name of Arthur Lee. Dumbarton has the mountain of Ben Arthur, and the town of Dumbarton itself is called *Castrum Arthuri* in

a record of 1367. The second group is north of the
Firth of Forth and the Wall of Antonine, in a district
which must always have been Pictish rather than
British. In Stirling according to the *Itinerarium* of
William of Worcester (c. 1478) '*rex Arthurus custo-
diebat le round table in Castro de Styrlyng, aliter
Snowden West Castle.*' This Round Table may be an
earthwork later called the King's Knot. At Larbert,
in the same county, a Roman building bears the name
of Arthur's O'on, and the *Furnus Arthuri* was a land-
mark in 1293. Arthur's Stone and Arthur's Fold are
at Coupar Angus and Arthur's Seat at Dunnichan,
both in Forfar. Even as far away as Kincardine, a
cairn in Garvock is Arthurhouse. Two localities in
Perth are linked with the end of Guinevere. Bury
Hill in Strathmore claims to be the castle to which
Mordred carried her off, and Mr Stuart Glennie was
told here how Arthur, when he recovered her, caused
her to be torn in pieces by wild horses, and how
parts of her body were buried in four places. 'Thae
auld histories are maistly lees, I'm thinking,' said
his informant. One of the four places must have
been Ganore's Grave at Meigle. Here the poet Gray
saw 'the tomb of Queen Wander, that was riven to
death by stoned horses for nae gude that she did—so
the woman here told me, I assure you.' There is in
fact in Meigle churchyard a worn carving, which
might be taken for a representation of a human body
tied to the wheels of a chariot and torn by wild
beasts. A writer of 1560 describes it more plausibly
as 'Ane goddess in ane caert and twa hors drawand

her.' The third Scottish group of localities is in the
eastern lowlands south of Forth. Geoffrey of Monmouth made Loth, Mordred's father, the eponymous
King of Lothian. Historically the district seems to
have been debatable ground between Pict and Briton
in the fifth and sixth centuries, until the growth of
Saxon Bernicia absorbed both elements. In Linlithgow is the Bed of Wallace near Bouden Hill. It was
so called, according to a local stone-breaker's account
to Mr Stuart Glennie, 'because the King was cockled
there.' But he added—and it is characteristic of the
folk—'It's mentioned in history that King Arthur's
wife was na' faithfu', an maybe it was her that was
ouer cosh wi' anither man on the tap there.' Edinburgh has long boasted its Arthur's Seat. Loth's
tomb is at Traprain in Haddington. The fragments
of Arthur's image of the Virgin, which the thirteenth
century *glossator* of Nennius locates in Wedale,
doubtless belonged to St Mary's church at Stowe on
the Edinburgh side of the Roxburgh boundary.
And now, as we near the Border, we get once more
a legend of the familiar southern type. As in Wales,
so under the Eildon Tree, just south of Melrose in
Roxburgh, Arthur sleeps in a cave until the appointed
day.

England, north of the Roman Wall, is of course
historically continuous with the region just traversed.
The slumber legend recurs at Sewingshields, where
castle vaults replace a cave as the locality, and at
Sneep in Northumberland. Near Sewingshields, too,
are Arthur's Chair on King's Crags, from which the

king threw a boulder at Guinevere on Queen's Crags, and Cumming's Cross, where inhospitable sons of Arthur attacked strangers on their return from his palace and robbed them of the royal gifts. In Malory's time, both Bamborough and Alnwick had been conjecturally identified with Lancelot's Joyous Gard. There is an Arthur's Hill in Newcastle, and an Arthur's Well at Waltoun-Crags; but when Brand wrote his history of Newcastle in 1839, this was regarded as the well in which St Paulinus baptized his converts. From the rest of England there is little to record. The slumber legend makes its last appearance at Richmond Castle in Yorkshire.[1] The folklore of the midlands and the south-east contributes nothing at all.

I do not suppose that this long catalogue is exhaustive. This matters the less, in that it can throw little light upon the location of an historical Arthur. It is too widespread, and indeed Arthurian localities are also to be traced in Brittany, with which an historical Arthur can have had nothing to do. Moreover, folk nomenclature of the nineteenth or even the sixteenth century is very poor evidence that the personalities which it uses are part of its primitive tradition. The imagination of the folk is impressed by its *mirabilia*, and readily invents stories to explain them. The names are the least permanent element of such stories. They are often, perhaps originally, anonymous, told of an indefinite fairy or giant, or of the devil. Then some named hero known to the

[1] A. Nutt in *Folk-Lore Journal*, i. 193.

folk acquires them, only to lose them to another. The Cornish Bodrugan affords a very good example. Here Carew found in possession Sir Bors, who is forgotten now. But Bodrugan has a headland, and a story of a hero who once took a spectacular leap from a chapel upon it, to escape his pursuers. It is told now of Henry of Bodrugan, who chose the wrong side at Bosworth Field. In the twelfth century it was told of Tristan. He, like Bors, has been forgotten, but the story endures. So, too, it has been with Arthur. Some at least of the Welsh cave legends have been transferred from him to one Owen Lawgoch and even to Owen Glendower; and the twelfth-century Arthur's Oven on Dartmoor has only reached the Ordnance surveyors as a vague King's Oven. The lapse of folk-memory is, indeed, as characteristic as its tenacity. When I passed Athelney last year, a Glastonbury car driver called my attention to the farmhouse in which 'Arthur' burnt the cakes. And this quality makes the folk readily susceptible to external suggestion. Mr Stuart Glennie's Linlithgow roadman substituted Arthur for Wallace because he had read history. After all, social groups are not watertight. Folk belief on the one hand, literary and antiquarian ideas on the other, interpenetrate. The schoolmaster is not entirely an invention of the nineteenth century. The Cornish vogue of Arthur, in particular, has been developed under external stimulus. Long before any folk-memories are recorded, the vagrant fancy of Geoffrey of Monmouth had put Arthur at Tintagel. And when an antiquarian came to Tintagel with Geoffrey's book in his pocket and asked for traces of the hero, one may be sure that the complaisance of the native guide would supply his need. A philological equation, right or wrong, between Camlan and the Camel, the misreading of a Latin inscription, possible traces of a ninth-century battle at Camelford; all would help. Once started, the tendency to find Arthur naturally spread. Davies Gilbert in 1838 already noted the Cornish habit of ascribing everything of unknown antiquity to the then famous hero. You can almost watch the process. Carew, although he saw the Latin inscription at Camelford and was evidently on the look-out for folk-memories, describes Tintagel entirely in terms of Geoffrey. He knows nothing of its *mirabilia*. Nor can there be much doubt that Dozmary Pool, which belonged in earlier folk-lore to the devil-ridden Tregeagle, owes its present Arthurian associations to the fancies of readers of Malory and Tennyson. The isolated stories of Cadbury Castle near the Camels look more like an independent Somerset tradition, although here also something is due to sixteenth-century archaeology and the identification with Camelot. The most one can say of the folk-memories is, I think, that they do not, in the main, run counter to the indications available from literary sources as to the districts in which the Arthurian legend probably originated and developed. And this does not help us much, as these districts are practically conterminous with the Celtic fringe in the west and south-west of the country. The popular vogue of Arthur in Scotland is indeed something of an exception, since the literary sources do not connect him with Strathclyde. And it is a little curious that mediaeval references to Arthur *mirabilia* as boundary marks are more frequently recorded in Scotland than elsewhere. This may be a mere accident of research. The chronicle tradition of Arthur was probably familiar in Scotland long before the earliest of them in 1293, although the extant romances in Northern English are all later. Why he should have aroused such interest in mediaeval Scotland is not quite clear, unless Scottish antiquarians, like some modern scholars, supposed the account of him in Nennius to be connected with the Bernician rather than the Kentish invasion. In any case the localities and stories gathered from the districts of ancient Pictland must reflect the late perversion of the legend by Fordun and Boece, which exalts the Pictish Lot and Mordred, and depreciates the characters of Arthur and Guinevere. The pejorative treatment of Guinevere as a wanton wife, for which there is little basis in Geoffrey or the earlier romances, is consistent with this. It must be added, however, that the sexual judgment of Guinevere by the folk is, characteristically enough, everywhere sterner than that of the exponents of *amour courtois*. In some parts of Wales, Professor Rhys tells us, to call a girl a Gwenhwyvar is to imply that she is no better than she ought to be; and he translates an old rhyme which runs:

> Guinevere Giant Ogurvan's daughter,
> Naughty young, more naughty later.

In Cornwall too, when the waves beat fiercely upon the rocks of Boskenna, the folk of Penzance say that it is the Jennifer weeping.

If, then, the folk-memories do not much help us to any precise geography for Arthur's activities, can we get anything better out of the battle names? Gildas gives no locality to his *obsessio Badonici montis*; the words that follow in one text, *qui prope sabrinum hostium habetur*, are a thirteenth-century gloss.[1] Nennius gives none to his *bellum in Monte Badonis*. Bede copies the wording of Gildas, and his ninth-century translator, who may be King Alfred, gives the rendering *Beadonescan dune*. Geoffrey of Monmouth treats his *urbs Kaerbadii, quae nunc Bado nuncupatur*, as Bath, and is probably followed both by the interpolator of Gildas and by *The Dream of Rhonabwy*, which describes Arthur as gathering his forces in the Severn Valley, before advancing to meet Osla Gyllellvawr at Badon. It seems to have been a guess by Camden which first transferred the site from Bath itself to Bannesdown or Bannerdown Hill a little further up the Avon. The identification of Badon with Bath has found recent supporters, notably in Mr E. W. B. Nicholson, who produces philological arguments for a British noun *bād*, yielding Badon in the sense of 'bathing place' as a Celtic name of the town called by the Romans *Aquae Sulis*. It may be so. But I think that Mr Nicholson's general view is prejudiced by a willingness to find something credible in the details of Geoffrey's story of the battle.

[1] *Record* ii.

Geoffrey represents the Saxons as defeated by Arthur in Lindsey, as then sailing round to Totnes, crossing Devon and Somerset and attacking Bath from the south-west, and finally as pursued by the victorious Britons to the Isle of Thanet. Mr Nicholson thinks that Wace's 'l'eve del Teigne' preserves a reading of Geoffrey corrupted in the known texts, and that the pursuit was to the river Teign in Devonshire. But even so the narrative must remain, in the light of Geoffrey's normal method of writing history, quite subjective. There is no evidence, literary or archaeological, for any use by the Saxon invaders of the island ports west of Southampton Water; and if there had been any such use, the whole history of Wessex would have been different. Indeed, it is very doubtful whether the Saxons were at any time far-flung pirates like the Danes who followed them. Their transmarine raids seem to have been limited to the *litus Saxonicum*, and there are those who think that the colonization itself was effected from an intermediate settlement in the Netherlands, rather than direct by a long sea voyage from the Cimbric peninsula. A confusion of Thanet with Cunetio and a dash for Bath from an advanced post in the Kennet valley is perhaps a more plausible conjecture. But it is on the whole safer to abandon any attempt to treat Geoffrey as a serious historical authority. We have, no doubt, to remember that British occupation of Bath appears to have terminated soon after the departure of the Romans. It is conceivable that the Saxons might have reached the town during the first fury of the invasions, when, as Gildas tells us, they raged from sea to sea and touched the western ocean. Serious effort to subdue the Avon and Severn valleys before the battle of Dyrham in 577 is unlikely, and no mere repulse of a vanguard raid would really fit in with Gildas' account of the *Mons Badonicus*. It was a disaster to the Saxons which came at the end of many years of settled warfare, and their victory left the Britons in peace for many years more. I think we must clearly look for Badon on the main line of the West Saxon advance, either along the Thames and the connected lateral valleys or on the borders of the Hampshire districts which the West Saxons seem to have occupied by a southwards movement from the Thames. Mr Guest long ago suggested Badbury Rings near Wimborne, which is not far from Charford, where the *Saxon Chronicle* claims a victory for Cerdic at about the date assigned by the *Annales Cambriae* to Badon. The chief difficulty about this is that philologists regard Badbury as a Saxon name, compounded of the familiar *burh*, a fort, and *Badda*, which may be a 'pet-form' of several Saxon personal names. It does in fact occur as the name of a Saxon moneyer. But a place not yet subdued by the Saxons is not likely to have had a Saxon name, and if it had, Gildas is not likely to have used it. The same difficulty attaches to other places in the available area which bear the name Badbury. There is a Badbury Hill with a camp in Great Coxwell, on the Berkshire ridge of high ground between the upper Thames valley and the

Vale of White Horse. Or one might very well think of the Saxons as pushing along the south side of the Vale of White Horse, in an endeavour to reach the Roman road from the south-east to Cirencester and Gloucester, which they afterwards mastered by another route through Salisbury and Barbury. All would be well until they came to Liddington Camp, close to which is a third Badbury. But if Arthur was posted here, they would have to fight him or leave him on their rear when they debouched into the Vale to cut the road. Another plausible spot is Bedwyn in the Kennet valley. It is close to Inkpen, and Inkpen protects the east end of the Wansdyke, which was almost certainly constructed or used by post-Roman Britons as a defence against enemies on the north. Here Mr Plummer has already proposed to locate a battle of Biedanheafde recorded by the *Saxon Chronicle* in 675. It was fought between rival Saxon kings, but it might very well be a 'second battle of Badon' which the *Annales Cambriae* put in 667. Here, too, philology is cold, preferring to derive Bedwyn from *bedewinde*, the Saxon name for a small species of convolvulus, which the philologists think must have grown very plentifully there. I have no doubt it did; it grows plentifully in any suitable soil.

Baydon, on the Roman road, south-east of Liddington Camp, Beedon in Berkshire, Bowden in Northamptonshire, and with some hesitation Bown Hill in Gloucestershire, are again assigned to Saxon personal names. The result of all this remains, once more, inconclusive. Geographically either Liddington

Castle or Inkpen would do well enough for Badon, and Badbury Rings, in view of its very southern position, perhaps rather less well. A defeat there would hardly stem the main western advance of the Saxons. Any one of the three identifications would justify us in regarding Arthur as holding the *massif* of the Wiltshire and Dorsetshire downs, and would be consistent with a battle of his predecessor Ambrosius at Wallop and a derivation from his name of Amesbury. This derivation philology does not condemn. Ambrosius may be also traceable in Amberley (Sussex), Ambrosden (Oxfordshire) and Ombersley (Worcester). I have no claims to be a philologist, but I sometimes doubt whether the Saxon derivation of Badbury, or rather of its first element, is impeccable. Why did so many different Baddas give their names to high fortified British places? There is, I think, a growing tendency in place-name study to leave rather more room than its founders left for a Celtic element. Is it possible that *Bad* represents some Celtic name adopted by the Saxons and perverted into something more consonant with their own linguistic habits?

The other battles in Nennius are even more elusive. He puts one at the mouth of a river Glein, four on a river Dubglas in the region of Linnuis, one on a river Bassas, one in the wood of Celidon, one at the fort of Guinnion, one in the City of the Legion, one on the river Tribruit, one at the hill of Agned. I have followed the *Harleian MS*. Others give Bregion or some variant as a second name for Agned, and it has been suggested that both names stood in an original list of twelve, and have been compressed to make room for an intrusive Badon. The Celtic names, as known to Nennius, may not be quite fairly represented by his manuscripts. Most of them are difficult to fix to the West Saxon area, even if we conceive of Arthur as operating north as well as south of Thames. Glein is a possible river name enough; there is a Glen in Northumberland, another in Lincolnshire, a Glyme in Oxfordshire. So is Dubglas (*du*, black; *glais*, stream, in Welsh). Douglas is common in Scotland and Ireland; there is none now in England, south of Lancashire. Of course Celtic names may have vanished from Anglicized regions, although river-names are more permanent than most. Celidon might be any forest; perhaps Chiltern, not claimed as a Saxon name, may represent it. Linnuis is probably Lindsey, and the City of the Legion must be either Chester or Caerleon. All three seem far afield for Arthur, and nothing plausible has been suggested in or near Wessex for Bassas, Guinnion, Tribruit, Agned or Bregion. It is hardly worth while guessing. Some scholars give Arthur a much wider range than Wessex. Mr Stuart Glennie, of course, treats him as a northern and not a southern hero. His identifications, largely selected from earlier conjectures, are the Glen in Northumberland, the Dunglass in Lothian (Linnuis), the hill (Bass) of Roughmute on the Carron, Tweeddale (Celidon), Dumbarton (*urbs Legionis*), Gala Water (Guinnion), the Forth (Tribruit), Edinburgh (Agned). Badon he puts at Bouden Hill in Linlithgow. Mr Alfred Anscombe, who emends the readings of the manuscripts very freely, finds the records of two distinct campaigns. In the first Arthur cleared the Roman Wall of Saxons, on the Lune (Glein) and the Douglas and at Baxenden (Bassas) in Lancashire, at a supposed forest of Celidon near Leeds, and at Binchester (Guinnion) in Durham. In the second he cleared the Welsh marches, fighting at Chester, the river Goyt (Tribruit) in Cheshire, and Leintwardine (Bregion) and Acornbury (Agned) in Herefordshire. Both these reconstructions seem to me out of court on historical grounds. Mr Stuart Glennie puts Arthur's activities wholly, and Mr Anscombe predominantly, in the north. But we have no reason to suppose that there was any serious Saxon interference with the northern British before Ida's Bernician advance in the second half of the sixth century, long after Arthur was in Avallon. Nennius treats all the battles as against the southern invaders. The *Urbs Legionis* is difficult, however, to fit into any southern theory; and it is open to us to fall back upon the agnostic conclusion, that the chronicler has brought together the dim memories of many battles, fought by many leaders, under Arthur's name.

As to the site of Camlan, there is very little to go upon. It might be the Camel at Camelford, or it might be the Cam near Cadbury. Many Celtic rivers could well bear the name of *cam*, 'the crooked.' Geoffrey of Monmouth chose the Camel. Whether he went upon folk-memories or merely upon etymology we do not know. And if there were folk-memories, they may have been perverted from a later battle between Ecgbert of Wessex and the Dumnonians in 825. The *Saxon Chronicle* puts it at 'Gafulford,' which historians incline to interpret as Camelford, although it may also be Galford in West Devon. There is no historical light upon Medraut. More than one of the contemporary kings censured by Gildas had obtained their dominions by violence. Maelgwn had dispossessed his uncle, but Arthur can hardly have been of Gwynedd. Constantine of Dumnonia and Aurelius Caninus, presumably of Wilts, had also 'rolled in the mud of parricide.' It is not certain, however, that Arthur was a king; the obscure words of Nennius rather suggest that he was not. We know no more of Arthur's real tomb than did William of Malmesbury.

CHAPTER VII

ARTHUR AND MYTHOLOGY

THE stories of Arthur, whether handed down in historical or literary form from Nennius onwards, or surviving in current folk-lore, contain obvious elements which do not properly belong to a Christian warrior and maintainer of the Roman tradition, engaged in repelling a barbarian invasion. Christianity has indeed made its own contribution to these elements in the protective image of the Virgin at Guinnion or Badon, afterwards supplemented, perhaps under crusading influence, by a cross brought from Jerusalem. But most of the marvels which cling to Arthur's name, even if they come to us through *Vitae Sanctorum*, are no part of the ecclesiastical order of ideas; and comparative mythology has not been slow to trace in them further examples of just that *detritus* of Celtic or other pre-Christian notions of the world and its governance which we found embedded in the *Mabinogi*. There is nothing surprising about this. It has already been pointed out that the least essential feature of a legend is its nomenclature, and it is natural enough that stories of forgotten mythological import, still enduring in the popular imagination, should settle upon the shoulders of historical heroes, who had, as Herodotus puts it, won their way to the marvellous. So simple

205

an explanation, however, has not always satisfied the
mythologists, and the legendary Arthur has sometimes been stressed to the point of overshadowing
or even eliminating his historic reality. Thus the late
Mr Alfred Nutt was inclined to regard Arthur as
a Brythonic equivalent of the Goidelic Finn, since
Finn too had a magical parentage and a wife who was
unfaithful to him with his nephew. So too Dr Kemp
Malone tells us that Arthur, with supernatural
belongings and the leader of the 'wild hunt,' is no
exception to the general rule that figures of Celtic
mythology become kings of Britain; and he conjectures that Arthur is really a doublet of a divine
Uthyr Ben, due to a confusion between the Welsh
uthr, 'cruel,' and a variant form *aruthr*, and to an
attempt in Cornwall to remedy the confusion by
making Arthur the son of Uther. I do not think that
these theories are worth serious pursuit, since they
rest upon the uncritical assumption that details, such
as Arthur's relationship to Uther or to Mordred,
which we find for the first time in Geoffrey of
Monmouth, can safely be treated as derived from
earlier Celtic legend. That is clearly not so, in view
of the arbitrary combinations to which Geoffrey
submits his material. A similar uncritical use, not
only of Geoffrey, but also of the later elaborations of
the romance-writers, renders valueless much of the
work of the late Professor Rhys. He is even capable
of quoting the fifteenth-century Malory as an
authority for mythological *data*. Professor Rhys
does not, indeed, surrender the historical Arthur. He

finds it, however, difficult to understand how one British leader should have become so famous above the rest, and should have attracted to himself so disproportionate a share of legend. It does not seem much of a difficulty, if Arthur really won, or was believed by Celtic bards on the testimony of Nennius to have won, the momentous battle of Badon. But it leads Professor Rhys to the ingenious solution that, in addition to the historical Arthur, there must also have been a Brythonic divinity Arthur, 'after whom the man may have been called, or with whose name his, in case it was of a different origin, may have become identical in sound owing to an accident of speech.' And he goes on to draw an analogy between the conflict of Arthur and Mordred for Guinevere and that of Airem and Mider in the Irish story of the *Wooing of Etain*. Airem is the High King of Ireland and his wife Etain is a fairy. But in an earlier incarnation she has been the wife of Mider King of the Fairies. Now Mider comes to claim her. He challenges Airem to a game of chess; the winner is to fix the stakes. Airem wins. He bids Mider undertake labours of planting and clearing and making a causeway; and by watching the fairies at their task learns the art of yoking oxen. Then Mider repeats his challenge, wins, and claims to put his arms round the queen and kiss her in mid-court. He carries her away to a fairy mount or *sid*. Presently Airem learns where the fugitives are, digs into the *sid*, and recovers Etain. Mider is clearly a mythological personage. He is one of the Tuatha De

Danann, the Celtic divinities who appear in Irish historical legend as a pre-Goidelic race, and in Irish folk-lore have become fairies. But as to the exact mythological significance of the Airem and Mider story and its Arthurian parallel, Professor Rhys is in doubt. He is a philologist, and comparative mythology is never more dangerous than when it calls in the aid of philology. He thinks that Etain may mean 'the shining one' and Gwenhwyvar 'the white phantom.' These names suggest the dawn. If so, we have to do with a nature myth, and must regard Arthur-Airem as a Celtic Zeus, the god of the lighted heaven, struggling for the dawn with Mider-Mordred, the god of darkness.

This, however, is only a flicker of the old 'solar' theory of mythological interpretation, to which Professor Rhys remains sentimentally attached. He makes a new start from the agricultural element represented by the yoking episode in the Irish story; and he finally arrives with some hesitation at the conclusion that the divinity, which he still believes to be inherent in the common Goidelic-Brythonic personality of Arthur-Airem, was that, not of a heaven god, but of a culture hero, bringing the gifts of civilization to men. Now the culture hero is in itself a fruitful mythological conception, and one which Professor Rhys has done much to establish. It is the characteristic feature of a stage reached by most European peoples in the development of their religious thought. The high gods dwell in their realm aloof, and with them it rests to bestow or to

withhold all the good of which man has need.
Primarily this is food, through success in hunting or
the fertility of herds and crops. But as the notion of
what is good expands, and comes to include such
elements as fire, iron, gold, craftsmanship, victory,
poetry, these too tend to be thought of as gifts of
the gods. Normally man attempts to bind the gods
to himself by such devices as sacrifice, ritual tendance
and prayer. But when he begins to reflect upon his
civilization and finds that much of it is permanent,
he comes to believe that some real or imagined
ancestor must have been in closer touch with the
gods than ordinary men, and must have won the
rudiments of this civilization for his successors. He
visited the remote and normally inaccessible Otherworld, where are all good things in inexhaustible
abundance, and by cajolery or violence obtained its
treasures from their friendly or reluctant keepers.
This is the culture hero. He taught men the uses of
agriculture and waymaking and song, and rid them
of giants and monsters with the magic weapons won
in his quest. He is a mediator between god and man,
and in time he comes to be thought of as himself in
some sense divine. Perhaps he was the son of a god;
and perhaps when his time on earth was ended, he
did not linger about his grave, like the ghosts of
common men, but went back to that happy Otherworld, which took shape, in accordance with varying
geographical conditions, in the parallel fancies of the
Land Overseas and the Hollow Hill. So the Otherworld assumed also the aspect of a kingdom of the

dead. Ultimately the conceptions of the god and the culture hero tended to approximate; the hero took over more and more of the divine functions, and became himself the object of a religious cult. Herakles and Asklepios in Greek, Odin in Teutonic mythology, are types; and although Celtic mythology has only reached us in broken fragments, there is sufficient ground for inferring that in it too the culture hero was a familiar figure. His traces are in the *Mabinogi* as well as in the Irish stories.

Once more Professor Rhys calls upon philology to support the claim that Arthur-Airem was a culture hero. There is an Aryan root *ar*, from which come various words indicative of ploughing, the Latin *arare*, the English *ear*, but which probably had the wider original significance of 'fitting together.' This might yield in Irish Airem, and might also yield an early Celtic Artor, in the sense of 'ploughman' or 'harnesser,' which in its turn might become in Welsh Arthur. Unfortunately, evidence for the actual existence of an early Celtic Artor is lacking. Professor Rhys finds support in the Mercurius Artaius of one Gaulish inscription, who may be identical with the Mercurius Cultor of another, and in the goddess Artio, of whom a figured representation has been found at Berne. It is likely enough that the Celtic culture hero was identified in Gallo-Roman inscriptions with Mercury. But it must be remembered that Gaul is not Britain, that Artaius may be merely an epithet derived from a place-name, and that Artio is much more likely to be related to another root *ar*, which appears in the Welsh *arth*, 'bear,' since side by side with the goddess is shown in the Berne figure a bear as her cult-symbol or attribute. Philology, then, hardly bears the weight of any identity of Arthur and Airem, or of the existence of Arthur as a Celtic mythological name which might be conflated with the Latin Artorius. Professor Rhys, who is always candid, has rather ruefully to admit that it 'only refers us to a root *ar* (or to several roots of that form) of widely divergent meanings.' It must be added that Arthur has also been claimed as a bear god.

Philology apart, it is not to be denied that there may be points of contact between the Arthurian and Irish stories. The pairs of names have at least a superficial resemblance, and this will be the greater if the Medyr of *Kulhwch and Olwen*, which seems to mean the 'marksman,' is, as is possible, only a variant of Medraut. There is not much to be made of the fact that Medyr, standing in Kelliwic, could hit through the legs a wren at Esgeir Oervel in Ireland; or of a parallel drawn by Professor Rhys between three Étains in Irish myth and three Gwenhwyvars in a Welsh triad, since nothing is known of the latter outside the triad, for which they may have been invented, and the former are made up of Airem's wife in her two incarnations, and a third Etain who was her daughter. But another triad, in which Medraut is said to have dragged Gwenhwyvar from her royal chair and struck her, does rather curiously recall the central episode of the

Wooing of Etain. There seems little justification for assuming any common origin for the stories, but the literary influence of Ireland upon Wales may have led to some contamination of details. Once more, it must be remembered that we do not know precisely what the pre-Galfridian Welsh narrative of Camlan was, or what part Gwenhwyvar played in it, and there is another version of her rape, apparently independent of Geoffrey, in which the agent is not called Medraut, but Melvas. This is first found in Caradoc's *Vita* of Gildas. Here Melvas is King of Somerset and Arthur recovers Gwenhwyvar from Glastonbury. The *Vita*, or some common source, must be behind the *Conte de la Charrete* of Chrétien de Troyes, in which the same story is told at great length, and the rescue of the queen is ascribed to Lancelot. Chrétien's ravisher is Meleagant. He is the son of Bagdemagus, whom Chrétien's continuator makes King of Goire with a capital at Bade. Presumably Bade is Bath. But Goire, from which it is said that none ever return, and which is only reached by a sword bridge and a bridge under water, has not unnaturally been claimed as a representation of the Otherworld. So far as Chrétien's own conception is concerned, this gets some support from an incidental reference in his *Erec* to Maheloas, *li sire de l'isle de voire*, where there is no thunder, or lightning-stroke, or tempest, no toad or serpent, or too much heat or winter. *L'isle de voire* has the characteristics of an Earthly Paradise, and its name suggests the boats and towers of glass which often figure in Celtic descriptions of the Otherworld, across the translucent wave. Meleagant son of Bagdemagus must be the Maelwys son of Baeddan of *Kulhwch and Olwen*; and his name, variously explained as 'the princely youth' or 'the prince of death,' has also been given an Otherworld connotation, which is difficult to reconcile with the suggestion of Professor Rhys that Maelwys in *Kulhwch and Olwen* ought to be spelt Maelyf or Maeluf, and that the hero intended was an Irishman of history, Maeluma son of Baedan mac Cairill. The list of Gwenhwyvar's abductors is not yet exhausted; as the schoolgirl wrote, she was a lady very much subject to the misfortune of being run away with. The tragical intrigue with Lancelot is a comparatively late development of romance. But in an English ballad, the place of Maelwys is taken by King Cornwall, in a late Welsh dialogue, if rightly interpreted, by Kei, in Heinrich von dem Türlin's *Diu Crône* by Gasozein, in Ulrich von Zatzikhoven's *Lanzelet* by Valerin. In both the German versions a prior claim, of betrothal or of pre-nuptial *liaison*, is put forward in justification of the rape, and this has been regarded as supporting the analogy with the reincarnated Etain. The argument can hardly be stressed. Nor must too much be made of the Otherworld character of the land of Goire. If it came from a legendary source, it would have been natural enough for Geoffrey and Caradoc to euhemerize it. But it may be merely romantic invention, perhaps influenced by the *Vita Merlini*. Perilous bridges are common enough in romances, and some scholars look upon them as of oriental rather than Celtic derivation. On *a priori* grounds, there is no reason why one of the feats of the culture hero should not have been the delivery of a queen from the Otherworld, in its aspect as a land of the dead. Even so, for example, Herakles rescued Alkestis; and the mortal visitants who stray or are lured into fairyland are just as often women as men. At the same time, there is nothing in either Geoffrey or Gildas to suggest that they are telling anything but an ordinary tale of human violence. A mediaeval chieftain, and in particular a Celtic mediaeval chieftain, might reasonably expect to be allowed to take his neighbour's wife without incurring the suspicion of Otherworld tendencies.

The deeds of Arthur, however, are not always, even by Geoffrey, limited to the normal range of human prowess. He fights against giants, on Snowdon and on Mont St Michel in the *Historia*, and on Brent Knoll in the Glastonbury story of Ider. He fights against monsters, the serpent of Carhampton in the *Vita Carantoci*, the *afanc* of Llyn Barfog in the fables of the Merionethshire mountains. The Vulgate *Mort Artu*, apparently drawing upon a tale which had made its way to Savoy, gives him another adversary in a monstrous cat called the Chapalu; and there are traces of a version in which this combat, and not that with Mordred at Camlan, proved his end. The Chapalu seems to be a derivative from the Palug's Cat of a poem in the *Black Book of Carmarthen*. It was there a Manx cat, and the hero of the episode was Kei; but a transference from one

heroic name to another has ceased to cause us
surprise. Obviously stories of giant and monster
slaying belong to the common form both of heroic
and of hagiographic legend. They may be interpreted at will as nature-myths of the sun dispelling
the mists of morning, or as reminiscences of conflicts
with prehistoric races or extinct fauna. But they fit
in well enough with the conception of the culture
hero, ridding the land of obstacles to civilization.
And there are other Arthurian features which look
still more like the culture hero. The traditional chase
of the great pig Troit, already known to Nennius,
recurs in an elaborate form in *Kulhwch and Olwen*,
where the Twrch Trwyth and another pig, Yskithyrwyn Benbaedd, are the objects of separate
quests. The tusk of one of them is to serve as a
razor and the other carries a comb and scissors
between his ears. These may reasonably be regarded
as instruments of civilization; and, indeed, the
clipping of hair was an initiation ceremony for the
Celts, comparable to knighthood. Similarly, a pig
hunted by Arthur in a triad left on the land the
agricultural boons of corn and honey. But the pig
itself, the chief domestic animal of the Celts, is one
of the gifts of civilization, and the winning of it by
a culture hero from the Otherworld may be traced
among the fragmentary themes of the *Mabinogi*.
Another triad, which describes an unsuccessful
attempt of Arthur to get pigs out of the guardianship
of Tristan, suggests that this exploit had attached
itself to him and may be at the bottom of all his pig-

hunts. Geoffrey of Monmouth naturally ignored these, but they may be faintly reflected in Merlin's prophetical designation of Arthur as *Aper Cornubiae*. *Kulhwch and Olwen* is rich in culture-myths. Agricultural tasks have to be wrought; magical food-giving vessels have to be achieved. These episodes perhaps belong to an independent story, with which that of Arthur's hunt has been conflated. But in the *Preiddeu Annwfn*, obscure as that poem is, we may dimly discern Arthur paying a visit to the Other-world, and finding there the Caldron of the Head of Hades, which is but one of many vessels of abundance or regeneration or inspiration known to mythologists. They are gear of the gods, and fortunate is the culture hero who can make himself master of one of them. It has been supposed that the Holy Grail was once such a talisman, and even that it may originally have been associated with Arthur; but that is too difficult a question to be entered upon here. In the forms in which we have the legend, Arthur and the Grail King are distinct. Nor does any food-giving significance appear to be attached to the Round Table. The origin and purport of this have been much debated. It seems to have come late into the Arthurian picture. Geoffrey has nothing of it. A latish Welsh poem gives Arthur a 'long' or 'great' table in Devon, but does not call it 'round.'[1] Conceivably there is a hint of it in the *Vita* of Carannog, where Arthur attempts to make a table of the saint's altar, but anything placed on it is flung

[1] Rhys, *Arthurian Legend*, 58; cf. F. Lot in *Rom.* xxviii. 343.

off. There is an inverted analogy here to the Carn Cabal of Nennius, any stone taken from which is replaced at night. The Round Table first clearly appears as such in the *Brut* of Wace, who says that it was established to prevent disputes for precedence among Arthur's followers. Wace probably got it from *li conteor et li fableor* whom he mentions. The normal mediaeval hall had of course its rectangular high table, but a circular arrangement seems to have been usual in Irish mead halls, and is indeed ascribed to the Celts of Gaul by Posidonius in the first century B.C. Nor are such brawls for precedence as Arthur desired to avoid unknown in Irish stories. I do not know that any more recondite explanation is needed. Otherwise, one might suggest that *li conteor et li fableor* were fashioning Arthur's court on the model of that of Charlemagne, and were recalling the episode in the *Pèlerinage de Charlemagne*, where the pilgrims find the church of the Last Supper, with twelve seats and in the midst a thirteenth *bien close et scellée*, in which the emperor seats himself with his twelve peers around him.

These traits of the culture hero are only fringe on the trappings of the warrior king. They have far less interest than that enduring myth of the undying Arthur. The place of Arthur's grave was unknown to the early Welsh bard and to William of Malmes-bury. But the fable of the hoped-for return was already *antiquitas naeniarum* to the historian, and although not traceable in Wales, was rooted in Cornwall and perhaps Brittany some years before he wrote. It was evidently familiar to Geoffrey. For some reason, literary or political, he ignores it in the set narrative of the *Historia*, and even in the *Prophecies*, as we have them, he passes it over lightly as an *exitus dubius*. Whether it was more prominent in the *Prophecies*, as originally issued, we cannot tell. The version incorporated in the *Historia* seems to link up the foreshadowed restoration of the Britons with a return, not of Arthur, but of Cadwallader. In the *Historia* itself Cadwallader is the last king of Britain before the final Saxon conquest, and there is a story of his death in exile at Rome, which really belongs to the English Ceadwalla. The Cadwallader of history was a seventh-century North Wales chieftain of whom little is known. The prophetic allusions to him are repeated in post-Galfridian Welsh poems, and he acquired the reputation of a saint. There does not appear to be any evidence that he was in fact looked to in popular belief as a deliverer. His coming is still the subject of prophecy in the *Vita Merlini*. But here Geoffrey also takes up the legend of Arthur where the *Historia* dropped it, and becomes more communicative. Taliesin reminds Merlin how, after the battle of Camlan, they two, with their steersman Barinthus, bore the wounded king over the sea to the Fortunate Isle, which is also the Isle of Apples, to be healed after long time by Morgen, who dwells there with her eight sisters. The description of the island clearly owes something to classical models; but indeed the Greek and the Celtic conceptions of the Otherworld seem to have been closely similar.

Geoffrey may have had in mind a specific Breton belief, recorded most fully by Pomponius Mela (c. 41–50 A.D.), who says that the island of Sena off the coast of Gaul was the home of nine virgin priestesses, shape-shifters, controllers of the sea and winds by their spells, and skilled alike in medicine and divination.[1] But Barinthus Geoffrey took from the *Navigatio Brendani*, a Christianized version of the Irish *imrama* or travel-tales, which are fundamentally narratives of Otherworld visits. The Fortunate Isle of the *Vita Merlini* must be the *insula Avallonis* of the *Historia*. There is no particular reason to suppose that Geoffrey invented this name. He makes one other use of it in the *Historia*, where Arthur's sword Caliburnus, the Caladbolg of the Irish culture hero Cuchulainn, is said to have been forged in Avallon; and there is a possible independent allusion to *tot l'or d'Avalon* in the French poem *Le Couronnement de Louis*, which was written in the middle of the twelfth century. The name Avalon is not unknown in Breton and French topography. But it may very well have been a Celtic designation of the Otherworld. Giraldus Cambrensis and others give alternative derivations of it from a personal name Avallo or Avalloc, and from *aval*, 'an apple'; and these become the basis for stories about Glastonbury, with which Avallon had been identified. Modern philology has suggested a third derivation from the Breton *avel*, 'air,' but this has not met with much support. Professor Rhys adopted Avalloc, and con-

[1] *De Chorographia*, iii. 5.

structed a hypothetical 'Celtic dark divinity' Avallach, of whom there is no mythological record, unless Aballac, who occurs at the beginning of certain Welsh genealogies as a son of Beli and Anna, the cousin of the Virgin Mary, can be pressed into the service. An origin in the apple seems probable enough and would be consistent with the *insula pomorum* of the *Vita Merlini* and with many Irish *imrama* and other stories, in which the apple is a characteristic fruit of the Otherworld. Morgen's name has also been matter for controversy. It has been compared with that of the Irish war goddess Morrigan, but there is nothing bellicose about Geoffrey's Morgen. Professor Rhys is happier here with the analogy of Muirgein, given as a baptismal name to the mermaid Liban in an Irish story. It would mean *Muri-gena*, 'the sea-born.' The Argante of Layamon might have the independent sense of 'brilliant,' but is more likely to be due to a scribal error. In many of the Irish stories the Otherworld is an isle of women, as well as an isle of apples, and the visitants are entangled in amorous adventures, like those of Odysseus with Circe or Calypso. If this was an element in the original notion of Avallon, Geoffrey has dropped it, and little significance can be attached to the thirteenth-century paraphrase of the *Vita Merlini* by the Pseudo-Gildas, with its *vivuntque simul, si credere fas est*. The euhemerizing Giraldus rejects the belief that Morgen was a *dea phantastica*, and turns her into a noble matron and a kinswoman of Arthur. The *Draco Normannicus* and

Chrétien de Troyes call her Arthur's sister; and in the hands of the romancers she takes on the aspect of the wicked enchantress, Morgain la Fée. But these developments belong to literature, not to mythology. One other personage of the *Vita Merlini* may have a touch of the Celtic Otherworld about him. This is Barinthus, perhaps a shadow of the sea god Manawyddan, who meets the travellers of the *imrama* upon the ocean wave.

The myth of Arthur in Avallon, then, is still that of a culture hero, now resting after his labours for mankind in the happy land. So far it has been a Land Overseas. But we must now consider a group of stories, divergent from Geoffrey and the ordinary romance tradition, in which the abode of Arthur seems to answer to the alternative conception of the Otherworld as a Hollow Hill. These stories have a curious uniformity about them, although some come from mediaeval legend and others from more recent folk-belief. The earliest record is in the *Otia Imperialia* of Gervase of Tilbury.[1] Gervase knows the ordinary fable of Avallon and Morgen. But he also tells, on the authority of natives, how in recent days a groom of the Bishop of Catania, following a strayed horse among the recesses of Mount Aetna in Sicily, came upon a fair plain full of all manner of delights. In it was a palace and in the palace a king lying on a bed. This was Arthur. He told the groom of his battle with Mordred, and of the healing of his wounds, which broke out afresh every year. And

[1] *Record* xxix.

221

then he sent him back with presents to the bishop, which many had seen and marvelled at. The *Otia Imperialia* dates from about 1211, but Gervase had been in Sicily as a follower of the Norman King William about 1190, and his story therefore agrees in its chronology with another reported a little later in the *Dialogus Miraculorum* of Caesarius of Heisterbach as an incident of the conquest of Sicily by the Emperor Henry VI in 1194.[1] But here the tone is rather different. Arthur is not seen. One of his retainers meets the groom, and sends a message to the owner of the horse, who is the dean of Palermo, to appear at Arthur's court in fourteen days. The dean mocks at the summons, but on the fourteenth day he dies. There are some other traces of the Sicilian legend, in particular a thirteenth-century poem which describes the advent of three Breton knights to Aetna to learn, if they might, the truth about Arthur. But it forms no part of the abundant native folk-lore of the mountain, and may be taken to have been introduced by the Norman conquerors or their Breton followers. With it probably came the name of the *Fata Morgana* for the mirage at Messina.

Against these far-flung stories of Aetna may be placed the Hollow Hill legends of our own country. They are thickest in Wales; that of the cave of Craig-y-Dinas in Glamorganshire may be taken as typical. A Welshman, crossing London Bridge with a hazel staff in his hand, is met by a stranger, who tells him that beneath the tree from which that staff

[1] *Record* xxx.

was cut lies a treasure hoard. They return to Wales together and find a cavern under the hazel. In the passage hangs a bell. It must not be touched, says the cunning man; if it is, the inmates of the cave will wake and ask, 'Is it day?' and the answer must be given, 'No, sleep thou on.' In the cave are warriors sleeping, and one wears a crown. It is Arthur, waiting until the bell gives the signal to rise and lead the Cymry to victory. Within the circle of warriors lie a heap of gold and a heap of silver; there is a taboo against taking from more than one of them. The Welshman accidentally strikes the bell, but gives the required answer, and escapes with his treasure. When it is exhausted, he pays a second visit. But this time he forgets to give the answer. The warriors take the gold from him, beat him, and send him forth a cripple. The cave can never be found again. Other caves boast the same story, sometimes fragmentary, and sometimes with variants. A bugle may replace the bell. There is not always a wizard guide; the discovery may be made, much as on Aetna, by a shepherd seeking his sheep. At Llandegai three women are seen in a coracle, as the visitant leaves the cave; the influence of the romances may be suspected here. On Snowdon Arthur's men are in the cave, but not Arthur himself. He lies under a cairn on the pass called Bwlch y Saethau, where he fell driving his foes up from Cwmllan, which has doubtless been taken for Camlan. In Anglesea the cave was Arthur's shelter in a war, not with Saxons, but with Goidels. The outlines of the legend have been variously blurred in the imagination of the folk. There is another outcrop of similar belief in the north of England. Beneath the Castle of Sewingshields, near the Roman wall in Northumberland, are vaults where Arthur sleeps with Guinevere and all his court and a pack of hounds. He waits until one blows the horn which lies ready on a table, and cuts a garter placed beside it with a sword of stone. Once a farmer, knitting on the ruins, followed his clew of wool which had fallen to a crevice and found the vault. He cut the garter and Arthur woke, but as he sheathed the sword, fell asleep again, with the words—

> O woe betide that evil day
> On which this witless wight was born,
> Who drew the sword—the garter cut,
> But never blew the bugle horn.

In another version Arthur says that, if the visitant will blow the horn and draw the sword, he will 'confer upon him the honours of knighthood, to last through time.' But the craven takes fright, goes to look for a comrade, and the entrance is lost. A similar adventure befell one Potter Thompson in the ruins of Richmond Castle in Yorkshire. He too was dismissed with contumely.

> Potter Thompson, Potter Thompson, hadst thou blown the horn,
> Thou hadst been the greatest man that ever was born.

It will be observed that the trend of the northern stories is other than that common in Wales. There a taboo forbids the ringing of the bell. Here the man who does not blow the horn has failed in a quest, just as did Perceval, when he omitted to ask the significance of the Grail, and so release the land from its enchantment. Finally, in far Somerset, there is the isolated example of Cadbury camp, where once again Arthur is in a hollow hill, although no human eye has ever been fortunate enough to look through the gates of his dwelling.

Comparative mythology has not been slow to point out that the Hollow Hill conception of Arthur's rest has many analogues, from the Christianized version of the Seven Sleepers of Ephesus onwards. That is very true. The pages of Grimm and of such modern historians of fairyland as Dr Hartland are rich in cave-bound personages, many of whom are destined national deliverers. Stories closely parallel to those of Wales are told in Ireland of Earl Gerald at Mullaghmast, of the O'Donoghue at Killarney, of Garry Geerlaugh at Ardee in Louth, of an unknown warrior in Donegal. They will all save Erin, one day or other. Once in seven years, Earl Gerald rides round the Curragh of Kildare. His horse, like Arthur's at Cadbury, has silver shoes. They were half an inch thick when he fell asleep. When they are worn as thin as a cat's ear, a miller's son with six fingers on each hand will blow a trumpet, and Gerald will do battle with the English. In Scotland, the heroes are Bruce on Rathlin Island, Finn and his folk in Inverness. In Sutherlandshire and in the Isle of Man they are anonymous. Europe knows the stories well. King Marko sleeps in Serbia and Bohemia, the robber chief Dobocz in the Carpathian hills, King Wenzel in Bohemia. But it is the Teutonic area which owns the greatest collection of such tales. They are told of Dietrich in Alsace, of Siegfried at Geroldseck, of Olger at Kronburg, of the founders of the Swiss Federation at Lucerne or on the Grütli, and of many others. Here too they are often anonymous, or of uncertain attribution. Frederick Barbarossa sleeps at the Kyffhaüser in Thuringia, sitting at a stone table. His beard has grown twice round the table; when the third circuit is completed, he will awake. He will hang his shield on a withered tree, which will break into leaf, and a better day will dawn. Once a shepherd piped to him. The emperor asked, 'Fly the ravens round the mountain still?' and when he was told that they did, replied, 'Then must I sleep another hundred years.' The piper was rewarded with the stand of a basin, which proved to be of pure gold. Frederick is in several other caves, notably on the Unterberg near Salzburg. Here too are the details of the beard and the withered tree. It will leaf again before the final battle, which will be Armageddon. Whether it did leaf again, I do not know. But the Kyffhaüser is also claimed for the Emperor Otto and a Marquis John, and the Unterberg for Charlemagne and even Charles V. Charlemagne is also in the Odenberg, which another version assigns to Odin. Once again we find the substance of topographical legends far more stable than their nomenclature. And of this the Welsh caves themselves furnish an example, for their ownership fluctuates between Arthur and a rather mysterious Owen Lawgoch, identified by Professor Rhys with Yvain de Galles, a fourteenth-century Welshman whom Froissart names as fighting for the French against the English. And in one case it is the fifteenth-century Owen Glendower, and in another a Hairy Man. Perhaps his claim is the oldest of all. Grimm thinks that the long beard points to the red-bearded Thor, or it may be Odin, although Charlemagne also was *à la barbe florie*. If Odin was the original Teutonic sleeper, we have come again upon the culture hero. Whether the leafing tree justifies us in thinking of a still earlier stratum of religious belief, in the priest king slain to bring back the *renouveau* of the year, may be left to speculation. In Gervase of Tilbury's story Arthur's wounds break out annually.

One other feature of Arthur must also be an inheritance from Odin, or from some Celtic equivalent. Odin is generally accepted as the original Teutonic leader of the 'furious host,' riding in the skies at night with his troop of dead souls. It is an old belief, familiar to Virgil and other Latin writers.

> Armorum sonitum toto Germania caelo
> Audiit.

And it is widespread, at least in western Europe. The riders have become ghostly warriors or huntsmen. In France they are *la mesnie Hellequin*, which seems to mean no more, philologically, than 'hell-rout.' Walter Map, at the end of the eleventh century, knew of the *phalanges noctivagae* in Hereford and the Welsh marches, as well as in Brittany. He calls them the *familia Herlethingi*, and connects them with a story of a King Herla. 'Hurlican' is still a name for a troublesome child in Dorsetshire. In mediaeval and popular belief the leadership of the 'wild hunt' has been transferred from Odin to many heroic personages. Among them are several of the cave sleepers. Dietrich rides and Charlemagne. Earl Gerald rides on May Day in Ireland. And Arthur, too, rode. After finishing his Sicilian story, Gervase of Tilbury adds that he had heard of similar occurrences in the woods both of Greater and of Lesser Britain. Foresters had told of companies of knights, met hunting beneath the full moon, with hounds and a din of horns; and these, when questioned, had declared themselves to be of Arthur's household. The belief is recorded in the *Mort Artu* of the Boron cycle. Half-way through the thirteenth century the preacher Étienne de Bourbon, expatiating on devils, says that they amuse themselves by taking the form of hunting or tilting knights, *qui dicuntur de familia Allequini vel Arturi*.[1] There is an echo in the sixteenth-century *Complaynt of Scotland*—

> Arthour knycht he raid on nycht
> With gyltin spur and candil lycht.

And there is a last faint survival in the tramplings heard during tempest by the Cadbury peasant on the forgotten road to Glastonbury. Perhaps Arthur rides

[1] *Record* xxxi.

no longer, but he still wanders, in the form of a bird.
Cervantes knew this, and gives it, as an English, not
a Spanish, superstition, in *Don Quixote*. An eighteenth century tourist was rebuked by a native for
shooting a raven on Marazion Green, because King
Arthur lived in that form. In modern Cornish folk-
lore, the bird is generally the red-legged Cornish
chough. A recent enquirer was told by a Delabole
quarryman that it was the nath or puffin.

It is to be observed that many of the cave stories
show a complication of motive. The denizens are
not merely waiting for the signal to awake; they are
also guardians of treasures, which the intruders may
or may not secure. And this feature affords a link
with innumerable other stories, which are of treasure
hunts pure and simple. They often take the form of
visits to caves, or more frankly to fairyland. There
are often taboos against excessive greed, which prove
too much for the frailty of human nature. And there
are illusions. A gift of what looks like rubbish is
made; it turns out to be gold. Alternatively, stolen
gold turns into dead leaves, when it is taken home.
The London Bridge opening from Craig-y-Dinas
recurs in an English tale of the Pedlar of Swaffham,
who is thus guided to a treasure in his orchard.[1] A
cave in Dinas Emrys knows nothing of Arthur. It
was Merlin who left a treasure here after his interview
with Vortigern. It will not be found until the destined heir comes, a youth with blue eyes and yellow
hair. A bell will guide him to the cave and it will

[1] Cf. *Antiquary* x. 302.

open at the touch of his foot. In analogous stories the secret will be revealed to a little girl or to a Goidel shepherd lad by a black sheep with a speckled head. Mythologically, I suppose we must say of the heroic cave sleepers that, while in one aspect they represent culture heroes resting in the Otherworld after their labours, in another they look more like the lords of the Otherworld themselves, to whom its treasures properly belong. And the first Celtic sleeper of whom we hear is certainly presented to us, not as a hero, but as a god. Plutarch, in the *De defectu Oraculorum*, quotes the report of one Demetrius, who had been sent by the emperor to get information about a number of uninhabited islands near Britain.[1]

There is, men said, an island in which Kronos is imprisoned with Briareus keeping guard over him as he sleeps; for, as they put it, sleep is the bond forged for Kronos. They add that around him are many deities, his henchmen and attendants.

What Celtic divine name, one wonders, did Demetrius turn into Kronos? Can it have been that of Cernunnos, the squatting horned divinity who appears on several Gallo-Roman altars? He must certainly have been a god of plenty, since his symbols are the torque and the cornucopia, and a sack from which pour forth what may be acorns and may be coins.

It is not possible fully to explain the Celtic expectation of Arthur by pointing to the *débris* of a

[1] *De defectu Oraculorum*, xviii.

culture hero. In the twelfth century it was a living political force and it had its later recrudescences. This is a problem of mass psychology, not of lingering pagan fancies. It has often happened in the course of history that the death of a great leader has been hardly accepted by those who had put their trust in him. Men thought that Harold had not really fallen at Senlac; he must still be living on, to make head one day against the Normans. Such beliefs spring up most naturally in the shock of exaltation and dismay due to some distant and imperfectly apprehended disaster. Frederick Barbarossa could not have been drowned in crossing a brook in Cilicia; nor could all the hopes of Portugal have vanished with Sebastian in the sands of Alcazar. Impostors were still claiming to be Frederick in the fourteenth century, and Sebastianism is said to be barely extinct to-day. There were many who held that Lord Kitchener was languishing in a German prison, long after the sinking of the *Hampshire*. But such cases are not quite similar to the Arthurian hope, which emerges, so far as we know, some centuries after Arthur had ceased to be. Perhaps the nearest analogy is once more to be found in Charlemagne, the rumour of whose resurrection from the dead is reported by the chronicler Ekkehard on the eve of the first Crusade. This was an enterprise organized with all the resources of ecclesiasticism, and it is not surprising that the literary activities, which had already woven fables of the emperor and his peers around so many monasteries and pilgrimage shrines, were able to make one final effort in the interests of the Holy Sepulchre. Some similar propaganda, working no doubt upon the dormant pagan fancies, must underlie the British hope. One may reasonably conjecture that it formed part of the reorganization of Breton independence, after the Norman invasions of the tenth century. Such sentiments outlive the causes which produce them.

But the flames which once burnt around the memory of Arthur have long ago sunk into grey ashes. He wakes no national passions now. He has been taken up, with Roland and with Hector, and with all who died fighting against odds, into the Otherworld of the heroic imagination. His deeds are the heritage of all peoples; not least of the English folk against whom he battled. To this outcome many men have worked; the good clerk Wace, Chrétien de Troyes, the unknown author of the *Lancelot* and the *Mort Artu*, our own Thomas Malory. But most of all are we bound to praise that learned and unscrupulous old canon of St George's in Oxford, Geoffrey of Monmouth. And withal we still do not know where is Arthur's grave.

Ubi nunc fidelis ossa Fabricii manent?

RECORDS

233

i

GALLIC CHRONICLES

(*a*) [From anonymous chronicle, ending 452, edited by T. Mommsen in *Chronica minora Saeculorum iv–vii* (*M.G.H.*), i. 652,
660.]

[s.a. 409–10.] Hac tempestate praeualetudine [*ex coni. ed.*
praeualente hostium multitudine] Romanorum uires funditus
attenuatae.

Britanniae Saxonum incursione deuastatae.

[s.a. 441–2.] Britanniae usque ad hoc tempus uariis
cladibus euentibusque latae in dicionem Saxonum rediguntur.

(*b*) [From anonymous chronicle, ending 511, *ibid.* i. 661.]

[s.a. 439–48.] Britanniae a Romanis amissae in dicionem
Saxonum cedunt.

ii

GILDAS

[From *De Excidio et Conquestu Britanniae* (c. 548), edited by T.
Mommsen in *Chronica minora Saeculorum iv–vii* (*M.G.H.*),
iii. 1.]

[Ch. xx.] Igitur rursum miserae mittentes epistolas reliquiae ad Agitium Romanae potestatis virum, hoc modo
loquentes: 'Agitio ter consuli gemitus Britannorum'; et post
pauca querentes: 'repellunt barbari ad mare, repellit mare ad
barbaros; inter haec duo genera funerum aut iugulamur aut
mergimur'; nec pro eis quicquam adiutorii habent. Interea
famis dira ac famosissima vagis ac nutabundis haeret, quae
multos eorum cruentis compulit praedonibus sine dilatione
victas dare manus, ut pauxillum ad refocillandam animam
cibi caperent; alios vero nusquam, quin potius de ipsis
montibus, speluncis ac saltibus dumis consertis continue re-
bellabant. Et tum primum inimicis per multos annos praedas in terra agentibus strages dabant.... Quievit parumper

inimicorum audacia nec tamen nostrorum malitia; recesserunt hostes a civibus nec cives a suis sceleribus. [Ch. xxi.] ... Revertuntur ergo impudentes grassatores Hiberni domos, post non longum temporis reversuri. Picti in extrema parte insulae tunc primum et deinceps requieverunt, praedas et contritiones nonnumquam facientes. In talibus itaque indutiis desolato populo saeva cicatrix obducitur. Fame alia virulentiore tacitus pullulante, quiescente autem vastitate tantis abundantiarum copiis insula affluebat, ut nulla habere tales retro aetas meminisset, cum quibus omnimodis et luxuria crescit. ... Ungebantur reges non per deum, sed qui ceteris crudeliores exstarent, et paulo post ab unctoribus non pro veri examinatione trucidabantur aliis electis trucioribus... [Ch. xxii.] Interea volente deo purgare familiam suam et tanta malorum labe infectam auditu tantum tribulationis emendare, non ignoti rumoris penniger ceu volatus arrectas omnium penetrat aures iamiamque adventus veterum ⟨hostium⟩ volentium penitus delere et inhabitare solito more a fine usque ad terminum regionem. Nequaquam tamen ob hoc proficiunt. ... Pestifera lues... feraliter insipienti populo incumbit, quae in brevi tantam eius multudinem remoto mucrone sternit, quantam ne possint vivi humare. Sed ne hac quidem emendantur. ... Initur consilium, quid optimum quidve saluberrimum ad repellendas tam ferales et tam crebras supra dictarum gentium irruptiones praedasque decerni deberet. [Ch. xxiii.] Tum omnes consiliarii una cum superbo tyranno[1] caecantur, adinvenientes tale praesidium, immo excidium patriae, ut ferocissimi illi nefandi nominis Saxones deo hominibusque invisi, quasi in caulas lupi, in insulam ad retundendas aquilonales gentes intromitterentur. ... Tum erumpens grex catulorum de cubili leaenae barbarae, tribus, ut lingua eius exprimitur, cyulis, nostra longis navibus, secundis velis, omine auguriisque, quibus vaticinabatur, certo

---

[1] *Avranches MS* 162 (12th cent.) adds: 'Vortigerno'; *Cambridge MS*, Ff. 1. 27 (13th cent.): 'Gurthigerno Britannorum duce'; probably glosses.

apud eum praesagio, quod ter centum annis patriam, cui proras librabat, insideret, centum vero quinguaginta, hoc est dimidio temporis, saepius vastaret, evectus, primum in orientali parte insulae iubente infausto tyranno terribiles infixit ungues quasi pro patria pugnaturus, sed eam certius impugnaturus. Cui supradicta genetrix, comperiens primo agmini fuisse prosperatum, item mittit satellitum canumque prolixiorem catastam, quae ratibus advecta adunatur cum manipularibus spuriis. . . . Igitur intromissi in insulam barbari, velut militibus et magna, ut mentiebantur, discrimina pro bonis hospitibus subituris, impetrant sibi annonas dari: quae multo tempore impertitae clauserunt, ut dicitur, canis faucem. Item queruntur non affluenter sibi epimenia contribui, occasiones de industria colorantes, et ni profusior eis munificentia cumularetur, testantur se cuncta insulae rupto foedere depopulaturos. Nec mora minas effectibus prosequuntur. [Ch. xxiv.] Confovebatur namque ultionis iustae praecedentium scelerum causa de mari usque ad mare ignis orientali sacrilegorum manu exaggeratus et finitimas quasque civitates agrosque populans non quievit accensus, donec cunctam paene exurens insulae superficiem rubra occidentalem trucique oceanum lingua delamberet. . . . Ita ut cunctae coloniae crebris arietibus omnesque coloni cum praepositis ecclesiae, cum sacerdotibus ac populo, mucronibus undique micantibus ac flammis crepitantibus, simul solo sternerentur. . . . [Ch. xxv.] Itaque nonnulli miserarum reliquiarum in montibus deprehensi acervatim iugulabantur: alii fame confecti accedentes manus hostibus dabant in aevum servituri, si tamen non continuo trucidarentur, quod altissimae gratiae stabat loco: alii transmarinas petebant regiones cum ululatu magno ceu celeumatis vice hoc modo sub velorum sinibus cantantes: 'dedisti nos tamquam oves escarum et in gentibus dispersisti nos': alii montanis collibus minacibus praeruptis vallatis et densissimis saltibus marinisque rupibus vitam suspecta semper mente credentes, in patria licet trepidi perstabant. Tempore igitur interveniente aliquanto, cum recessissent domum crudelissimi praedones,...duce Ambrosio Aureliano viro modesto, qui solus forte Romanae gentis tantae tempestatis collisione occisis in eadem parentibus purpura nimirum indutis superfuerat, cuius nunc temporibus nostris suboles magnopere avita bonitate degeneravit, vires capessunt, victores provocantes ad proelium: quis victoria deo annuente cessit. Ex eo tempore nunc cives, nunc hostes vincebant...usque ad annum obsessionis Badonici montis[1], novissimaeque ferme de furciferis non minimae stragis, quique quadragesimus quartus ut novi orditur annus mense iam uno emenso, qui et meae nativitatis est.

iii

BEDE

(*a*) [From *De Temporibus* (703), edited by T. Mommsen in *Chronica minora Saeculorum iv–vii* (*M.G.H.*), iii. 303.]

Marcianus Ann. vii. Anglorum gens in Brittaniam venit.

(*b*) [From *De Temporum Ratione* (725), edited by T. Mommsen, *ibid.*]

A[nno] M[undi] mmmmccccx [= 459] Marcianus et Valentinianus an. vii. Gens Anglorum sive Saxonum Britaniam tribus longis navibus advehitur quibus dum iter prosperatum domi fama referret, mittitur exercitus fortior qui iunctus prioribus primo hostes quos petebatur abigit; deinde in socios arma vertens totam prope insulam ab orientali eius plaga usque ad occidentalem igni vel ense subigit conficta occasione, quod pro se militantibus Brittones minus sufficienter stipendia darent.

(*c*) [From *Historia Ecclesiastica* (731), edited by C. Plummer, i. 30, 352.]

[Lib. i. ch. 15.] Anno ab incarnatione Domini ccccxlviiii Marcianus cum Valentiniano xlvi ab Augusto regnum adeptus, vii annis tenuit. Tunc Anglorum sive Saxonum

---

[1] Badonici montis] *Cambridge MS*, Ff. 1. 27, adds the gloss: 'qui prope Sabrinum hostium habetur.'

gens, invitata a rege praefato [Vurtigerno] Brittaniam tribus longis navibus advehitur. . . . At ubi hostilis exercitus exterminatis dispersisque insulae indigenis domum reversus est, coeperunt et illi paulatim vires animosque resumere, emergentes de latibulis, quibus abditi fuerant, et unanimo consensu auxilium caeleste precantes, ne usque ad internicionem usquequaque delerentur. Utebantur eo tempore duce Ambrosio Aureliano, viro modesto, qui solus forte Romanae gentis praefatae tempestati superfuerat, occisis in eadem parentibus regium nomen et insigne ferentibus. Hoc ergo duce vires capessunt Brettones, et victores provocantes ad proelium, victoriam ipsi Deo favente suscipiunt. Et ex eo tempore nunc cives, nunc hostes vincebant, usque ad annum obsessionis Badonici montis, quando non minimas eisdem hostibus strages dabant, xlmo circiter et iiiio anno adventus eorum in Brittaniam.

[Lib. v. ch. 24 (*Recapitulatio Chronica*).] Anno ccccxlviiii Marcianus cum Valentiniano imperium suscipiens, vii annis tenuit, quorum tempore Angli a Brettonibus accersiti Brittaniam adierunt.

iv

NENNIUS

[From *Historia Britonum* (early in 9th cent.), edited by T. Mommsen in *Chronica minora Saeculorum iv–vii* (*M.G.H.*), iii. 111.]

[Ch. lvi.] In illo tempore Saxones invalescebant in multitudine et crescebant in Brittannia. Mortuo autem Hengisto Octha filius eius transivit de sinistrali parte Britanniae ad regnum Cantorum et de ipso orti sunt reges Cantorum. Tunc Arthur pugnabat contra illos in illis diebus cum regibus Brittonum, sed ipse dux erat bellorum.[1] Primum bellum fuit

---

[1] Tunc...bellorum] *Vatican MS* 1964 (11th cent.) reads: 'Tunc belliger Arthur cum militibus Bryttanniae atque regibus contra illos pugnabat, et licet multi ipso nobiliores essent, ipse tamen duodecies dux belli fuit victorque bellorum.' After *bellorum* two glosses appear in some 13th cent. MSS: (*a*) 'Mab Uter Britannice, filius horribilis Latine, quoniam a puericia sua crudelis fuit.' (*b*) 'Artur Latine translatum sonat ursum horribilem vel malleum ferreum, quo confringuntur mole leonum.'

in ostium fluminis quod dicitur Glein. Secundum et tertium et quartum et quintum super aliud flumen, quod dicitur Dubglas et est in regione Linnuis. Sextum bellum super flumen, quod vocatur Bassas. Septimum fuit bellum in silva Celidonis, id est Cat Coit Celidon. Octavum fuit bellum in castello Guinnion, in quo Arthur portavit imaginem sanctae Mariae perpetuae virginis super humeros suos et pagani versi sunt in fugam in illo die et caedes magna fuit super illos per virtutem domini nostri Iesu Christi et per virtutem sanctae Mariae virginis genetricis eius. Nonum bellum gestum est in urbe Legionis. Decimum gessit bellum in litore fluminis, quod vocatur Tribruit.[1] Undecimum factum est bellum in monte, qui dicitur Agned.[2] Duodecimum fuit bellum in Monte Badonis, in quo corruerunt in uno die nongenti sexaginta viri de uno impetu Arthur;[3] et nemo prostravit eos nisi ipse solus, et in omnibus bellis victor extitit. Et ipsi, dum in omnibus bellis prosternebantur, auxilium a Germania petebant et augebantur multipliciter sine intermissione et reges a Germania deducebant, ut regnarent super illos in Brittannia usque ad tempus quo Ida regnavit, qui fuit Eobba filius. Ipse fuit primus rex in Beornica.

[Ch. lxxiii.] Est aliud mirabile in regione quae dicitur Buelt. Est ibi cumulus lapidum et unus lapis superpositus super congestum cum vestigio canis in eo. Quando venatus est porcum Troynt, impressit Cabal, qui erat canis Arthuri

---

[1] Tribruit] *Vatican MS*: 'Trahtreuroit.'

[2] qui dicitur Agned] *Vatican MS*: 'qui nominatur breguoin ubi illos in fugam vertit quem nos cat bregion appellamus.' *Cotton MS Caligula* A. viii: 'qui dicitur agned cat bregomion.'

[3] The following gloss appears in some 13th cent. MSS: 'Nam Artur Hierosolymum perrexit et ibi crucem ad quantitatem salutiferae crucis fecit et ibi consecrata est, et per tres continuos dies ieiunavit, vigilavit et oravit coram cruce dominica, ut ei dominus victoriam daret per hoc lignum de paganis, quod et factum est. Atque secum imaginem sanctae Mariae detulit, cuius fracturae adhuc apud Wedel in magna servantur veneratione. Wedale est villa in provincia Lodonesiae, nunc vero iuris episcopi Sancti Andreae Scotiae sex miliaria ab occidentali parte ab illo quondam nobili monasterio de Melros.'

militis, vestigium in lapide, et Arthur postea congregabat
congestum lapidum sub lapide, in quo erat vestigium canis
sui, et vocatur Carn Cabal. Et veniunt homines et tollunt
lapidem in manibus suis per spatium diei et noctis et in crastino
die invenitur super congestum suum.

Est aliud miraculum in regione quae vocatur Ercing.
Habetur ibi sepulcrum iuxta fontem, qui cognominatur
Licat Anir, et viri nomen, qui sepultus est in tumulo, sic
vocabatur Anir. Filius Arthuri militis erat, et ipse occidit
eum ibidem et sepelivit. Et veniunt homines ad mensurandum
tumulum in longitudine aliquando sex pedes, aliquando novem,
aliquando duodecim, aliquando quindecim. In qua mensura
metieris eum in ista vice, iterum non invenies eum in una
mensura, et ego solus probavi.

v

ANNALES CAMBRIAE

[From *Annales* (10th cent.), edited from *Harleian MS* 3859 (11th
or 12th cent.), by E. Phillimore in *Y Cymmrodor* ix. 141 and
J. Loth, *Les Mabinogion*, ii. 370.]

[*Computus.*] A mundi principio usque ad Constantinum
et Rufum ⟨457⟩ quinque milia sexcenti quinquaginta octo
anni reperiuntur. Item a duobus geminis Rufo et Rubelio
⟨29⟩ usque in Stilichonem consulem ⟨400⟩, cccti septuaginta
tres anni. Item a Stilichone usque ad Valentinianum filium
Placide ⟨425⟩ et regnum Guorthigirni, viginti octo anni.
Et a regno Guorthigirni usque ad discordiam Guitolini et
Ambrosii, anni sunt duodecim, quod est Guoloppum, id est,
Catguoloph. Guorthigirnus autem tenuit imperium in
Brittannia, Theodorio et Valentiniano consulibus ⟨425⟩, et
in quarto anno regni sui Saxones ad Brittanniam venerunt,
Felice et Tauro consulibus ⟨428⟩, quadringentesimo anno ab
incarnatione ⟨passione?⟩ domini nostri Iesu Christi.

Ab anno quo Saxones venerunt in Brittanniam et a
Guorthigirno suscepti sunt, usque ad Decium et Valerianum

⟨Aetium et Valentinianum = 446?⟩ anni sunt sexaginta
novem ⟨xix?⟩. . . .

An' lxxii ⟨518⟩. Bellum Badonis in quo Arthur portavit
crucem domini nostri Iesu Christi, tribus diebus et tribus
noctibus, in humeros suos, et Brittones victores fuerunt. . . .

An' xciii ⟨539⟩. Gueith Camlann in qua Arthur et
Medraut corruerunt; et mortalitas in Brittannia et in Hibernia
fuit. . . .

An' ciii ⟨549⟩. Mortalitas magna in qua pausat Mailcun
rex Guenedotae. . . .

An' cxxvi ⟨572⟩. Gildas obiit. . . .
An' cxxix ⟨575⟩. Bellum Armterid. . . .
An' clxxxii ⟨628⟩. Etguin baptizatus est. Et Run filius
Urbgen baptizavit eum. . . .

An' ccxxi ⟨667⟩. Primum Pasca apud Saxones celebratur.
Bellum Badonis secundo. Morcant moritur.

An' ccclxv ⟨811⟩. Elbodg, archiepiscopus Guenedotae
regione, migravit ad Dominum.

vi

LIFE OF ST GOEZNOVIUS

[From *Legenda Sancti Goeznovii* (1019?), printed from 15th cent.
    MS by A. De La Borderie, *L'Historia Britonum et L'Historia
    Britannica avant Geoffroi de Monmouth* (1883) and *Histoire de
    Bretagne*, ii. 525.]

In Legenda sancti Goeznovii. Venerabili domino et patri
in Christo Eudoni episcopo, fratribusque cum eo in Christi
servicio congerentibus Guillelmus, eorum presbiter, in Domino
salutem, anno ab Incarnatione Domini M° nono decimo, qui
est xxiiii^{us} episcopatus tui, domine episcope. [§ 1] Legimus
in Ystoria Britanica quod, cum Britani sub Bruto et Corineo
Albidiam, quam vocaverunt Britaniam, cum insulis circum-
adiacentibus virtute sibi subiugassent, crescente eorum
multitudine et regno prosperato in conspectu eorum, Conanus
Meriadocus, vir catholicus et bellicosus, cum infinita

multitudine eorumdem, qui in tantum excreverat quod una eos regio minime capiebat, in sinum Armoricum Galliae transfretavit. Cuius prima sedes fuit iuxta fluvium Guilidonam in finibus Plebis Columbae [Plougoulm], in loco qui adhuc dicitur Castrum Meriadoci. Is cum suis Britonibus totam terram illam ab utroque mari usque ad civitatem Andegavorum cum omni territorio Nannetensi et Redonico in virtute laudabili acquisivit, interfectis omnibus indigenis qui adhuc pagani erant, unde et Pengouet, quod sonat Canica capita, vocabantur. Mulieribus autem tantummodo linguas resecantes, ne per eas lingua Britannica mutaretur, eis ad coniugia et ad alia servicia, prout temporis exigebat necessitas, utebantur. Ecclesiis itaque per loca ad laudandum Deum edificatis, terra illa tota, per plebes et tribus, divina gratia minor Britannia dicta est. Et ita Armorici et insulani Britones, eisdem legibus utentes et fraterna dilectione sese tractantes, tanquam populus unius sub uno regionis imperio multo tempore regebantur. [§ 3] Processu vero temporis, Vortigernus rex usurpativus, ad praestandum sibi pro defensione regni maioris Britaniae quod iniuste tenebat subsidium, viros bellicos de Saxoniae partibus evocavit, et eos in regno socios sibi fecit. Qui, cum essent pagani, et viri diabolici, humanum sanguinem ex sua propria natura effundere affectantes, multa mala erogabant Britonibus. Quorum superbia postmodum per magnum Arturum Britonum regem fuit ad tempus repressa, eis pro parte maxima ab insula repulsis et servire coactis. Sed eodem Arturo, post multas victorias quas in Britannicis et Gallicis partibus praeclare gessit, ab humanis tandem actibus evocato, via iterum patuit Saxonibus, qua in insulam remearent, et facta est maxima oppressio Britonum et ecclesiarum eversio persecutioque sanctorum. Et haec persecutio multorum regum temporibus, tam Saxonum quam Britonum sibi invicem concertantium, perduravit. Qui Saxones, licet ab Anglia, antiquissima civitate Saxoniae, sibi et insulae nomen imposuerint, et se Anglos sive Anglicos vocaverint, a Britonibus tamen usque in hodiernum diem Saxones appellantur. Ea tempestate, multi sancti viri sponte se martirio offerebant; alii, consilio evangelico adherentes, relicta Britania maiore quae nunc est Patria Saxonis, in hanc minorem Britaniam transfretabant, quidam ut tyrannidem evaderent paganorum, quamplures vero secretius ut et devotius, relictis omnibus, gratum et placitum exiberent in locis solitariis Domino famulatum.

vii

LIFRIC OF LLANCARFAN

[From *Vita Cadoci* (c. 1075), printed from *Cotton MS Vesp.* A. xiv (early 13th cent.) by W. J. Rees, *Lives of the Cambro-British Saints*, 22.]

[*Prologus.*] Ubi Gundleius [rex Gundliauc in Demetia] corpore incolumis cum praenotata virgine [Gladusa filia Brachani], licet plurima strage, maestus praeliando cum adversariis, terminos terrae suae attigisset, ecce tres heroes strenui, Arthurus cum duobus equitibus suis, Cei videlicet et Bedguir, super cacumen supradicti collis cum alea ludentes consedere. Illis enimvero cernentibus regem cum puella sibi appropinquantem, Arthurus ilico libidine in amorem adolescentulae nimium succensus, ac iniqua cogitatione plenus, consodalibus inquit: Scitote me vehementer in concupiscentiam puellae huius quam ille miles equitando devehit accendi. At illi prohibentes eum dixerunt: Absit a te tantum scelus patrari; nos enim soliti sumus inopes anxiosque iuvare, quocirca huic angustato praelio certaminis concurrentes citius subveniamus. At ille: Quum ambo mavultis ei succurrere quam puellam mihi ab eo violenter diripere, pergite obviam eis, ac quis illorum sit heres diligenter huius terrae sciscitamini. Illis autem confestim abeuntibus, et pro regis precepto sciscitantibus, Gundleius respondit: Testante Deo et omnibus Brittanorum peritissimis, istius terrae heredem me esse profiteor. Reversisque nuntiis ad dominum suum, retulerunt quae ab illo audierant. Tum Arthuro sociisque eius armatis, in hostes Gundleii irruunt, eosque versis tergis cum magna confusione ad patrium solum fugaverunt. Tunc Gundleius per patrocinium Arthuri triumphans ad suum palatium cum praescripta virgine Gladusa perrexit....

[Ch. 18.] *De altercatione inter Sanctum Cadocum [filium Gundleii] et regem Arthurum pro cuiusdam reconciliatione....* Dux quidam Brittanorum fortissimus, vocabulo Ligessauc, filius Eliman, cognomento quoque Lauhiir, id est longa manus, tres milites Arthurii regis illustrissimi Brittanniae trucidavit. Ceterum Arthurio quaquaversum eum persequente, nusquam tutum locum repperit, nullusque ipsum tutari ob praedicti regis pavorem ausus fuit; donec tandem creberrima fuga fatigatus ad virum Dei profugus pervenit. Qui ipsius miseratus labores benignius illum suscepit, in Domino confidens, Arthurium vero nil metuens, secundum illum Dominicum preceptum: Nolite timere eos qui corpus occidunt, animam autem non possunt occidere, sed potius eum timete qui potest animam et corpus mittere in gehennam. Mansit itaque cum eo in regione Guunliauc, Arthurio nesciente, septem annis securus. Quibus evolutis rursus praelibato regi proditus, idem demum placitandi causa, quod vi cum viro Dei nullatenus auderet contendere, cum plurima militum copia ad amnem Oscam pervenit. Directis ergo legatis ad regem, vir Dei sciscitatur ab eo si controversiam in sagacium iudicum arbitrio statueret. At ille adquievit. Sanctus namque Cadocus, de diversis eiusdem patriae partibus tribus ad se principalibus proceribus, David videlicet et Teliauno et Dochu, Keneder et Maidoc, accersitis, cum pluribus aliis clericis et senioribus totius Brittanniae iudicibus insimul coadunatis, usque ad ripam praegrandis fluminis Oscae, ipso praecedente, pariter convenerunt. Ibi quoque more hostium ex utraque fluvii parte causam amaris verbis agitantes diutius utrinque litigaverunt. Post hanc autem altercationis intercapedinem, eruditiores ex iudicibus viri decreverunt Arthurium pro redemtione uniuscuiusque virorum

necatorum tres boves optimas debere suscipere. Alii vero
centum vaccas illi in pretium praescriptorum virorum tri-
buendas sanxerunt, a priscis enim temporibus apud Brittones
huiusmodi iudicium ac istud pretium de regum ducumque
ministris constitutum erat. Hoc accepto, Arthurius insultans
uni coloris vaccas renuit; verum discolores accipere voluit,
scilicet in anteriori parte rubei, in posteriori vero candidi,
coloris distinctas plurima tergiversatione gestivit. Illi quippe
quo huiuscemodi coloris pecora repperirentur penitus ignorantes, quid consilii super his caperent haesitabant; quocirca
vir Dei in trium personarum nomine imperavit iuvenibus de
concilio quatenus novem, sive velut quidam fatentur centum,
iuvencas ad se minare, cuiuscunque coloris forent. Ut autem
pernotata animalia prae oculis ipsius et aliorum Dei famulorum
adducta fuerunt, divino magnatio, ex prava Arthurii cupidine,
in praelibatis coloribus pro benivolo iustorum precatu ac
desiderio, statim mutata fuere. Intuente autem totius cleri
comitatu plerisque aliis Dei fidelibus a beato viro illo con-
gregatis hoc miraculo, gavisi sunt gaudio magno, Deum valde
glorificantes. Porro vir Dei consuluit quatenus iure prae-
memoratas boves agere deberet. Et responditur ex altrinsecus
iudicum cunctis: Jus quidem est te ipsas ad vadi medium
gregatim compellere. Compulsit igitur illas eotenus occur-
reruntque eis Arthurius, Chei et Bedguur ceteris in littore
sedentibus; at Chei et Bedguur gliscentes eas manibus ad litus
alterum per cornua trahere; sed extemplo inter ipsorum
manus, cunctis videntibus, divino nutu, in filicis fascibus
transfiguratae sunt. Quod prodigium Arthurius aspectans, ut
sibi dimittetur iniuria quam illi irrogaverat beatum virum
humiliter flagitavit. Largitus est autem illi veniam delicti,
iuxta illud evangelicum: Dimittite et dimittetur vobis. Inito
igitur praelibatus rex cum agmine suo consilio, refugium eius
per septem annos totidemque menses eidemque numeri dies
protelavit. Si quis vero alienigena praefinito tempore de
Sancti Cadoci pago repatriare gestiens ad aliquam mundi
plagam discesserit seu transfretaverit, si forte valida vi pro-

cellarum ac sinistri flatus tempestate ingruente in illius portum videlicet Barren appulsus fuerit, adque ad pristinum refugium sui locum denuo remeaverit, secundum seniorum traditionem usque ad ultimum vitae suae terminum, servitio ipsius deputandus ac alacriter recipiendus est. Hoc Arthurus universique duces eiusdem cum totius Brittaniae senioribus corroborantes dixerunt: Nos quoque in omnium auditu verba sanctionis huius contestamur, et quicunque ea praevaricatus fuerit, addat super eum Deus omnes plagas in veteri et nova lege scriptas, nomenque eius de libro vitae deleatur. Qui vero haec custodierit, omnibus veteris et novi testamenti benedictionibus repleatur et super illum descendant et maneant, nec non ipsius anima in requie consistat eterna. Peracto vero consilio, omnes vaccae quae in filicum manipulis fuerunt conversae in suis bostaribus incolumes apud earundem possessores sunt repertae. Ab illo enim die locus Brittanico fatu Trefredinauc, villa filicis, vocatur. Illud quoque vadum, circa quod placitum erat, Rithguutebou nuncupatur.

viii

LIFE OF ST CARANNOG

[From *Vita Carantoci* (c. 1100?), edited from *Cotton MS Vesp.*
A. xiv (early 13th cent.) by F. Lot in *Romania*, xxx. 1.]

[§ 3.] Et postea venit iterum ad suam propriam regionem Keridiciaun, ad suam speluncam cum clericis multis, et ibi multas virtutes fecit quas enumerare aliquis non potest. Et dedit ei Christus altare honorificabile de excelso, cujus nemo intelligebat colorem. Et postea ad Sabrinam amnem venit ut navigaret et misit altare in mare, quod et precedebat ubi Deus volebat illum venire. [§ 4.] In istis temporibus Cato et Arthur regnabant in ista patria, habitantes in Dindraithov; et venit Arthur circuiens ut inveniret serpentem validissimum, ingentem, terribilem, qui vastaverat duodecim partes agri Carrum. Et venit Carantocus et salutavit Arthurum, qui gaudens accepit benedictionem ab illo. Et interrogavit Carantocus Arthurum utrum audisset ubi applicuisset altare suum, et Arthur respondit: Si habuero precium nuntiabo tibi. Et ille dixit: Quid precium postulas? Ille respondit: Ut deducas serpentem qui in prope est tibi ut videamus si servus Dei es. Tunc beatus Carantocus perrexit et oravit ad Dominum, et ilico venit serpens cum sonitu magno, quasi vitulus ad matrem currens, inclinavitque caput suum ante servum Dei, quasi servus obediens domino suo humilis corde et lenis oculis. Et misit stolam suam circa collum ejus et deduxit illum quasi agnum, nec exaltavit pennas neque angulas, et erat collum ipsius quasi collum tauri septem annorum, quod vix poterat stola circumdare. Deinde perrexerunt una ad arcem et salutaverunt Catonem et bene suscepti sunt ab eo. Et duxit illum serpentem in media aula et cibavit illum coram populo, et conati sunt occidere illum. Non reliquit eum occidi quia dixit quod ex verbo Dei venisset ut deleret peccatores qui in Carrum erant et ut ostenderet virtutem Dei per illum. Et postea perrexit extra portam arcis et Carantocus dissolvit eum, [et] imperavit illi ut discedens nemini noceret nec reverteretur amplius, et exivit, haesitque, sicut ante dixit ordinatio Dei. Et accepit altare, quod cogitaverat Arthur in mensam facere, sed quidquid apponebatur super illam jactabatur in longinquo. Et postulavit rex ab illo ut reciperet Carrum in sempiterno graphyo et postea edificavit ecclesiam ibi. [§ 5.] Postea venit vox illi de coelo ut mitteret altare in mare. Deinde misit Catonem [et] Arthurum ut interrogarent de altari, et nunciatum est illis quod in ostium Guellit appulerat. Et dixit rex: Iterum date illi duodecim partes agri ubi altare inventum esset. Postea venit Carantocus et edificavit ibi ecclesiam, et vocata est civitas Carrov.

ix

LIFE OF ST ILLTUD

[From *Vita Iltuti* (c. 1100?), printed from *Cotton MS Vesp.* A. xiv
by W. J. Rees, *Lives of the Cambro-British Saints*, 158.]

Audiens interea miles magnificus [Iltutus, filius Bicani et
Rieingulid filiae Anblaud Britanniae regis] Arthurii regis
sui consobrini magnificentiam cupivit visitare tanti victoris
curiam, deseruit quam vocamus Ulteriorem Britanniam, et
pervenit navigando ubi vidit maximam militum abundantiam.
Ibidem quoque receptus honorifice, et munificatus ad desi-
derium militare; impleto autem desiderio capiendi munera,
recessit gratissimus a regali curia.

x

LIFE OF ST PADARN

[From *Vita Paterni* (12th cent.), printed from *Cotton MS Vesp.*
A. xiv by W. J. Rees, *Lives of the Cambro-British Saints*, 188.]

Cum autem Paternus esset in ecclesia requiescens post
tantum laborem marinum, deambulabat quidam tirannus
regiones altrinsecus, Arthur nomine; qui quodam die venit
ad cellam Sancti Paterni episcopi. Et dum Paternum allo-
queretur, aspexit tunicam, quam confossus zelo avaritiae
petivit ut sua fieret; respondens Sanctus ait: Non habitu
cuiuslibet maligni haec tunica condigna est; sed habitu
clericatus. Ille baccando monasterium exivit; iterumque
indignando revertitur ut tolleret tunicam contra comitum
sanctorum consilia. Unus autem discipulorum Paterni videns
illum in furore revertentem cucurrit ad Sanctum Paternum
et ait: Tirannus qui hinc antea exivit, revertitur insultans,
subiiciens plantis terram placat. Respondit Paternus: Immo
absorbeat eum tellus. Cum dicto statim terra aperit sinum
suae profunditatis, absorbetque Arthurum adusque mentum;
qui illico agnoscens suum reatum, incipit Deum pariter

Paternumque laudare, donec veniam petens, terra illum
sursum emitteret; ab illo loco Sanctum flexis genibus poposcit
indulgentiam, cui Sanctus indulsit. Paternum sibi sempiter-
num accepit patronum, ac sic discessit.

xi

HERMANN OF TOURNAI

[From *De Miraculis S. Mariae Laudunensis* (1146), Bk. ii, printed
in Migne, *Patrologia Latina*, clvi. 983.]

[Ch. xv.] Exinde [de Essecestra] venimus [1113] in
provinciam quae vocatur Danavexeria, ubi ostenderunt nobis
cathedram et furnum illius famosi secundum fabulas Britannorum regis Arturi, ipsamque terram eiusdem Arturi esse
dicebant.... In villa quae Bomine vocatur....[Ch. xvi.]...
Quidam etiam vir ibidem manum aridam habens, coram
feretro pro sanitate recipienda vigilabat. Sed, sicut Britones
solent iurgari cum Francis pro rege Arturo, idem vir coepit
rixari cum uno ex famulis nostris, nomine Haganello, qui
erat ex familia domni Guidonis Laudunensis archidiaconi,
dicens adhuc Arturum vivere. Unde non parvo tumultu
exorto, cum armis ecclesiam irruunt plurimi, et nisi praefatus
Algardus clericus obstitisset, paene usque ad sanguinis effu-
sionem ventum fuisset. Quam rixam coram feretro suo
factam credimus Dominae nostrae displicuisse, nam idem
vir manum habens aridam, qui pro Arturo tumultum fecerat,
sanitatem non recepit.

xii

WILLIAM OF MALMESBURY

[From *De Rebus Gestis Regum Anglorum* (c. 1125), edited by W.
Stubbs (R.S.), i. 11; ii. 342.]

[*Lib.* i. § 8.] Sed, eo [Guortimero] extincto, Britonum
robur emarcuit, spes imminutae retro fluxere; et iam tunc
profecto pessum issent, nisi Ambrosius, solus Romanorum

superstes, qui post Wortigernum monarcha regni fuit, intumescentes barbaros eximia bellicosi Arturis opera pressisset. Hic est Artur de quo Britonum nugae hodieque delirant; dignus plane quem non fallaces somniarent fabulae, sed veraces praedicarent historiae, quippe qui labantem patriam diu sustinuerit, infractasque civium mentes ad bellum acuerit; postremo, in obsessione Badonici montis, fretus imagine Dominicae matris, quam armis suis insuerat, nongentos hostium solus adorsus incredibili caede profligarit.

[*Lib.* iii. § 287.] Tunc [1066–87] in provincia Walarum, quae Ros vocatur, inventum est sepulchrum Walwen, qui fuit haud degener Arturis ex sorore nepos. Regnavit in ea parte Britanniae quae adhuc Walweitha vocatur: miles virtute nominatissimus, sed a fratre et nepote Hengestii, de quibus in primo libro dixi, regno expulsus, prius multo eorum detrimento exilium compensans suum; communicans merito laudi avunculi, quod ruentis patriae casum in plures annos distulerint. Sed Arturis sepulcrum nusquam visitur, unde antiquitas naeniarum adhuc eum venturum fabulatur. Ceterum, alterius bustum, ut praemisi, tempore Willelmi regis repertum est supra oram maris, quatuordecim pedes longum; ubi a quibusdam asseritur ab hostibus vulneratus, et naufragio eiectus; a quibusdam dicitur a civibus in publico epulo interfectus. Veritatis ergo notitia labat in dubio, licet neuter eorum defuerit famae suae patrocinio.

xiii

HENRY OF HUNTINGDON

(*a*) [From *Historia Anglorum* (c. 1129), ii. 18, edited by T. Arnold (R.S.), 48.]

Arthurus belliger, illis temporibus dux militum et regum Britanniae, contra illos [Saxones] invictissime pugnabat: duodecies dux belli fuit, duodecies victor bellatorum.... Haec autem bella et loca bellorum narrat Gildas historiographus. Quae tamen omnia loca nostrae aetati incognita sunt; quod providentia Dei factum esse putamus, ad despectum popularis aurae, laudis adulatoriae, famae transitoriae.

(*b*) [From *Chronica* of Robert de Torigny (c. 1139–85), edited by R. Howlett in *Chronicles of the Reigns of Stephen, Henry II and Richard I* (R.S.), iv. 64. The passages in square brackets are Richard's glosses on Henry's letter (1139), as found in *Arundel MS* 48 and *Bibl. Nat. MS Lat.* 6042 of his *Historia Anglorum.*]

[Huic prologo subiiciam unam epistolam Henrici archidiaconi . . . quam epistolam, sicut in ea reperitur, cum Romam idem Henricus pergeret, me ei praebente copiam exemplaris totius historiae Britonum, apud Beccum excerpsit . . .]. Incipit Epistola Henrici Archidiaconi ad Warinum De Regibus Britonum. Quaeris a me, Warine Brito, vir comis et facete, cur patriae nostrae gesta narrans a temporibus Iulii Caesaris, inceperim, et florentissima regna, quae a Bruto usque ad Iulium fuerunt, omiserim. Respondeo igitur tibi quod nec voce nec scripto horum temporum saepissime notitiam quaerens invenire potui. Tanta pernicies oblivionis mortalium gloriam successu diuturnitatis obumbrat et exstinguit. Hoc tamen anno [qui est ab incarnatione Domini MCXXX nonus], cum Roman proficiscerer [cum Theobaldo Cantuariensi archiepiscopo] apud Beccensem abbatiam [apud Beccum, ubi idem archiepiscopus abbas fuerat] scripta rerum praedictarum stupens inveni. [Siquidem Robertum de Torinneio, eiusdem loci monachum, virum tam divinorum quam secularium librorum inquisitorem et coacervatorem studiosissimum, ibidem conveni. Qui cum de ordine historiae de regibus Anglorum a me editae me interrogaret, et id quod a me quaerebat libens audisset, obtulit mihi librum ad legendum de regibus Britonum, qui ante Anglos nostram insulam tenuerunt.] Quorum excerpta, ut in epistola decet, brevissime scilicet, tibi dilectissime, mitto. . . . Inter eundem tamen et in ipso actu tot vulnera recepit (Arturus), quod et ipse procubuit. Mortuum tamen fuisse Britones parentes tui negant, et eum venturum solenniter expectant [licet parentes sui Britones mortuum fore denegent, et venturum adhuc sollenniter expectent].... Haec sunt quae tibi [Warine Brito carissime] brevibus promisi; quorum si prolixitatem desideras, librum grandem Gaufridi Arturi quem apud Beccum inveni quaeras, ubi praedicta diligenter et prolixe tracta videbis [apud Beccense coenobium inveni, diligenter requiras, ubi praedicta satis prolixe et elucenter reperies]. Vale.

xiv

GEOFFREY OF MONMOUTH

(*a*) [From *Historia Regum Britanniae* (c. 1135?) in text of *Cotton* *MS Titus* C. xvii (12th cent.), ff. 1, 23 v.; 33 v.; 41, 46 v.]

[i. 1.] Incipit prologus in historia[m] Britonum. Dum mecum multa et de multis saepius animo reuoluens in historiam regum Britanniae inciderem, in mirum contuli quod, infra mentionem quam de eis Gildas et Beda luculento tractatu fecerant, nichil de regibus qui ante incarnationem Christi inhabitauerant, nichil etiam de Arturo caeterisque compluribus qui post incarnationem successerunt reperissem, cum et gesta eorum digna eternitate laudis constarent, et a multis populis quasi inscripta iocunde et memoriter praedicarentur. Talia mihi et de talibus multitotiens cogitanti, obtulit Gwalter Oxinefordensis archidiaconus, uir in oratoria arte atque in exoticis historiis eruditus, quendam Brittanici sermonis librum uetustissimum, qui a Bruto primo rege Brittonum usque ad Cadualadrum filium Cadwallonis actus omnium continue et ex ordine perpulchris orationibus proponebat. Rogatu itaque illius ductus, tametsi infra alienos ortulos falerata uerba non collegerim, agresti tamen stilo propriisque calamis contentus codicem illum in Latinum sermonem transferre curaui. Nam si ampullosis dictionibus paginam illinissem, tedium legentibus ingererem, dum magis in exponendis uerbis quam in historia intelligenda ipsos commorari oporteret. Opusculo igitur meo Rodberte dux

Claudiocestriae[1] faueas, ut sic doctore te, te monitore corri-
gatur, quod non ex Gaufridi Monemutensis fonticulo censeatur
extortum,[2] sed sale Mineruae tuae conditum illius dicatur
editio, quem Henricus rex illustris Anglorum generauit,[3]
quem philosophia liberalis artibus erudiuit, quem innata
probitas in militia militibus praefecit, unde Britannia tibi
nunc temporibus nostris, ac si alterum Henricum adepta,
interno congratulatur affectu.[4]

[vii. 1.] Nondum autem ad hunc locum historiae perue-
neram, cum de Merlino diuulgato rumore compellebant me
undique contemporanei mei prophetias ipsius edere; maxime
autem Alexander Lincolniensis episcopus uir summae religionis et prudenciae. Non erat alter in clero siue in populo,
cui tot nobiles famularentur, quos mansueta pietas ipsius et
benigna largitas in obsequium suum alliciebat. Cui cum
satisfacere praeeligissem, prophetias transtuli et ei cum
huiusmodi litteris direxi.

[vii. 2.] Coegit me, Alexander Lincolniensis praesul,
nobilitatis tuae dilectio prophetias Merlini de Britannico in
Latinum transferre antequam historiam perarassem quam de
gestis regum Britannorum inceperam. Proposueram enim

1 Rodberte dux Claudiocestriae] *Bern MS 568*: 'Stephane rex Anglie.'

2 extortum] *Cambridge Univ. MS Ii. 1. 14*: 'exortum.'

3 quem...generauit] *Bern MS*: 'cuius Henricus illustris rex Anglorum
awnculus extitit.'

4 affectu] *Bern MS, Cambridge Univ. MS Ii. 1, 14* and others add:
'Tu quoque Roberte consul Claudiocestrie (*Cambridge*, Galeranne consul
Mellenti) altera regni nostri columna operam adibeas tuam ut utriusque
moderatione communicata editio in medium producta et pulcrius
elucescat. Te etenim ex illo celeberrimo rege Henrico progenitum
(*Cambridge*, ex illius celeberimi regis Karoli stirpe progenitum) mater
philosophia in gremio suo excepit scientiarumque suarum subtilitatem
edocuit ac deinde ut in militaribus clareres exercitiis ad castra regum
derexit, ubi commilitones tuos audacter supergressus et terror hostium
insistere et protectio tuorum esse paternis auspiciis addidicisti. Fidelis
itaque protectio tuorum existens me tuum uatem codicemque ad oblec-
tamentum tuum editum sub tutela tua recipias ut sub tegmine tam
patule arboris recubans calamum muse mee coram inuidis atque improbis
tuto modulamine resonare queam.'

illam prius perficere istudque opus subsequenter explicare, ne dum uterque labor incumberet, sensus meus ad singula minus fieret. At tamen quoniam securus eram ueniae, quam discretio subtilis ingenii tui donaret, agrestem calamum meum labellis apposui, et plebeia modulatione ignotum tibi interpretatus sum sermonem. Admodum autem ammiror, quia id pauperi stilo dignatus eras committere, cum tot doctiores virga potestatis tuae coerceat, qui sublimior[i]s carminis delectamento aures Mineruae tuae mulcerent. Et ut omnes philosophos totius Britanniae insulae praeteream, tu solus es, quod non erubesco fateri, qui prae cunctis audaci lyra caneres, nisi te culmen honoris ad caetera negotia vocaret. Quoniam ergo placuit ut Gaufridus Monemotensis fistulam suam in hoc uaticinio sonaret, modulationibus suis fauere non diffugias, et si quid inordinate siue uiciose protulerit ferula camenarum in rectum aduertas concentum.

[vii. 4.] Mox ille [Merlinus] ait... Montes itaque eius [Britanniae] ut ualles aequabuntur, et flumina uallium sanguine manabunt. Cultus religionis delebitur, et ruina ecclesiarum patebit. Praeualebit tandem oppressa, et saeuitiae exterorum resistet. Aper etenim Cornubiae succursum praestabit, et colla eorum sub pedibus suis conculcabit. Insulae Oceani potestati ipsius subdentur, et Gallicanos saltus possidebit. Tremebit Romulea domus saeuitiam ipsius, et exitus eius dubius erit. In ore populorum celebrabitur, et actus eius cibus erit narrantibus. Sex posteri eius sequentur sceptrum. Sed post ipsum exurget Germanicus uermis.... Terminus illi positus est, quem transuolare nequibit.... Populus namque in ligno et ferreis tunicis superueniet, qui uindictam de nequitia ipsius sumet. Restaurabit pristinis incolis mansiones, et ruina alienigenarum patebit. Germen albi draconis ex ortulis nostris abradetur, et reliquiae generationis eius decimabuntur. Iugum perpetuae seruitutis ferent, matremque suam ligonibus et aratris uulnerabunt. Succedent duo dracones, quorum alter inuidiae spiculo suffocabitur, alter uero sub umbra nominis redibit. Succedet leo iustitiae, ad cuius rugitum Gallicanae

turres et insulani dracones tremebunt.[1] . . . Deinde reuertentur
ciues in insulam. Nam discidium alienigenarum orietur.
Niueus quoque senex in niueo equo fluuium Perironis
diuertet, et cum candida uirga molendinum super ipsum
metabitur. Cadualadrus Conanum uocabit, et Albaniam in
societatem accipiet. Tunc erit strages alienigenarum: tunc
flumina sanguine manabunt: tunc erumpent Armorici fontes
et diademate Bruti coronabuntur. Replebitur Cambria
laetitia, et robora Cornubiae uirescent. Nomine Bruti
uocabitur insula, et nuncupatio extraneorum peribit. . . .

[ix. 11.] Tunc inuitatis probissimis quibusdam ex longe
positis regnis, coepit [Arturus] familiam suam augmentare:
tantamque facetiam in domo sua habere, ita ut aemulationem
longe manentibus populis ingereret. Unde nobilissimus
quisque incitatus nichili pendebat se, nisi sese uel in induendo,
siue in arma ferendo, ad modum militum Arturi haberet.

[ix. 13] Ad tantum etenim statum dignitatis Britannia tunc
reducta erat, quod copia diuitiarum, luxu ornamentorum,
facetia incolarum, caetera regna excellebat. Quicunque uero
famosus probitate miles in eadem erat, unius coloris uestibus
atque armis utebatur. Facetae etiam mulieres consimilia
indumenta habentes nullius amorem habere dignabantur nisi
tertio in militia probatus esset. Efficiebantur ergo castae et
meliores, et milites amore illarum probiores.

[xi. 1.] De hoc quidem, consul auguste, Gaufridus Monumetensis tacebit. Sicut in praefato Britannico sermone
inuenit, et a Waltero Oxenefordensi in multis historiis
peritissimo uiro audiuit, uili licet stilo, breuiter tamen pro-
palabit, quae praelia inclitus ille rex post uictoriam istam in
Britanniam reuersus cum nepote suo commiserit.

[xi. 2.] Sed et inclytus ille Arturus letaliter uulneratus
est, qui illinc [de flumine Cambula] ad sananda uulnera sua
in insulam Auallonis euectus Constantino cognato suo et filio

---

[1] tremebunt] At the end of a passage about Henry I, here omitted,
later MSS insert: 'Vae tibi Neustria, quia cerebrum leonis in te effundetur,
dilaceratisque membris a patrio solo eliminabitur.'

Cadoris ducis Cornubiae diadema Britanniae concessit, ab incarnatione domini dxlij.

[xii. 20.] Reges autem eorum qui ab illo tempore in Gwaliis successerunt Caradoco Lancarbanensi contemporaneo meo in materiam scribendi permitto; reges uero Saxonum Willelmo Malmesburiensi et Henrico Huntendunensi, quos de regibus Britonum tacere iubeo, cum non habeant librum illum Britannici sermonis, quem Walterus Oxenefordensis archidiaconus ex Britannia aduexit, quem de historia eorum ueraciter editum in honore praedictorum principum hoc modo in Latinum sermonem transferre curaui.

(*b*) [From *Vita Merlini* (c. 1150), edited from *Cotton MS Vesp. E. iv* (13 cent.) by J. J. Parry.]

[1–12]
 Fatidici uatis rabiem musamque iocosam
 Merlini cantare paro; tu corrige carmen,
 Gloria pontificum calamos moderando Roberte.
 Scimus enim quia te perfudit nectare sacro
 Philosophia suo fecitque per omnia doctum,
 Vt documenta dares dux et preceptor in orbe.
 Ergo meis ceptis faueas uatemque tueri
 Auspicio meliore uelis quam fecerit alter,
 Cui modo succedis merito promotus honori.
 Sic etenim mores, sic uita probata genusque
 Vtilitasque loci clerus populusque petebant,
 Vnde modo felix Lincolnia fertur ad astra.

[908–940]
 Insula pomorum que fortunata uocatur
 Ex re nomen habet quia per se singula profert.
 Non opus est illi sulcantibus arua colonis;
 Omnis abest cultus nisi quem natura ministrat;
 Vltro fecundas segetes producit et uuas,
 Nataque poma suis pretonso germine siluis;
 Omnia gignit humus uice graminis ultro redundans.
 Annis centenis aut ultra uiuitur illic.

Illic iura nouem geniali lege sorores
Dant his qui ueniunt nostris ex partibus ad se,
Quarum que prior est fit doctior arte medendi,
Exceditque suas forma prestante sorores.
Morgen ei nomen, didicitque quid utilitatis
Gramina cuncta ferant ut languida corpora curet.
Ars quoque nota sibi qua scit mutare figuram
Et resecare nouis quasi Dedalus aera pennis.
Cum uult est Bristi, Carnoti siue Papie;
Cum uult in uestris ex aere labitur horis.
Hancque mathematicam dicunt didicisse sorores
Moronoe, Mazoe, Gliten, Glitonea, Gliton,
Tyronoe, Thiten, cithara notissima Thiten.
Illuc post bellum Camblani uulnere laesum
Duximus Arcturum nos conducente Barintho,
Equora cui fuerant et celi sydera nota.
Hoc rectore ratis cum principe uenimus illuc,
Et nos quo decuit Morgen suscepit honore,
Inque suis talamis posuit super aurea regem
Strata, manuque sibi detexit uulnus honesta,
Inspexitque diu; tandemque redire salutem
Posse sibi dixit, si secum tempore longo
Esset et ipsius uellet medicamine fungi.
Gaudentes igitur regem commisimus illi,
Et dedimus uentis redeundo uela secundis.

[953–970]
Non dum desierat cum talia protulit alter:
Ergo necesse foret populo transmittere quemdam
Et mandare duci festina naue redire,
Si iam conualuit, solitis ut uiribus hostes
Arceat, et ciues antiqua pace reformet.
Non, Merlinus ait, non sic gens illa recedet,
Ut semel in uestris ungues infixerit ortis:
Regnum namque prius populosque iugabit et urbes,
Viribus atque suis multis dominabitur annis.

Tres tamen ex nostris magna uirtute resistent,
Et multos periment, et eos in fine domabunt:
Set non perficient, quia sic sententia summi
Judicis existit, Britones ut nobile regnum
Temporibus multis amittant debilitate,
Donec ab Armorico ueniet temone Conanus
Et Cadualadrus Cambrorum dux uenerandus,
Qui pariter Scotos, Cambros et Cornubienses
Armoricosque uiros sociabunt federe firmo.

[1525-29]

Duximus ad metam carmen; uos ergo Britanni
Laurea serta date Gaufrido de Monumeta.
Est etenim uester, nam quondam prelia uestra
Vestrorumque ducum cecinit scripsitque libellum,
Quem nunc Gesta uocant Britonum celebrata per orbem.

[*In a later hand*]

Explicit vita Merlini Calidonii per Galfridum Mone-
mutensem.

xv

ORDERICUS VITALIS

[From *Historia Ecclesiastica* xii. 47 (1134-5), edited by A. Le
Prévost, iv. 486.]

Ecce Ambrosii Merlini prophetia, quam tempore Guorti-
gerni regis Britanniae vaticinatus est, per DC⟨C⟩ annos in
pluribus manifeste completa est. Unde libet mihi quaedam
huic opusculo inserere, quae temporibus aetatis nostrae
videntur competere. Contemporaneus quippe beato Germano
...fuit....Si quis haec et alia de casibus Britonum plenius
nosse desiderat, Gildae Britonis historiographi, et Bedae
Anglici libros legat, in quibus de Guortemiro et fratribus
ejus, et de forti Arturo, qui xii bella contra Anglos fecit,
luculenta narratio legentibus emicat....Jam dictus vates
seriatim quae futura erant insulis Septentrionis praedixit,
typicisque locutionibus memoriae litterarum tradidit...

[Follows Geoffrey of Monmouth, *Hist.* vii. 4, from 'Populus' to 'cives in insulam,' omitting the allusion to Henry I's death in Neustria]...Hanc lectiunculam de Merlini libello excerpsi, et studiosis, quibus ipse propalatus non est, quantulamcumque stillam propinavi, cujus aliquam partem in rebus gestis intellexi. Plura vero, ni fallor, cum moerore seu gaudio experientur adhuc nascituri. Historiarum gnari ejus dicta facile poterunt intelligere, qui noverint ea quae contigerunt Hengist et Catigirno, Pascent et Arturo, Aedelberto ac Edwino, Oswaldo et Osvio, Cedwal et Elfredo, aliisque principibus Anglorum et Britonum usque ad tempora Henrici et Gritfridi, qui dubia sub sorte adhuc imminentia praestolantur, quae sibi divinitus ineffabili dispositione ordinantur. Nam luce clarius patet callenti quod de duobus filiis Guillelmi dicitur: Succedent, inquit, duo dracones, domini scilicet libidinosi et feroces, quorum alter invidiae spiculo (id est: Guillelmus Rufus) in venatione sagitta suffocabitur; alter (id est: Rodbertus dux) sub umbra carceris, stemma pristini nominis (id est: ducis) gerens, peribit. Succedet leo justitiae (quod refertur ad Henricum) ad cujus rugitum Gallicanae turres et insulani dracones contremiscunt, quia ipse divitiis et potestate transcendit omnes qui ante illum in Anglia regnaverunt. Sic caetera sophistae liquido discutiant. Multa possem explanando dicere, si commentarium niterer ut scirem super Merlinum edere.

xvi

SUGER, ABBOT OF ST DENIS

[From *Gesta Ludovici Regis, cognomento Grossi* (1138–45), edited by A. Molinier (1887), 45.]

[Ch. xv.] Ea tempestate [c. 1109], ad partes Normannorum contigit devenisse regem Anglorum Henricum [i], virum fortissimum, pace et bello clarum. Cuius admirabilem et paene per universum orbem declaratam excellentiam ille etiam agrestis vates, Anglorum sempiterni eventus mirabilis spectator et relator, Merlinus, tam eleganter quam veraciter,

summo praeconio commendat, ac in eius laude voce prophetica
erumpens ex abrupto, ut vatum mos inolevit: Succedet, inquit,
leo iustitiae...aquila eius super montem Aravium nidifi-
cabit. Quae tota tanti et tam decrepiti vaticinii usque adeo
et personae eius strenuitati et regni administrationi adap-
tantur, ut nec unum iota, nec unum verbum ab eius con-
venientia dissentire valeat, cum ex hoc etiam quod in fine de
catulis eius dicitur, manifeste appareat filios eius et filiam
naufragatos et a maritimis piscibus devoratos et convertibiliter
phisice transformatos illius vaticinium pro certo verificasse.

xvii

ALFRED OF BEVERLEY

[From *Annales* (c. 1149), edited by T. Hearne (1716), *Praefatio*.]

Ferebantur tunc temporis per ora multorum narrationes
de historia Britonum, notamque rusticitatis incurrebat, qui
talium narrationum scientiam non habebat....Quid plura?
Quaesivi historiam, et ea vix inventa, lectioni eius intentissime
studium adhibui....De praefata historia quaedam deflorare
studui, ea videlicet quae fidem non excederent, et legentem
delectarent, et memoriae tenacius adhaererent, et quorum
veritatem etiam ceterarum historiarum collatio roboraret.

xviii

GEOFFREY GAIMAR

[From *Lestorie des Engles* (c. 1150), edited by T. D. Hardy and
    C. T. Martin (R.S.).]

[l. 6442] [Gaimar] purchaca maint esamplaire,
            Liures Engleis, e par gramaire,
            E en Romanz, e en Latin,
            Ainz ken pust traire a la fin.
            Si sa dame [Custance] ne li aidast,
            Ia a nul jor nel acheuast.

Ele enveiad a Helmeslac
Pur le liuere Walter Espac.
Robert li quens de Gloucestre
Fist translater icele geste,
Solum les liueres as Waleis
Kil aueient des Bretons reis.
Walter Espec la demandat,
Li quens Robert li enveiat.
Puis la prestat Walter Espec
A Raoul le fiz Gilebert.
Dame Custance lenpruntat
De son seignur, kele mult amat.
Geffrai Gaimar cel liuere escrit,
Les translad anfes i mist
Ke li Waleis ourent leisse;
Kil aueit ainz purchace,
V fust a dreit v fust a tort,
Le bon liuere de Oxeford,
Ki fust Walter larcediaen,
Si en amendat son liuere bien.
E del estorie de Wincestre
Fust amende ceste geste,
De Wassingburc vn liuere Engleis
V il trouad escrit des reis,
E de tuz les emperurs
Ke de Rome furent seignurs
E de Engleterre ourent trev;
Des reis ki dels ourent tenv:
De lur vies, e de lur plaiz,
Des auentures e des faiz;
Coment chescons maintint la terre,
Quel amat pes, e liquel guere.
De tut le plus pout ci trouer,
Ki en cest liuere volt esgarder,
E ki ne creit co ke io di,
Demand a Nicole de Trailli.

xix

ROBERT DE TORIGNY

[From *Chronica* (c. 1139–85), edited by R. Howlett in *Chronicles of the Reigns of Stephen, Henry II and Richard I* (R.S.), iv. 168.]

[s.a. 1152.] Gaufridus Arthur, qui transtulerat historiam de regibus Britonum de Britannico in Latinum, fit episcopus Sancti Asaph in Norgualis.

xx

CARADOC OF LLANCARFAN

[From *Vita Gildae* (before 1156?), edited by T. Mommsen in *Chronica minora Saeculorum iv–vii* (*M.G.H.*), iii. 107.]

[Ch. v.] Contemporaneus Gildas vir sanctissimus fuit Arturi regis totius majoris Britanniae, quem diligendum diligebat, cui semper cupiebat obedire. Confratres tamen xxiii resistebant regi rebelli praedicto, nolentes pati dominum, sed crebro fugabant et expellebant a saltu et bello. Hueil major natu belliger assiduus et miles famosissimus nulli regi obedivit, nec etiam Arthuro. Affligebat eundem, commovebat inter utrumque maximum furorem. A Scotia veniebat saepissime, incendia ponebat, praedas ducebat cum victoria ac laude. Unde rex universalis Britanniae audiens magnanimum juvenem talia fecisse et aequalia facere persecutus est victoriosissimum juvenem et optimum, ut aiebant et sperabant indigenae, futurum regem. In persecutione autem hostili et in conventu bellico in insula Minau interfecit juvenem praedatorem. Post illam interfectionem Arthurus victor remeavit, gaudens maxime quod superaverat suum fortissimum hostem. Gildas Britonum historiographus tunc remanens in Hibernia studium regens et praedicans in civitate Ardmaca audivit fratrem suum ab Arthuro rege interfectum fuisse. Doluit ab auditu, flevit cum gemitu, ut frater carissimus pro carissimo fratre; oravit pro spiritu fraterno cotidie,

orabat insuper pro Arthuro fratris sui persecutore et inter-
fectore. . . . Interea. . . Gildas. . . venit ad Britanniam. . . .
Pernoctavit honorifice receptus a Cadoco venerabili abbate
in Carbana valle. . . . Audito adventu Gildae Sapientis ab
Arthuro rege et primatibus totius Britanniae episcopis et
abbatibus, convenerunt innumerabiles ex clero et populo, ut
Arthurum pacificarent ex supra dicto homicidio. At ille, sicut
primitus fecerat, cognito rumore de obitu fratris, indulsit
inimico, veniam postulanti osculum dedit, et benignissimo
animo benedixit osculanti. Hoc peracto rex Arthurus dolens
et lacrimans accepit ab episcopis adstantibus paenitentiam et
emendavit in quantum potuit, donec consummavit vitam.

[Ch. x.] Gildas. . . ascendit naviculam et ingressus est
Glastoniam. . . Melvas rege regnante in aestiva regione.
Susceptus vir suscipiendus a Glastoniense abbate docuit
confratres et diversas plebes seminans semen seminandum
caelestis doctrinae. Ibi scripsit historias de regibus Britanniae.
Glastonia, id est Urbs Vitrea, quae nomen sumpsit a vitro,
est urbs nomine primitus in Britannico sermone [Ynis-
gutrin?]. Obsessa est itaque ab Arturo tyranno cum innu-
merabili multitudine propter Guennuvar uxorem suam
violatam et raptam a praedicto iniquo rege, et ibi ductam
propter refugium inviolati loci propter munitiones arundineti
et fluminis ac paludis causa tutelae. Quaesiverat rex rebellis
reginam per unius anni circulum, audivit tandem illam
remanentem. Illico commovit exercitus totius Cornubiae et
Dibneniae; paratum est bellum inter inimicos. Hoc viso,
abbas Glastoniae comitante clero et Gilda Sapiente intravit
medias acies, consuluit Melvas regi suo pacifice, ut redderet
raptam. Reddita ergo fuit, quae reddenda fuerat, per pacem
et benivolentiam. His peractis duo reges largiti sunt abbati
multa territoria, qui venerunt ad templum sanctae Mariae
visitandum et orandum confirmante abbate fraternitatem
dilectam pro pace habita et pro beneficiis quae fecerant et
amplius quae facturi erant. Inde redierunt reges pacificati
promittentes veneranter obedire reverentissimo abbati Glasto-

niensi et numquam violare sanctissimum locum nec etiam
subjacentia loco principali.

[Ch. xiv.] Ynisgutrin nominata fuit antiquitus Glastonia
et adhuc nominatur a Britannis indigenis; ynis in Britannico
sermone insula Latine; gutrin vero vitrea. Sed post adventum
Angligenarum et expulsis Britannis, scilicet Walensibus,
revocata est Glastigberi ex ordine primi vocabuli, scilicet
glas Anglice vitrum Latine, beria civitas, inde Glastiberia,
id est Vitrea Civitas.

> Nancarbanensis dictamina sunt Caratoci:
> qui legat, emendet: placet illi compositori.

xxi

ÉTIENNE DE ROUEN

[From *Draco Normannicus* (1167–8), edited by R. Howlett in
Chronicles of the Reigns of Stephen, Henry II and Richard I
(R.S.), ii. 695.]

*Quod post haec Henricus rex contra quosdam Britonum
principes sibi rebelles cum valida manu pergit.*

[l. 945]
> Arturi dapifer, Rollandus, consul et idem
> Tunc Britonum, regi dirigit ista suo.

*Epistola Rollandi...ad Arturum olim Britanniae regem
missa, qui tunc apud antipodes degebat.*

> Arturo regi trino Rollandus: In armis
> Efferus Henricus pellit ad arma tuos.
> Providus ergo tuis, quorum tu solus haberis
> Et rex et dominus, auxiliare cito.
> Aut par te venias, aut mittas huc legiones,
> Aut iuveni manda bella necemque. Vale....

Epistola Arturi...ad Henricum...

[l. 1161]
> Saucius Arturus petit herbas inde sororis,
> Avallonis eas insula sacra tenet.

Suscipit hic fratrem Morganis nympha perennis,
  Curat, alit, refovet, perpetuumque facit.
Traditur antipodum sibi ius; fatatus, inermis,
  Belliger assistit, proelia nulla timet.
Sic hemispherium regit inferius, nitet armis,
  Altera pars mundi dimidiata sibi....
Planius haec qui scire cupit, mea gesta revolvat,
  Quae Monumetensis vera loquendo canit....

xxii

ALAIN DE LILLE

[From *Prophetia Anglicana Merlini Ambrosii Britanni* (1167–83),
  lib. i. p. 17 (ed. 1603).]

Et addit: Exitus eius dubius erit. Verissime quidem, sicut
hodieque probat varia hominum de morte ejus [Arturi] et
vita opinio. Quod si mihi non credis, vade in Armoricum
regnum, id est, in minorem Britanniam et praedica per
plateas et vicos Arturum Britonem more ceterum mortuorum
mortuum esse, et tunc certe re ipsa probabis, veram esse
Merlini prophetiam, qua ait: Arturi exitium dubium fore;
si tamen immunis evadere inde potueris, quin aut maledictis
audientium opprimaris, aut certe lapidibus obruaris.

xxiii

PSEUDO-WILLIAM OF MALMESBURY

[From interpolations (12th–13th cent.), in *De Antiquitate Glastoniensis Ecclesiae* (1129–39), edited by T. Hearne with
  Historia of Adam of Domerham (1727).]

[p. 16.] Legitur in antiquis Britonum gestis, quod a
boreali Britanniae parte venerunt in occidentem duodecim
fratres, et tenuerunt plurimas regiones...quas proavus eorum
Cuneda tenuerat. Nomina eorum....Glasteing. Hic est
ille Glasteing, qui per mediterraneos Anglos, secus villam

quae dicitur Escebtiorne, scrofam suam usque ad Wellis, et
a Wellis per inviam et aquosam viam, quae Sugewege, id est,
Scrofae via, dicitur, sequens porcellos suos, iuxta ecclesiam, de
qua nobis sermo est, lactentem sub malo invenit, unde usque
ad nos emanavit, quod mala mali illius Ealdcyrcenas epple, i.
veteris ecclesiae poma, vocantur: sus quoque Ealdecyrce suge
idcirco nominabatur, quae cum ceterae sues quatuor pedes
habeant, mirum dictu, ista habuit octo. Hic igitur Glasteing,
postquam insulam illam ingressus eam multimodis bonis vidit
affluentem, cum omni familia sua in ea venit habitare,
cursumque vitae suae ibidem peregit. Ex cuius progenie et
familia ei succedente locus ille primitus dicitur populatus.
Haec de antiquis Britonum libris sunt.

[p. 17.] *De diversis nominibus eiusdem insulae.* Haec itaque
insula primo Ynswytrin a Britonibus dicta, demum ab
Anglis terram sibi subjugantibus, interpretato priore vocabulo,
dicta est sua lingua Glastinbiry; vel de Glasteing, de quo
praemisimus. Etiam insula Avalloniae celebriter nominatur,
cujus vocabuli haec fuit origo. Supradictum est quod Glasteing
scrofam suam sub arbore pomifera juxta vetustam ecclesiam
invenit, ubi quia primum adveniens poma in partibus illis
rarissima repperit, insulam Avalloniae sua lingua, id est,
insulam pomorum, nominavit. Avalla enim Britonice poma
interpretatur Latine. Vel cognominatur de quodam Avalloc,
qui ibidem cum suabus filiabus, propter loci secretum, fertur
inhabitasse.

[p. 42.] Praetermitto de Arturo, inclito rege Britonum,
in cimiterio monachorum inter duas piramides cum sua conjuge
tumulato, de multis etiam Britonum principibus. Idem
Arturus, anno incarnacionis Dominicae dxlii in Cornubia,
juxta fluvium Cambam, a Mordredo letaliter vulneratus est,
qui inde, ad sananda vulnera sua, in insulam Avallonis est
evectus, et ibidem defunctus in aestate circa Pentechosten,
fere centenarius, aut circiter.[1]

[1] A gloss in *T.C.C. MS* R. 5, 33 adds an extract from Giraldus Cambrensis, *Speculum Ecclesiae* (cf. No. xxvi (d)).

[p. 47.] *De illustri Arturo.* Legitur in gestis illustrissimi regis Arturi, quod cum in quadam festivitate natalis Domini apud Karliun strenuissimum adolescentem, filium scilicet regis Nuth, dictum Ider, insigniis militaribus decorasset, et eumdem, experiendi causa, in montem Ranarum, nunc dictum Brentecnol, ubi tres gigantes malefactis famosissimos esse didicerat, contra eosdem dimicaturum duxisset, idem tiro, Arturum et suos comites ignorantes praecedens, dictos gigantes fortiter aggressus, mira caede trucidavit. Quibus peremptis, Arturus adveniens, dictum Ider nimio labore deficientem et sui omnino inpotem in extasi collapsum inveniens, eumdem quasi defunctum cum suis lamentabatur. Rediens ergo ad sua cum ineffabili tristicia, corpus, quod exanime existimabat, ibidem reliquit, donec vehiculum ad illud reportandum illuc destinasset. Sese etiam necis ejus causam reputans, quia tardius ad auxilium ejus venerat, cum demum Glastoniam adveniret, ibidem quater viginti monachos pro anima ejusdem instituit, possessiones[1] et territoria ad eorum sustentacionem, aurum et argentum, calices et alia ornamenta ecclesiastica largiens abundanter.

xxiv

PETER OF BLOIS

[From *De Confessione* (c. 1190), printed in Migne, *Patrologia Latina*, ccvii. 1088.]

Saepe in tragoediis et aliis carminibus poetarum, in ioculatorum cantilenis describitur aliquis vir prudens, decorus, fortis, amabilis et per omnia gratiosus. Recitantur etiam pressurae vel iniuriae eidem crudeliter irrogatae, sicut de Arturo et Ganganno[2] et Tristanno fabulosa quaedam referunt histriones, quorum auditu concutiuntur ad compassionem audientium corda, et usque ad lacrimas compunguntur.

[1] Glosses in *T.C.C. MS* R. 5, 33 show that the monks claimed 'Brentemareys, Poweldone, cum multis aliis terris in confinio sitis' as of Arthur's donation (Hearne 47, 96). [2] Gauganno?

XXV

RALPH OF COGGESHALL

[From *Chronicon Anglicanum* (1187–1224), edited by J. Stevenson (R.S.), 36.]

[s.a. 1191.] Hoc autem anno inventa sunt apud Glastinge-beriam ossa famosissimi Arturi, quondam regis Britanniae, in quodam vetustissimo sarcophago recondita, circa quod duae antiquae pyramides stabant erectae, in quibus literae quaedam exaratae erant, sed ob nimiam barbariem et deformationem legi non poterant. Inventa sunt autem hac occasione. Dum enim ibidem terram effoderent ut quemdam monachum sepelirent qui hunc locum sepulturae vehementi desiderio in vita sua praeoptaverat, reperiunt quoddam sarcophagum, cui crux plumbea superposita fuerat, in qua ita exaratum erat; 'Hic jacet inclitus rex Arturius, in insula Avallonis sepultus.' Locus autem ille olim paludibus inclusus, insula Avallonis (id est insula pomorum), vocitatus est.

xxvi

GIRALDUS CAMBRENSIS

[From *Opera*, edited by J. S. Brewer and J. F. Dimock (R.S.).]

(*a*) [From *Itinerarium Kambriae* (c. 1191), i. 5 (*Opera*, vi. 57).]

Notandum autem quod in his Urbis Legionum partibus fuit diebus nostris vir quidam Kambrensis, cui nomen Meilerius, futurorum pariter et occultorum scientiam habens. ... Librum quoque mendosum, et vel falso scriptum, vel falsum etiam in se continentem inspiciens, statim, licet illiteratus omnino fuisset, ad locum mendacii digitum ponebat. Interrogatus autem qualiter hoc nosset, dicebat daemonem ad locum eundem digitum suum primo porrigere. ... Contigit aliquando, spiritibus immundis nimis eidem insultantibus, ut Evangelium Johannis ejus in gremio poneretur: qui statim tanquam aves evolantes, omnes penitus evanuerunt. Quo sublato postmodum, et Historia Britonum a Galfrido Arthuro tractata, experiendi causa, loco ejusdem subrogata, non solum corpori ipsius toti, sed etiam libro superposito, longe solito crebrius et taediosius insederunt.

(*b*) [From *De Instructione Principum* (1193–9), Distinctio i (*Opera*, viii. 126).]

Arthuri quoque Britonum regis inclyti memoria est non supprimenda, quem monasterii Glastoniensis egregii, cuius et ipse patronus suis diebus fuerat praecipuus et largitor ac sublevator magnificus, historiae multum extollunt.... Huius autem corpus, quod quasi phantasticum in fine et tanquam per spiritus ad longinqua translatum, neque morti obnoxium fabulae confinxerant, his nostris diebus apud Glastoniam inter lapideas pyramides duas, in coemiterio sacro quondam erectas, profundius in terra quercu concava reconditum, et signatum miris indiciis et quasi miraculosis, est inventum, et in ecclesiam cum honore translatum marmoreoque decenter tumulo commendatum. Unde et crux plumbea lapide supposito, non superius ut [nostris] solet diebus, [sed] inferiori potius ex parte infixa, quam nos quoque vidimus, namque tractavimus litteras has insculptas et non eminentes et exstantes, sed magis interius ad lapidem versas, continebat: 'Hic jacet sepultus inclitus rex Arthurus cum Wenneveria uxore sua secunda in insula Avallonia.' Occurrunt hic autem notabilia plurima; habuerat enim uxores duas, quarum ultima simul cum ipso sepulta fuerat, et ossa ipsius cum ossibus viri simul inventa, sic distincta tamen, ut duae partes sepulchri, versus caput scilicet, ossibus viri continendis deputatae fuissent, tertia vero versus pedes ossa muliebria seorsum contineret; ubi et trica comae muliebris flava cum integritate pristina et colore reperta fuit, quam ut monachus quidam avide manu arripuit et sublevavit, tota statim in pulverem decidit. Cum autem aliqua indicia corporis ibi inveniendi ex scripturis suis, aliqua ex litteris pyramidibus impressis, quanquam nimia plurimum antiquitate deletis, aliqua quoque per visiones et

269

revelationes bonis viris et religiosis factas, maxime tamen et
evidentissime rex Angliae Henricus secundus, sicut ab
historico cantore Britone audierat antiquo, totum monachis
indicavit, quod profunde, scilicet in terra per xvi pedes ad
minus, corpus invenirent, et non [in] lapideo tumulo sed in
quercu cavata. Ideoque tam profunde situm corpus, et quasi
absconditum fuerat, ne a Saxonibus post necem ipsius insulam
occupantibus, quos tanto opere vivens debellaverat et fere ex
toto deleverat, posset nullatenus inveniri; et ob hoc etiam
litterae, veritatis indices, cruci impressae interius ad lapidem
versae fuerunt, ut et tunc temporis quod continebat occul-
tarent, et quandoque tamen pro locis et temporibus id pro-
palarent. Quae nunc autem Glastonia dicitur, antiquitus
insula Avallonia dicebatur. Est enim quasi insula tota
paludibus obsita, unde dicta est Britannice Inis [*MS* emin]
Avallon, id est, insula pomifera. Pomis enim, quae aval
Britannica lingua dicuntur, locus ille quondam abundabat.
Unde et Morganis, nobilis matrona et partium illarum
dominatrix atque patrona, necnon et Arthuro regi sanguine
propinqua, post bellum de Kemelen Arthurum ad sanandum
ejusdem vulnera in insulam quae nunc Glastonia dicitur
deportavit. Dicta quoque quondam Britannice Inis [*MS* eius]
gutrin fuerat, hoc est, insula vitrea; ex quo vocabulo super-
venientes postea Saxones locum illum Glastingeburi vocita-
bant. Glas enim lingua eorum vitrum sonat, et buri castrum,
civitas, appellatur. Sciendum etiam quod ossa reperta corporis
Arthuri tam grandia fuerunt, ut et illud poetae completum
in his videri posset:

> Grandiaque effossis mirabitur ossa sepulchris
>
> [*Georg.* i. 497].

Os enim tibiae ipsius appositum [tibiae] longissimi viri loci,
quem et nobis abbas ostendit, et juxta pedem illius terrae
affixum, large tribus digitis trans genu ipsius se porrexit. Os
etiam capitis tanquam ad prodigium vel ostentum capax erat
et grossum, adeo ut intercilium et inter oculos spatium
palmalem amplitudinem large contineret. Apparebant autem

in hoc vulnera decem aut plura, quae cuncta praeter unum majus caeteris, quod hiatum grandem fecerat, quodque solum letale fuisse videbatur, in solidam convenerant cicatricem.

(*c*) [From *Descriptio Kambriae* (c. 1200), i. 7; ii. 7 (*Opera*, vi. 179, 216).]

[i. 7.] Wallia vero non a Walone duce, vel Wendoloena regina, sicut fabulosa Galfridi Arthuri mentitur historia; quia revera neutrum eorum apud Kambros invenies; sed a barbarica potius nuncupatione nomen istud inolevit.... [ii. 7.] Gloriantur [Britones] ad invicem, praedicant, et confidentissime jactant, toto quod mirum est in hac spe populo manente, quoniam in brevi cives in insulam revertentur; et juxta Merlini sui vaticinia, exterorum tam natione pereunte quam nuncupatione, antiquo in insula tam nomine quam omine Britones exultabunt.

(*d*) [From *Speculum Ecclesiae* (c. 1216), Dist. ii. ch. 8–10 (*Opera*, iv. 47). The omitted passages are mostly mutilated in the MS. A Welsh translation printed in *Revue Celtique*, xxxiii. 432 shows that they contained nothing material.]

[Ch. viii.] *De monacho* [*quodam tricam*] *muliebrem manu tractante, in Arthuri sepulchro repertam, et nimis impudenter* [*eius ruinam*] *accelerante.* [Porro] au[tem regn]ante nostris in Anglia [diebus] Henrico secundo, contigit ut apud Glastonense coenobium quondam nobile sepulchrum Arthuri, dicto rege monente et abbate loci eiusdem Henrico (qui ad cathedram Wigorniensem translatus postea fuit) procurante, diligenter quaesitum, in coemeterio sacro a sancto Dunstano dedicato, inter duas pyramides altas et literatas, in Arthuri memoriam olim erectas, multis laboribus effoderetur, et corpus eiusdem in pulverem et ossa redactum ab imis ad auram et statum digniorem transferretur. Inventa fuit in eodem sepulchro trica muliebris, flava et formosa, miroque artificio conserta et contricata, uxoris scilicet Arthuri, viro ibidem consepultae. Verum ut in ipsam, inter astantes plurimos... [monachus quidam acceleravit]...nimis [impudenter] et inverecunde, ut tricam illam prae caeteris arripere posset, in imum fossae profundae se praecipitem dedit....Monachus iste muliebrem tricam, firmos extricantem animos et infirmos intricantem, prae caeteris rapere cunctis, et impudicae mentis indicio manu tractare curavit. Et licet capilli imputribiles esse dicantur, quia nihil in se corpulentum, nihil humidum habent admixtum, tamen simul ut erectam, et diligenter inspectam manu tenuit, multis intuentibus et obstupentibus in pulverem illico decidit minutissimum, et tanquam in atomos, sicut dividi sic et discerni nescias, subito conversa disparuit....Cunctis praefiguravit esse caduca, et mundanam pulchritudinem omnem vanos oculos ad intuendum seu perpetrandum illicita perstringentem esse momentaneam et vanitati obnoxiam. Quoniam, ut ait philosophus, formae nitor rapidus est et velox, et vernalium florum mutabilitate fugacior. [Ch. ix.] *De sepulchro regis Arthuri ossa eius continente, apud Glastoniam nostris diebus invento, et plurimis circiter haec notabilibus occasionaliter adiunctis.* Porro quoniam de rege Arthuro et eius exitu dubio multa referri solent et fabulae confingi, Britonum populis ipsum adhuc vivere fatue contendentibus, ut fabulosis exsufflatis, et veris ac certis asseveratis, veritas ipsa de caetero circiter haec liquido pateat, quaedam hic adiicere curavimus indubitata veritate comperta. Post bellum de Ke[melen]....Arthuro ibi mortaliter vulnerato, corpus eiusdem in insulam Avaloniam, quae nunc Glastonia dicitur, a nobili matrona quadam eiusque cognata et Morgani vocata, est delatum, quod postea defunctum in dicto coemeterio sacro, eadem procurante, sepultum fuit. Propter hoc enim fabulosi Britones et eorum cantores fingere solebant, quod dea quaedam phantastica, scilicet et Morganis dicta, corpus Arthuri in insulam detulit Avalloniam ad eius vulnera sanandum. Quae cum sanata fuerint, redibit rex fortis et potens, ad Britones regendum, ut ducunt, sicut solet; propter quod, ipsum expectant adhuc venturum, sicut Judaei Messiam suum, maiori etiam fatuitate et infelicitate, simul ac infidelitate decepti....Avallonia vero dicta est, vel ab aval

Britannice, quod pomum sonat, quia locus ille pomis et pomeriis abundaret, vel a [A]vallone quodam, territorii illius quondam dominatore. Item solet antiquitus locus ille Britannice dici Inis Gutrin, hoc est, insula vitrea, propter amnem scilicet, quasi vitrei coloris in marisco circumfluentem; et ob hoc dicta est postmodum a Saxonibus terram occupantibus, lingua eorum, Glastonia. Glas enim Anglice vel Saxonice vitrum sonat. Patet ex his igitur quare insula, et quare Avallonia, et quare Glastonia dicta. Patet et hoc quoque, quo pacto dea phantastica Morganis a fabulatoribus nuncupata. Notandum hic etiam, quod licet abbas praenominatus...[aliqua]...ex litteris in illam inscriptis, quamquam antiquatis tamen et fere omnino vetustate deletis, maximam habuit praedictum regem Henricum ad haec evidentiam. Dixerat enim ei pluries, sicut ex gestis Britonum et eorum cantoribus histori[c]is rex audierat, quod inter pyramides duas, quae postmodum erectae fuerant in sacro coemeterio, sepultus fuit Arthurus, valde profunde propter metum Saxonum, quos ipse frequenter expugnaverat, et ab insula Britannica prorsus eiecerat, et quos Moderedus nepos eius pessimus contra ipsum post revocaverat, ne in mortuum etiam vindicis animi vitio desaevirent, qui totam iam insulam post mortem ipsius iterum occupare contenderant. Propter eundem etiam metum in lapide quodam lato, tanquam ad sepulchrum a fodientibus invento, quasi pedibus vii...[crux plum]bea, non superiori [sed poti]us inferiori parte lapidis inserta, literas has inscriptas habens: Hic iacet sepultus inclytus rex Arthurius, in insula Avallonia, cum Wennevereia uxore sua secunda. Crucem autem hanc extractam a lapide, dicto abbate Henrico ostendente, prospeximus, et literas has legimus. Sicut autem crux inferius lapidi inserta fuit, sic et crucis eiusdem pars literata, ut occultior esset, versus lapidem versa fuit; mira quidem industria et hominum tempestatis illius exquisita prudentia, qui corpus viri tanti, dominique sui, perpetuique loci illius patroni, ratione turbationis instantis, totis nisibus tunc occultare volebant, et tamen ut aliquo in posterum

tempore, tribulatione cessante, per literarum saltem cruci
insertarum et quandoque repertarum indicia propalari possent,
procurarunt. [Ch. x.] *Quod rex Arthurus, praecipuus
Glastoniensis ecclesiae [patronus fu]it....* Sic Arthuri corpus
inventum, non in sepulchro marmoreo, ut regem decebat
tam eximium, non in saxeo, aut Pariis lapidibus exsecto, sed
potius in ligneo, ex quercu ad hoc cavato, et xvi pedibus aut
pluribus in terra profundo, propter festinam magis quam
festivam tanti principis humationem, tempore nimirum turbationis urgentis id exigente. Dictus autem abbas, corpore
reperto, monitis quoque dicti regis Henrici marmoreum ei
sepulchrum fieri fecit egregium, tanquam patrono loci illius
praecipuo, qui scilicet ecclesiam illam prae caeteris regni
cunctis plus dilexerat, terrisque largis et amplis locupleta-
verat....

xxvii

BENEDICT OF PETERBOROUGH

[From *Gesta Regis Ricardi* (c. 1192), edited by W. Stubbs (R.S.),
ii. 159.]

[6 March, 1191.] Rex autem Angliae dedit ei [Tancredo
regi Siciliae] gladium optimum Arcturi, nobilis quondam
regis Britonum, quem Britones vocaverunt Caliburnum.

xxviii

WILLIAM OF NEWBURGH

[From *Prooemium* to *Historia Rerum Anglicarum* (1196–8), edited
by R. Howlett in *Chronicles of the Reigns of Stephen, Henry II
and Richard I* (R.S.), i. 11.]

Quidam nostris temporibus, pro expiandis his Britonum
maculis, scriptor emersit, ridicula de eisdem figmenta con-
texens, eosque longe supra virtutem Macedonum et Romanorum impudenti vanitate attollens. Gaufridus hic dictus est,
agnomen habens Arturi, pro eo quod fabulas de Arturo, ex

priscis Britonum figmentis sumptas et ex proprio auctas, per superductum Latini sermonis colorem honesto historiae nomine palliavit: qui etiam maiori ausu cuiusdam Merlini divinationes fallacissimas, quibus utique de proprio plurimum adiecit, dum eas in Latinum transfunderet, tanquam authenticas et immobili veritate subnixas prophetias, vulgavit.... Sane divinationum Merlini perspicua fallacia est in his quae in regno Anglorum contigisse noscuntur post mortem praenominati Gaufridi, qui divinationum illarum nenias ex Britannico transtulit; quibus, ut non frustra creditur, ex proprio figmento multum adiecit. Porro ad ea, quae vel ante ipsum vel in diebus eius evenerunt, taliter sua, quod utique facile poterat, temperavit figmenta, ut congruam possent interpretationem recipere. Praeterea in libro suo, quem Britonum historiam vocat, quam petulanter et quam impudenter fere per omnia mentiatur, nemo nisi veterum historiarum ignarus, cum in librum illum inciderit, ambigere sinitur. Nam qui rerum gestarum veritatem non didicit, fabularum vanitatem indiscrete admittit. Omitto quanta de gestis Britonum ante Iulii Caesaris imperium homo ille confinxerit, vel ab aliis conficta tanquam authentica scripserit.... Cuncta, quae homo ille de Arturo et eius vel successoribus vel, post Vortigirnum, praedecessoribus scribere curavit, partim ab ipso, partim et ab aliis constat esse conficta; sive effrenata mentiendi libidine, sive etiam gratia placendi Britonibus, quorum plurimi tam bruti esse feruntur, ut adhuc Arturum tanquam venturum exspectare dicantur, eumque mortuum nec audire patiantur.... Sed quantum mera historiae veritas hoc loco compositae praeiudicet falsitati, vel lippienti mentis acie clare videri potest. Ipsum autem Arturum facit praeclarum et spectabilem super omnes homines, tantumque illum in gestis vult esse, quantum sibi libuit fingere.... Quippe in orbe nostro nunquam talia contigerunt. Quomodo enim historiographi veteres, quibus ingenti curae fuit nihil memorabile scribendo omittere, qui etiam mediocria memoriae mandasse noscuntur, virum incomparabilem, eiusque acta supra modum

insignia, silentio praeterire potuerunt?...Cum ergo nec
tenuem de his veteres historici fecerint mentionem, liquet a
mendacibus esse conficta quaecunque de Arturo atque Merlino,
ad pascendam minus prudentium curiositatem, homo ille
scribendo vulgavit. Et notandum, quod eundem Arturum
postea refert in bello letaliter vulneratum, regno disposito, ad
curanda vulnera sua abiisse in illam, quam Britannicae fingunt
fabulae, insulam Avallonis: propter metum Britonum non
audens eum dicere mortuum, quem adhuc vere bruti Britones
exspectant venturum. De successoribus vero Arturi pari
impudentia mentitur;...Ut ergo eidem Bedae, de cuius
sapientia et sinceritate dubitare fas non est, fides in omnibus
habeatur; fabulator ille cum suis fabulis incunctanter ab
omnibus respuatur.

xxix

GERVASE OF TILBURY

[From *Otia Imperialia* (c. 1211), Bk. ii, extracted by J. Stevenson
in edition of Ralph of Coggeshall (R.S.), 438, and Bk. iii,
extracted by F. Liebrecht (1856), 12.]

[Bk. ii.] Arcturus vulneratur, omnibus hostibus ab ipso
peremptis. Unde secundum vulgarem Britonum traditionem
in insula Davalun ipsum dicunt translatum, ut vulnera
quotannis [recrudiscentia] sub interpolata sanatione curentur
a Morganda fatata; quem fabulose Brittones post data
tempora credunt rediturum in regnum.

[Bk. iii.] In Sicilia est mons Aetna....Hunc autem
montem vulgares Mongibel appellant. In huius deserto
narrant indigenae Arturum magnum nostris temporibus
apparuisse. Cum enim uno aliquo die custos palafredi
episcopi Catanensis commissum sibi equum depulveraret,
subito impetu lascivae pinguedinis equus exiliens ac in
propriam se recipiens libertatem fugit. Ab insequente
ministro per montis ardua praecipitiaque quaesitus non
inventus, timore pedissequo succrescente, circa montis opaca

perquiritur. Quid plura? arctissima semita sed plana est inventa; puer in spatiosissimam planitiem iucundam omnibusque deliciis plenam venit, ibique in palatio miro opere constructo reperit Arturum in strato regii apparatus recubantem. Cumque ab advena et peregrino causam sui adventus percontaretur, agnita causa itineris, statim palafridum episcopi facit adduci, ipsumque praesuli reddendum ministro commendat, adiiciens se illic antiquitus, in bello cum Modredo nepote suo et Childerico duce Saxonum pridem commisso, vulneribus quotannis recrudescentibus, saucium diu mansisse. Quinimo, ut ab indigenis accepi, exenia sua ad antistitem illum destinavit, quae a multis visa et a pluribus fabulosa novitate admirata fuerunt. Sed in sylvis Britanniae maioris aut minoris consimilia contigisse referuntur, narrantibus nemorum custodibus, quos forestarios, quasi indaginum ac vivariorum ferinorum aut regiorum nemorum [custodes], vulgus nominat, se alternis diebus circa horam meridianam et in primo noctium conticinio, sub plenilunio luna lucente, saepissime videre militum copiam venantium et canum et cornuum strepitum, qui sciscitantibus se de societate et familia Arturi esse affirmant.

XXX

CAESARIUS OF HEISTERBACH

[From *Dialogus Miraculorum* (c. 1240), edited by J. Strange (1851), xii. 12.]

Eo tempore quo Henricus Imperator subiugavit sibi Siciliam, in Ecclesia Palermensi quidam erat Decanus, natione ut puto Theutonicus. Hic cum die quadam suum qui optimus erat perdidisset palefredum, servum suum ad diversa loca misit ad investigandum illum. Cui homo senex occurrens, ait: Quo vadis, aut quid quaeris? Dicente illo, equum domini mei quaero; subiunxit homo: Ego novi ubi sit. Et ubi est, inquit. Respondit: In monte Gyber; ibi eum habet dominus meus Rex Arcturus. Idem mons flammas evomit sicut Vulcanus. Stupente servo ad verba illius, subiunxit: Dic domino tuo ut ad dies quatuordecim illuc veniat ad curiam eius solemnem. Quod si ei dicere omiseris, graviter punieris. Reversus servus, quae audivit domino suo exposuit, cum timore tamen. Decanus ad curiam Arcturi se invitatum audiens et irridens, infirmatus die praefixo mortuus est. Haec Godescalcus canonicus Bonnensis nobis retulit, dicens se eodem tempore ibidem fuisse.

xxxi

ÉTIENNE DE BOURBON

[From *Tractatus de diversis materiis praedicabilibus* (1251–60), printed by A. Lecoy de la Marche, *Anecdotes Historiques d'Étienne de Bourbon* (1877), 321.]

Item aliquando [ludificant daemones transmutando se] in similitudinem militum venantium vel ludentium, qui dicuntur de familia Allequini vulgariter vel Arturi. Audivi quod, cum quidam rusticus circa Montem Cati portaret facem lignorum ad lunam, vidit infinitam multitudinem canum venaticorum quasi post praedam latrantium, post infinitam multitudinem peditum et equitum. Et cum quaereret ab uno illorum qui essent, respondit quod essent de familia regis Arturi, ad cuius curiam propinquam venirent, ut ibi bene sibi esset. Et visum fuit dicto rustico quod sequeretur eos, et quod intraret in maxima et nobilissima palatia, et [videret] milites et dominas ludentes et choreizantes, comedentes et bibentes nobilia fercula, et in fine dictum est ei quod iret ad lectum, et quod ductus esset in camera ad lectum pretiosissime ornatum, in qua iacebat quaedam domina visa mirabiliter speciosa, cum qua cum intrasset et obdormisset, invenit se, in mane excitatus, super facem lignorum turpiter iacentem et ludificatum.

xxxii

MATTHEW PARIS

[From *Historia Anglorum* (c. 1253), edited by F. Madden (R.S.), iii. 124.]

[s.a. 1252.] Anno quoque sub eodem milites Angliae, ut exercitio militari peritiam suam et strenuitatem experirentur, constituerunt, non ut in hastiludio, quod Torneamentum dicitur, sed potius in illo ludo militari, qui Mensa Rotunda dicitur, vires suas attemptarent. Duo igitur milites electissimi, Ernaldus scilicet de Munteinni et Rogerus de Lemburne, dum se lanceis mutuo impeterent, Ernaldus letaliter vulneratus, praeceps cadens obiit interfectus, qui in militari exercitio nulli in Anglia secundus censebatur.

xxxiii

WAVERLEY ANNALS

[From *Annales de Waverleia*, edited by H. R. Luard in *Annales Monastici* (R.S.), ii. 389, 401.]

[s.a. 1278.] Item in solemnitate Paschali fuit dominus Eadwardus rex et regina apud Glastoniam, et ibi dominus rex tumbam regis Arthuri fecit aperire, et ossa dicti regis extrahi jussit et colligi, et in thesauraria dicti monasterii decenter fecit deponi, quousque possit honestius dicta ossa alicubi collocare.

[s.a. 1283.] Item corona famosi regis Arthuri, qui apud Wallenses a longo tempore in maximo honore habebatur, cum aliis iocalibus pretiosis domino regi est oblata; et sic Wallensium gloria ad Anglicos, licet invite, est translata.

[1 Aug. 1284.] Item convenerunt comites, barones, milites de regno Angliae, ac etiam multi proceres transmarini, circa festum beati Petri quod dicitur ad Vincula, ad rotundam tabulam apud Neuvin iuxta Snaudone praeconizatam in choreis et hastiludiis ad invicem colludentibus in signum triumphi contra Wallensium proterviam expediti.

xxxiv

ADAM OF DOMERHAM

[From *Historia de Rebus Gestis Glastoniensibus* (c. 1278–91), edited by T. Hearne (1727), 341, 587.]

Rex [Ricardus]...praefecit in abbatem Henricum de Soliaco, priorem de Bermundesie, virum de regia stirpe progenitum....Hic, de inclito rege Arturo decentius locando frequenter admonitus (requieverat enim, iuxta vetustam ecclesiam, inter duas piramides lapideas, quondam nobiliter insculptas, sexcentis quadraginta et octo annis) quadam die locum cortinis circumdans, fodere praecepit....Abbas igitur et conventus, suscipientes eorum exuvias, cum gaudio in maiorem transtulerunt ecclesiam, in mausoleo, nobiliter insculpto, intrinsecus bipertito, collocantes. Regium videlicet corpus per se ad caput tumbae, reginam ad pedes, s[eu] in orientali parte; ubi usque in hodiernum diem magnifice requiescunt. Hoc autem epitaphium tumbae inscribitur:

> His iacet Arturus, flos regum, gloria regni,
> Quem mores, probitas, commendant laude perhenni.
> Arturi iacet hic coniux tumulata secunda,
> Quae meruit coelos virtutum prole fecunda.

[s.a. 1277–78.] Dominus Edwardus rex Angliae illustris, cum domina Alienora consorte sua, venit Glastoniam... sanctum Pascha celebraturus....Die vero Martis proxima sequente...in crepusculo fecit Dominus Rex aperiri sepulcrum incliti Regis Arturi. Ubi in duabus cistis, imaginibus et armis eorum depictis, ossa dicti regis mirae grossitudinis, et Gwunnarae reginae mirae pulcritudinis, separatim invenit. Ymago quidem reginae plene coronata; ymaginis regis corona fuit prostrata, cum abscicione sinistrae auriculae, et vestigiis plagae unde moriebatur. Inventa eciam fuit scriptura super hiis singulis manifesta. In crastino vero, videlicet die Mercurii, Dominus Rex ossa Regis, Regina ossa Reginae, in singulis palliis preciosis involuta, in suis cistis recludentes, et

280

sigilla sua opponentes, praeceperunt idem sepulcrum ante maius altare celeriter collocari, retentis exterius capitibus et genis utriusque propter populi devotionem.

XXXV

WILLIAM RISHANGER

[From *Chronica* (c. 1300–27), edited by H. T. Riley (R.S.), 94.]

[s.a. 1279.] Illustris miles, Rogerus de Mortuo Mari, apud Kelingwurthe ludum militarem, quem vocant Rotundam Tabulam, centum militum ac tot dominarum, constituit; ad quam, pro armorum exercitio, de diversis regnis confluxit militia multa nimis.

xxxvi

MONK OF MALMESBURY

[From *Vita Edwardi Secundi auctore Malmesberiensi* (c. 1325), edited by W. Stubbs in *Chronicles of Edward I and Edward II* (R.S.), ii. 218.]

[s.a. 1315.] Porro ex dictis Merlini prophetae sperant adhuc Angliam recuperare. Hinc est quod frequenter insurgunt Walenses, effectum vaticinii implere volentes; sed quia debitum tempus ignorant saepe decipiuntur et in vanum laborant.

xxxvii

RANULPH HIGDEN

[From *Polychronicon* (1327–42), edited by J. R. Lumby (R.S.), v. 332.]

Ceterum de isto Arthuro, quem inter omnes chronographos solus Gaufridus sic extollit, mirantur multi quomodo veritatem sapere possint quae de eo praedicantur, pro eo quod si Arthurus, sicut scribit Gaufridus, terdena regna acquisivit, si regem Francorum subjugavit, si Lucium procuratorem reipublicae apud Italiam interfecit, cur omnes historici Romani, Franci, Saxonici, tot insignia de tanto viro omiserunt, qui de minoribus viris tot minora retulerunt.

xxxviii

ADAM MURIMUTH

(*a*) [From *Continuatio Chronicarum* (1338–47), edited from *Harleian MS* 3836 by E. M. Thompson (R.S.), i. 155.]

[s.a. 1344.] Die uero Jouis sequente post hastiludia domicellorum dominus rex fecit coenam magnam in qua suam rotundam tabulam inchoauit, et iuramenta quorundam comitum et baronum et militum quos uoluit esse de dicta tabula rotunda recepit, sub certa forma ad dictam rotundam tabulam pertinente. Et praefixit diem rotundae tabulae tenendae ibidem in festo Pentecostes proxime tunc futuro, et omnibus praesentibus dedit licentiam cum gratiarum actionibus ad propria remeandi. Ordinauit etiam postea quod ibidem fieret una nobilissima domus, in qua posset dicta rotunda tabula teneri in termino assignato; ad quam faciendam caementarios et carpentarios ceterosque artifices deputauit, et tam ligna quam lapides prouideri praecepit, non parcendo laboribus uel expensis. A quo opere fuit postea ex certis causis cessatum.

(*b*) [From later compilation (c. 1361) in *Cotton MS Nero* D. x, *ibid.* i. 232.]

In castello de Wyndelsore...oblato libro, dominus rex, tactis sacrosanctis, corporale praestitit iuramentum, quod ipse ad certum tempus ad hoc limitatum, dummodo sibi facultas arrideat, mensam rotundam inciperet, eodem modo et statu quo eam dimisit dominus Arthurus quondam rex Angliae, scilicet ad numerum trecentorum militum, et eam foueret et manuteneret pro uiribus, numerum semper inaugendo.

BIBLIOGRAPHICAL NOTE

[*Arch.* (Herrig's Archiv für das Studium der neueren Sprachen und Literaturen); *C.R.* (Celtic Review); *E.E.T.S.* (Early English Text Society); *E.H.R.* (English Historical Review); *E.S.* (Englische Studien); *F.L.* (Folk-Lore); *G.G.A.* (Göttingische gelehrte Anzeigen); *J.G.P.* (Journal of English and Germanic Philology); *M.G.H.* (Monumenta Germaniae Historica); *M.L.N.* (Modern Language Notes); *M.L.R.* (Modern Language Review); *M.P.* (Modern Philology); *N.A.* (Neues Archiv); *P.M.L.A.* (Publications of the Modern Language Association of America); *P.Q.* (Philological Quarterly); *R.C.* (Revue Celtique); *R.E.S.* (Review of English Studies); *R.R.* (Romanic Review); *Rom.* (Romania); *S.A.T.F.* (Société des Anciens Textes Français); *S.P.* (Studies in Philology of the University of North Carolina); *Z.C.P.* (Zeitschrift für Celtische Philologie); *Z.D.P.* (Zeitschrift für Deutsche Philologie); *Z.F.L.* (Zeitschrift für Französische Sprache und Literatur); *Z.R.P.* (Zeitschrift für Romanische Philologie); *Y.C.* (Y Cymmrodor).]

The most complete survey of the whole Arthurian theme is J. D. Bruce, *The Evolution of Arthurian Romance from the Beginnings down to the Year* 1300 (1923), which has a full bibliographical list. This book appeared when most of my own study had been finished, but has been invaluable in its later stages. I agree in the main with Dr Bruce's views as to the literary problems involved, but many scholars attribute a much greater share, both in the *Historia* of Geoffrey of Monmouth and in the romances, to Celtic tradition.

Other books of inclusive range are R. H. Fletcher, *The Arthurian Material of the Chronicles* (1906); W. Lewis Jones, *King Arthur in History and Legend* (1911); E. Windisch, *Das Keltische Britannien bis zu Kaiser Arthur* (1912); E. F. W. M. Van der Ven Ten-Bensel, *King Arthur in English Literature* (1925).

An historical background can be found in J. H. Ramsay, *The Foundations of England* (1898); C. Oman, *England before the Norman Conquest* (1910); K. Norgate, *England under the Angevin*

Kings (1887); H. W. C. Davis, *England under the Normans and Angevins* (1905); and for Wales, J. E. Lloyd, *A History of Wales* (1912); J. Rhys and D. Brynmor-Jones, *The Welsh People* (1900); H. Williams, *Christianity in Early Britain* (1912); J. Chevalier, *Essai sur la Formation de la Nationalité et les Réveils Religieux au Pays de Galles* (1923).

CHAPTER I (*The Early Tradition*)

The editions of Gildas, Bede, Nennius, the *Annales Cambriae*, William of Malmesbury, Henry of Huntingdon, and Hermann of Laon are given under *Records*. Mommsen's text of Gildas is re-produced, with a not very good translation, by H. Williams (1899–1901, *Cymmrodorion Record Soc.*). The *Chartres MS* of the *Historia Britonum* is separately edited by L. Duchesne in *Nennius Retractatus* (1894, *R.C.* xv. 174).

The nature and relations of the early documents, together with the chronological problems dealt with in ch. v, have been the subject of many dissertations, comprising *inter alia*—A. de la Borderie, *L'Historia Britonum attribué à Nennius* (1883); G. Heeger, *Die Trojanersaga der Britten* (1886); H. Zimmer, *Nennius Vindicatus* (1893); J. B. Bury, *Life of St Patrick* (1905); H. M. Chadwick, *Origin of the English Nation* (1907); and papers by J. Loth (*Rom.* xviii. 281); T. Mommsen (*N.A.* xix. 285); H. Zimmer (*N.A.* xix. 436, 667); L. Traube (*N.A.* xxiv. 721); L. Duchesne (*R.C.* xvii. 1); R. Thurneysen (*Z.D.P.* xxviii. 80; *Z.C.P.* i. 157; *E.S.* xxii. 285); E. W. B. Nicholson (*Z.C.P.* iii. 104; vi. 439; viii. 121; *C.R.* ii. 369); A. Anscombe (*Z.C.P.* i. 274; iii. 492; vi. 339; vii. 419; *Eriu*, iii. 117); A. W. Wade-Evans (*C.R.* i. 291; ii. 46, 126; ix. 35, 314; x. 215, 322; *YC.* xxii. 124); W. W. Newell (*P.M.L.A.* xx. 622); A. O. Anderson (*C.R.* viii. 149); F. Lot (*Mélanges Bémont*, 1); H. Howorth (6 *Archaeologia Cambrensis*, xvii. 87, 321; xviii. 199); A. G. van Hamel (Hoops's *Real-Lexicon f. Germ. Altertumskunde*); F. Liebermann (*Tout Essays*, 25); G. H. Wheeler (*E.H.R.* xli. 497).

CHAPTER II (*Geoffrey of Monmouth*)

Facts bearing on Geoffrey's life are furnished by W. Lewis Jones (1899, *Cymmrodorion Soc. Trans.*); H. L. D. Ward (*Cat. of B. M.*

Romances, i. 203); H. Salter, *G. of M. and Oxford (E.H.R.* xxxiv. 382); P. Marchegay, *Chartes Anciennes du Prieuré de Monmouth* (1879); A. W. Haddan and W. Stubbs, *Councils and Ecclesiastical Documents,* i. 360; and the article by H. R. Tedder in *D.N.B.* The *Gwentian Brut* is in 3 *Archaeologia Cambrensis,* x. 124. The *Liber Landavensis* is edited by J. G. Evans and J. Rhys (1893).

The editions of Ordericus, Suger, Alain de Lille and Alfred of Beverley are given in *Records.*

The text of the *Historia* (1854) by San Marte (pseud. of A. Schulz) follows that of J. A. Giles (1844), which is based on the 16th cent. editions and is of no critical value. A translation by S. Evans is in the *Everyman Library.* The Berne dedication was made known (1858) by F. Madden (*Archaeological Journal,* xv. 299), and the Meulan dedication by A. Griscom (1926, *Speculum,* i. 129), who has undertaken a study of some of the MSS, of which there are about 200. An imperfect list is given by T. D. Hardy (*Materials Relating to the History of Great Britain* (1862), i. 341). Those in the Brit. Mus. are described by Ward; that at Leyden by L. V. Delisle (*Bibl. de l'École des Chartes,* lxxi. 511). The chief dissertations are H. Tausendfreund, *Vergil und G. v. M.* (1913); P. Feuerherd, *G. of M. und das Alte Testament* (1915); H. Brandenburg, *G. v. M. und die frühmittelenglischen Chronisten* (1918); H. Matter, *Englische Gründungssagen* (1922); and papers by H. L. D. Ward (*Anglia,* xxiv. 381); A. Leitzmann (*Arch.* cxxxiv. 373); F. Liebermann (*Arch.* cxliv. 31); R. H. Fletcher (*P.M.L.A.* xvi. 461); A. Sayce (*YC.* x. 207); F. Petrie (*Proc. of Brit. Acad.* viii. 251; *History,* iv. 34); R. W. Chambers (*History,* iii. 225; iv. 34); E. K. Chambers (*R.E.S.* i. 431).

The text of the *Vita Merlini* by J. J. Parry (1925, *Illinois Studies,* x. 3) supersedes those of W. H. Black (1830), F. Michel and J. Wright (1837), A. F. Gfrörer (1840) and San Marte (1853). Dissertations are W. E. Mead, *Outlines of the History of the Legend of Merlin* (1899, in Pt iv of *E.E.T.S.* ed. of prose *Merlin*); F. Lot, *Études sur Merlin* (1900, reprint from *Annales de Bretagne,* xv); H. L. D. Ward (*Cat. of B.M. Romances,* i. 278); E. Anwyl (in A. Hastings, *Encycl. of Religion and Ethics*); R. Taylor, *The Political Prophecy in England* (1911); and papers by H. L. D. Ward (*Rom.* xxii. 504); F. Lot (*Rom.* xlv. 1); A. de Jubainville (*Revue des*

Bibliography

Questions Historiques, v. 559); A. C. L. Brown (*R.C.* xxii. 339); H. G. Leach (*M.P.* viii. 607); G. H. Maynadier (1913, *Kittredge Papers*); M. Gaster (*F.L.* xvi. 407); J. J. Parry (*M.P.* xxii. 413; *P.Q.* iv. 193).

The imitation of John of Cornwall is printed in C. Greith, *Spicilegium Vaticanum* 99 and H. de la Villemarque, *Myrdhinn* (1862), 417.

CHAPTER III (*Sources of Geoffrey*)

The Welsh bardic organization is described by Lloyd and by Rhys and Brynmor-Jones (cf. ch. i). Welsh texts of the *Four Books* are in the series of *Welsh Texts* (1887–1915) by J. Rhys and J. G. Evans.

The translations of Arthurian poems by Prof. Rhys are in his *Arthurian Legend* (1891) and Dent's edition (1893) of Malory. The earlier translations in W. F. Skene, *The Four Ancient Books of Wales* (1868) cannot be relied upon. Conflicting views as to the date of the earlier poems are in J. Morris-Jones, *Taliessin* (1918, *YC.*) and J. G. Evans, *Taliesin, or The Critic Criticised* (1924, *YC.*). The studies of J. Loth are in *R.C.* xxi. 28, 328, and his *Contributions à l'Étude des Romans de la Table Ronde* (1912) and his translation of *Les Mabinogion* (ed. 2, 1913). This contains the early triads as well as the prose stories. Lady Charlotte Guest's *The Mabinogion* (ed. A. Nutt, 1902) is an English version of the stories. There are dissertations by J. Rhys (*Cymmrodorion Trans.* 1894–5); E. Anwyl (*Z.C.P.* i. 277; ii. 124; iii. 123); W. J. Gruffyd (*Cymmrodorion Trans.* 1912–13); J. Baudis (*F.L.* xxvii. 31).

The editions of the *Vitae Sanctorum* are given in *Records*.

Much of the controversy as to the insular or continental origin of the *matière de Bretagne* (cf. ch. v) also bears upon the origin and authenticity of Geoffrey's *Liber*.

The Cornish element in the *Historia* is discussed by F. Lot (*Rom.* xxviii. 342; xxx. 11); and the early relations between Cornwall and Brittany in A. de la Borderie, *Histoire de Bretagne*, i–iii (1896–9), and in studies of the migration by J. Loth, *L'Émigration Bretonne en Armorique* (1883); T. Hodgkin (*Cornwall Polytechnic Soc. Reports*, N.S. i. 443); W. Edwards (*YC.* xi. 61).

CHAPTER IV (*The Acceptance of Arthur*)

The editions of Gaimar, William of Newburgh, Ralph of Coggeshall, Giraldus Cambrensis, Étienne de Rouen, Adam of Domerham, the *De Antiquitate Glastoniae*, Higden and the minor chronicles cited are given in *Records*.

The *Gesta Regum Britanniae* of the Pseudo-Gildas is edited by F. Michel (1862, *Cambrian Archaeological Association*), and the Welsh *Bruts* by J. G. Evans (1890). The latter, with the continuation (*Brut y Tywysogion*) ascribed to Caradoc of Llancarfan, are discussed by E. Phillimore (*YC*. xi. 133), and A. Griscom (*YC*. xxxv. 49; xxxvi. 1). The fragmentary French *Bruts* are printed in K. Hoffmann und K. Vollmöller, *Der Münchener Brut* (1877) and O. Wendeburg, *Über die Bearbeitung von G. v. M. in Harl. MS* 1605 (1881). Wace is inadequately edited by Le Roux de Lincy (1836–8). Dissertations are A. Ulbrich, *Über die Verhältnis von Wace zu G. v. M.* (1908, *Romanische Forschungen*, xxvi); A. B. Hopkins, *The Influence of Wace on Crestien de Troies* (1913); L. Waldner, *Wace's Brut und seine Quellen* (1914); J. H. Philpot, *Maistre Wace* (1925); and papers by E. Du Méril (Ebert's *Jahrbuch*, i. 1); B. Ten Brink (Ebert's *Jahrbuch*, ix. 241); G. Paris (*Rom.* ix. 592); H. L. D. Ward (*Cat. of B.M. Romances*, i. 260); K. Norgate (*D.N.B.*).

Layamon is edited by F. Madden (1847). Dissertations are P. Wuelcker, *Ueber die Quellen L.'s* (1876, Paul und Braune's *Beiträge*, iii. 524); R. Imelmann, *L., Versuch über seine Quellen* (1906); R. Seyger, *Beiträge zu L.'s Brut* (1912); L. Bartels, *Handschriften von L.'s Brut* (1913); F. L. Gillespy, *L.'s Brut* (1916, *California Univ. Publ.* iii. 361); and papers by B. S. Monroe (*J.G.P.* vii. 139); A. C. L. Brown (*M.P.* i. 95); R. H. Fletcher (*P.M.L.A.* xviii. 91); J. D. Bruce (*M.L.N.* xxvi. 65); H. L. D. Ward (*Cat. B.M. Romances*, i. 268); J. W. Hales (*D.N.B.*).

Translations from Wace and Layamon are in *Arthurian Chronicles* (*Everyman Library*).

The history of Glastonbury may be studied in R. Willis, *Architectural History of Gl.* (1866); E. A. Freeman, *English Towns and Districts* (1883); T. S. Holmes, *Wells and Gl.* (1908); F. B. Bond, *Architectural History of Gl.* (1925). The *De Antiquitate* and the exhumation are discussed by W. W. Newell, *William of Malmesbury on the Antiquity of Gl.* (1903, *P.M.L.A.* xviii. 459); F. Lot, *Gl. and Avalon* (1898, *Rom.* xxvii. 528) and *Mélanges Bretonnes* (1907); J. Armitage Robinson, *Somerset Historical Essays* (1921) and *Two Gl. Legends* (1926); and in papers by A. Holtzmann (*Germania*, xii. 257); G. Baist (*Z.R.P.* xix. 326); R. Thurneysen (*Z.R.P.* xx. 316); T. Lewis and J. D. Bruce (*R.C.* xxxiii. 432).

The Round Table jousts and their relation to the Order of the Garter are discussed in N. H. Nicolas, *Observations on the Institution of the Garter* (1846, *Archaeologia*, xxxi. 1); L. F. Mott, *The Round Table* (*P.M.L.A.* xx. 237); W. St J. Hope, *Windsor Castle* (1913); F. H. Cripps-Day, *History of the Tournament* (1918); R. Withington, *English Pageantry* (1918), i. 89.

The Arthurian foundation of Cambridge is claimed by Nicholas Cantelupe (ob. 1441) in *De Antiquitate et Origine Univ. Cant.* (ed. Hearne with Sprott's *Chronicle* in 1719).

John of Fordun's *Scotichronicon* is edited by W. F. Skene (1871–2). Hector Boece's *Scotorum Historia* was printed in 1527 and the adaptation of it in Scottish by John Bellenden (1536) was edited by T. Maitland, *History and Chronicles of Scotland* (1821). An English version forms part of R. Holinshed's *Chronicles* (ed. 1807–8, v. 136).

Polydore Virgil's *Anglica Historia* was printed in 1534. Leland's *Assertio Inclytissimi Arturii* (1544) is edited, with R. Robinson's translation (1582), by W. E. Mead (1925, *E.E.T.S.*). His *Codrus, sive Defensio Gallofridi Monumetensis* is in T. Hearne's edition of his *Collectanea*, v.

The Winchester Round Table is described by E. Smirke (1846, *Proc. of Arch. Institute at Winchester*) and T. W. Shore (1900–2, *Proc. of Hampshire Field Club*).

CHAPTER V (*Arthur and the Round Table*)

I can only give the chief texts and a few dissertations; Bruce's bibliographical list is full.

Early records of Arthurian names on the continent are given and discussed by P. Rajna, *Gli eroi Brettoni nell' onomastica italiana del secolo xii* (*Rom.* xvii. 161, 355); H. Zimmer (1890, *G.G.A.* 831); I. Sanesi, *Storia di Merlino* (1898), xii; L. Suchier and A. Birch-

Hirschfeld, *Gesch. der Franz. Lit.* (1900), 141; G. Paris, *Mélanges de Litt. Franç.* (1912), 46; E. Faral, *Recherches sur les Sources Latines des Contes et Romans* (1913), 396.

The Modena relief is described by W. Foerster, *Ein neues Artus-dokument* (1898, *Z.R.P.* xxii. 243, 526); B. Colfi (4 *Atti e Memorie di Storia per le Provincie Modenesi*, ix); G. Bertoni, *Atlante del Duomo di Modena*, Pl. x); A. K. Porter, *Lombard Architecture*, i. 436; iii. 44; E. Faral, *Sources Latines*, 395; R. S. Loomis (*J.G.P.* xxiii. 284; *M.L.N.* xl. 67).

The *lais* of Marie de France are edited by K. Warnke (ed. 2, 1900), and E. Höpffner (1921), and translated by E. Rickert (1901). Dissertations are F. Lot (*Rom.* xxiv. 513; xxviii. 321); J. Bédier (*Rev. des deux Mondes*, cvii. 835); J. C. Fox (*E.H.R.* xxv. 303; xxvi. 317); E. Winkler (*Sitzungsberichte of Vienna Acad. Phil.-Hist. Klasse*, clxxxviii); L. Foulet (*Z.R.P.* xxix. 19; xxx. 698; *M.L.N.* xx. 109; xxi. 46; xxii. 161; xxiii. 205).

The romances, other than the *Conte del Graal*, of Chrétien de Troyes, are edited by W. Foerster in a larger form (1884–1912), and a smaller form (1909–13), with a *Wörterbuch* (1914), the intro-duction to which gives the latest statement of the editor's views. Criticism of these will be found in the dissertations on the origins of Arthurian romance cited below. The *Ivain* is studied by R. Zenker, *Forschungen zur Artusepik* (1921); A. C. L. Brown, *Iwain* (1903) and papers in *P.M.L.A.* xx. 673; *M.P.* ix. 109; *R.R.* iii. 143; W. A. Nitze (*M.P.* vii. 267; xii. 145); L. B. Morgan (*M.P.* vi. 331); G. L. Hamilton (*R.R.* ii. 315; v. 213); O. M. Johnston (*Z.F.L.* xxxi. 157). There is no critical edition of the *Conte del Graal*. The text of the *Mons MS* was printed by C. Potvin (1866–71), and that of Chrétien's part from *B.N. MS* 794, by G. Baist (1912). From the vast literature on the Grail I can only note, as useful introductions, A. Nutt, *Studies on the Legend of the Holy Grail* (1888); R. Heinzel, *Über die Französischen Gralromane* (1891); J. L. Weston, *The Legend of Sir Perceval* (1906–9); R. H. Griffith, *Sir Perceval of Galles* (1911); A. C. L. Brown, *The Grail and the English Sir Perceval* (*M.P.* xvi. 553; xvii. 361; xviii. 201, 661; xxii. 79, 113); W. Golther, *Parzival und der Gral* (1925).

J. Bédier has edited the *Tristan* of Thomas (1903–5, *S.A.T.F.*), with a full study of the romances, and two poems on *La Folie*

Tristan (1907, *S.A.T.F.*), and E. Muret the *Tristan* of Beroul (1903, *S.A.T.F.*, 1913, *Classiques Fr.*). Among the most important dissertations are W. Golther, *Tristan und Isolde* (1907); J. Loth, *Contributions à l'Étude des Romans de la Table Ronde* (1912), with papers in *R.C.* xxxiv. 365; xxxvii. 317; G. Schoepperle, *Tristan and Isolt* (1913); and papers by E. Brugger (*Arch.* cxxix. 134, 375; cxxx. 117; *M.P.* xxii. 159); F. M. Warren (*M.L.N.* xxiv. 37); C. Appel (*Z.R.P.* xli. 219); R. S. Loomis (*M.L.R.* x. 304; xiv. 38; xvii. 24; *Illinois Univ. Studies*, ii. 247; *R.R.* viii. 196; *M.L.N.* xxxix. 319).

The miscellaneous French verse romances are analysed and the editions given by Bruce, ii. 175, and G. Paris, *Hist. Littéraire de France*, xxx (1888), 1. *The Legend of Sir Gawain* is discussed by J. L. Weston (1897).

The minstrel and the *trouvère* are studied in E. K. Chambers, *Mediaeval Stage* (1903) and E. Faral, *Les Jongleurs en France* (1910).

Many of the works already cited deal with the general problems of Arthurian origins—the sources of Geoffrey. The significance of the terms *Britannia, Britones, Bretagne, Breton*, the extent of Celtic influence on the *Matière de Bretagne*, the channels of transmission, the hypothetical pre-Chrétien French poems. To these may be added E. Faral, *Recherches sur les Sources Latines des Contes et Romans Courtois du moyen âge* (1913), and papers by H. Zimmer (*G.G.A.* xii.; *Z.F.L.* xii. 231; xiii. 1); W. Golther (*Z. f. vergleichende Literaturgeschichte*, N.F. iii. 211); M. Wilmotte (*Moyen Âge*, iv. 186); F. Putz (*Z.F.L.* xiv. 161); J. Loth (*R.C.* xiii. 475); F. Lot (*Rom.* xxiv. 321, 497; xxv. 1; xxvii. 529; xxviii. 1, 321; xxx. 1; xlv. 16; xlvi. 39); E. Brugger (*Z.F.L.* xx. 79; xxvii. 69; xxviii. 1); R. S. Loomis (*J.G.P.* xxiii. 582). The controversy on the relations of Chrétien's romances to their Welsh analogues is described by Bruce, ii. 62.

The identity of Bleheris is specially considered by J. L. Weston (*Rom.* xxxiii. 338; xxxiv. 100); E. Owen (*R.C.* xxxii. 5); W. J. Gruffyd (*R.C.* xxxiii. 180); F. Lot (*Rom.* xxviii. 336); R. S. Loomis (*M.L.N.* xxxix. 319).

The Robert de Boron poems are in F. Michel, *Le Roman du Saint Graal* (1841); the prose versions and *Perceval* continuation from the *Didot MS* in E. Hucher, *Le Saint Graal* (1875–8); the Perceval from the *Modena MS* in J. L. Weston, *Legend of Sir Perceval* (1906–9); and the *Merlin* with a *suite* independent of the *Vulgate* in G. Paris et J. Ulbrich, *Merlin* (1886, *S.A.T.F.*). The prose *Joseph* is also edited by G. Weidner (1881). Dissertations are W. Hoffmann, *Die Quellen des Didot-Perceval* (1905); H. O. Sommer, *Messire Robert de Borron und der Verfasser des D.-P.* (1908), and papers by E. Wechssler (*Z.R.P.* xxiii. 135) and E. Brugger (*Z.F.L.* xxxvi. 7); A. Pauphilet (1925, *Lot Mélanges*, 603).

The *Lanzelet* of Ulrich von Zatzikhoven is edited by K. Hahn (1845). *The Legend of Sir Lancelot du Lac* (1901) and *The Three Days' Tournament* (1902) are studies by J. L. Weston.

The *Vulgate* cycle is edited by H. O. Sommer (1908–16), and in part by pupils of E. Wechssler (1911–16) and J. D. Bruce, *Mort Artu* (1910). Dissertations, which also deal largely with the related cycles, are G. Paris, *Études sur les Romans de la Table Ronde* (*Rom.* x. 465; xii. 459); E. Brugger, *L'Enserrement Merlin* (*Z.F.L.* xxix. 56; xxx. 169; xxxi. 239; xxxiii. 145; xxxiv. 99; xxxv. 1); H. O. Sommer, *The Structure of Le Livre d'Artus* (1914); F. Lot, *Étude sur le Lancelot en Prose* (1918); A. Pauphilet, *Études sur la Queste del Saint Graal attribuée à Walter Map* (1921).

The prose *Tristan* cycle and the late Boron cycle are unedited. The former is studied by E. Löseth, *Le Roman en Prose de Tristan* (1890), and E. Vinaver, *Études sur le Tristan en Prose* (1925), and the latter by E. Wechssler, *Über die verschiedenen Redaktionen des R. de B. zugeschriebenen Graal-Lancelot-Cyklus* (1895); E. Vettermann, *Die Balendichtungen und ihre Quellen* (1918); and papers by A. Pauphilet (*Rom.* xxxvi. 591) and H. O. Sommer (*Rom.* xxxvi. 369, 543; *M.P.* v. 55, 181, 291; *Z.R.P.* xxxii. 327).

The standard edition of Malory's *Morte Darthur* is by H. O. Sommer (1889–91); there are others by E. Strachey (*Globe*), I. Gollancz (*Temple*), and J. Rhys (*Everyman*). Dissertations are V. D. Scudder, *Le Morte Darthur of Sir Thomas Malory and its Sources* (1921), and E. Vinaver, *Le Roman de Tristan et Iseut dans l'Œuvre de Thomas Malory* (1925). The English stanzaic *Morte Arthur* is edited by J. D. Bruce (1903, *E.E.T.S.*) and S. B. Hemingway (1912), and its relation to Malory discussed by J. D. Bruce in *Anglia*, xxxiii. 67.

Bibliography

The *Perlesvaus* is edited in vol. i of C. Potvin's *Conte du Graal*, and in part by J. T. Lister (1921), and translated by S. Evans as *The High History of the Holy Grail* (1898). Dissertations are W. A. Nitze, *The Old French Grail Romance, Perlesvaus* (1902), with papers in *M.P.* i. 247; xvii. 151, 605; *S.P.* xv. 7; E. Wechssler (*Z.R.P.* xx. 80).

The bibliography of the English Arthurian romances is treated, even more fully than by Bruce, in J. E. Wells, *Manual of the Writings in Middle English* (1916, with supplements of 1919, 1923 and 1927). The most important, *Sir Gawain and the Green Knight*, is edited by R. Morris and I. Gollancz (1864–1912 and 1923, *E.E.T.S.*) and by J. R. R. Tolkien and E. V. Gordon (1925), and elaborately studied by G. L. Kittredge (1916).

CHAPTER VI (*The Historicity of Arthur*)

Attempts at pedigree-making are A. S. Scott-Gatty (2 *Genealogist*, xviii. 209; xix. 73) and A. Anscombe (*YC.* xxiv. 75; xxix. 151; *Archiv f. Celtische Lexicographie*, i. 187, 513; ii. 147; iii. 57). *Artorius* is studied by K. Malone (*M.P.* xxii. 367).

The end of the Roman domination in Britain is considered by E. A. Freeman, *Western Europe in the Fifth Century* (1904); F. Sagot, *La Bretagne Romaine* (1911); F. Haverfield, *The Romanisation of Roman Britain* (ed. 4, 1923) and *The Roman Occupation of Britain* (1924); E. Foorde, *The Last Age in Roman Britain* (1925). The views of J. B. Bury in *The Notitia Dignitatum* (*Journ. of Roman Studies*, x. 131) and *Hist. of the Later Roman Empire* (1923) are criticized by R. G. Collingwood (*J. of R.S.* xii. 74).

The Saxon invasion is well discussed by Oman and Chadwick. Dissertations are H. H. Howorth (*E.H.R.* xiii. 668); W. H. Stevenson (*E.H.R.* xiv. 32); F. Lot (*Rev. Historique*, cxix. 1). On the datings of Gildas, Nennius and the *Annales Cambriae*, cf. ch. i supra. The archaeological evidence is collected by E. T. Leeds, *The Archaeology of the Anglo-Saxon Settlements* (1913) and *The West Saxon Invasion and the Icknield Way* (1925, *History*, x. 97) and G. Baldwin Brown, *The Arts in Early England*, iii, iv (1915). The views of P. T. Godsal, *The Storming of London* (1908) and *The Conquests of Ceawlin* (1924), and A. F. Major, *Early Wars of Wessex* (1913) are strategical speculations.

The *Anglo-Saxon Chronicle* is edited by J. Earle and C. Plummer (1892–9), and the *Vita Germani* of Constantius of Lyon (c. 480) by W. Levison in *Script. Rer. Merovingarum* (*M.G.H.*), vii. 225; it is discussed by W. Levison (*N.A.* xxix. 95) and in *Analecta Bollandiana*, xxiii.

Arthurian localities are collected in J. A. Bennett, *Camelot* (*Proc. Somerset Arch. Soc.* xxxvi. 1); H. St G. Gray, *Trial Excavations at Cadbury Castle* (*P.S.A.C.* lix. 1); R. Carew, *Survey of Cornwall* (1602); R. Hunt, *Popular Romances of the West of England* (3rd ed. 1881); W. H. Dickinson, *King Arthur in Cornwall* (1900); J. Rhys, *Celtic Folklore* (1901); J. S. Stuart Glennie, *Arthurian Localities* (1869, in *E.E.T.S. Merlin*); the *Denham Tracts* (1892–5, *F.L.S.*); F. J. Snell, *King Arthur's Country* (1926). To the bibliographical list in vol. i of the *Survey of English Place-Names* (1924) may be added the Bucks and Beds vols of that *Survey* and T. F. G. Dexter, *Cornish Names* (1926). W. H. P. Greswell, *Dumnonia and the Valley of the Parret* (1922) is a rather rambling account of the ancient kingdom. Special studies of the Arthurian battles are E. Guest, *The Early English Settlements in South Britain* (1849, in *Origines Celticae*, ii. 147); E. W. B. Nicholson, *Mons Badonicus and Geoffrey of Monmouth* (1896, *Academy*); P. T. Godsal, *Mons Badonicus: the Battle of Bath* (1914); A. Anscombe (*Z.C.P.* v. 103); A. de la Borderie (*R.C.* vi. 1). E. Thomas, *The Icknield Way* (1913) is useful on topography.

CHAPTER VII (*Arthur and Mythology*)

Mythological speculations are in J. Rhys, *Celtic Heathendom* (1888) and *Arthurian Legend* (1891); L. A. Paton, *Fairy Mythology of the Arthurian Romances* (1903); A. Nutt (*F.L.Record*, iv.; *R.C.* xii. 188); K. G. T. Webster, *Arthur and Charlemagne* (*E.S.* xxxvi. 337); K. Malone, *The Historicity of Arthur* (*J.G.P.* xxiii. 463); G. S. Loomis, *Arthur in Avalon* (1923, *Vassar Mediaeval Studies*); and in many of the papers given under ch. v. Much of the analogous Irish material is described in K. Meyer and A. Nutt, *Voyage of Bran* (1895–7). What little is known of Celtic religion can be studied in G. Dottin, *Manuel de l'Antiquité Celtique* (ed. 2, 1915) and the works there cited.

Arthur's fight with the cat is studied by E. Freymond (1899, *Gröber Festgabe*) and the origins of the Round Table by A. C. L. Brown, *The R. T. before Wace* (1900); L. F. Mott (*P.M.L.A.* xx. 231); J. L. Weston (1910, *Wilmotte Mélanges*); L. H. Loomis (*P.M.L.A.* xli. 771).

The *Pèlerinage de Charlemagne* is edited by E. Koschwitz (ed. 4, 1903), and studied by J. Bédier, *Légendes Épiques*, iv (1913), 130.

The Sicilian Arthur legends are discussed in A. Graf, *Miti, Leggende e Superstizioni del Medio Evo* (ed. 2, 1895), 461. The editions of Gervase of Tilbury, Caesarius of Heisterbach and Étienne de Bourbon are given in *Records*.

Much of the material on cave-legends is in J. Grimm, *Teutonic Mythology* (tr. 1880–3); it is analysed by E. S. Hartland, *Science of Fairy Tales* (1891).

The Wild Hunt is considered by O. Driesen, *Der Ursprung des Harlekin* (1904); Raynaud (1890, *Études dédiées à G. Paris*); F. Lot (*Rom.* xxxii. 423).

SUBJECT INDEX

Subject Index

Brent, 118–21
Brittany, 57, 90, 110, 135, 148, 193, 232
Broceliande, 138, 160, 165
Brut y Tywysogion, 21
Bruts: Welsh, 54; French, 101–5; English, 105
Brutus, 31

Cabal, 6, 72, 188
Cadbury, 184
Cadoc, St, 81; *extracts*, 243
Cadwallader, 26, 30, 41, 50, 97, 218
Caerleon, 20, 23, 37–9, 85, 107, 188
Caesarius of Heisterbach, 222; *extract*, 277
Caldrons of enchantment, 61, 68, 216
Caliburn (Caledvwlch, Excalibur), 36, 39, 72, 219
Camelford, 186, 195, 204
Camelot, 184, 195
Camlan (Camlann, Camblanus, Kemelen), 15, 39, 49, 59, 63, 76–9, 89, 91, 186, 195, 203
Caradoc of Llancarfan, 21, 41, 84; *extracts*, 262
Carannog, St, 82; *extract*, 246
Cave legends, 188–93, 221–30
Caxton, William, 130
Celtic elements in romance, 146–55, 165
Cerdic, 179
Cernunnos, 230
Chapalu, 214
Charlemagne, 38, 57, 72, 86, 120, 155, 217, 226, 231
Chrétien de Troyes, 136–47
Classical elements in romance, 154
Conan, 26, 40, 49
Conan Meriadoc, 33, 93
Consul (earl), 34, 37, 47

Cordelia (Kreurdilad, Kreiddylat), 32, 67, 74
Cornwall, 57, 91, 185
Culture legends, 68, 70, 80, 208–10, 215–7, 221
Cumbria, Arthurian localities in, 189
Cuneglassus, 180

Danavexeria, 18
Draco Normannicus, 110; *extracts*, 264
Dream of Rhonabwy, 77
Dumnonia, 12, 66, 92, 116, 184, 204

Edward I, 124–5, 128
Edward II, 124
Edward III, 128
Elbodugus (Elfodd), 6, 15
English Arthurian romances, 166
Étienne de Bourbon, 228; *extract*, 278
Étienne de Rouen, 110; *extracts*, 264

Filius Urbagen, 8, 13
Finn, 206
Folk elements in romance, 68, 71, 74, 135, 157
Folk memory, 183, 188, 193–5, 205
Fordun, John, 129
Four Ancient Books of Wales, 59

Gaimar, Geoffrey, 54; *extract*, 260
Galahad (Gwalhavet), 73, 161–2
Gallic Chronicles, 175, 177; *extracts*, 234
Gawain (Walwen, Gwalchmei), 17, 37, 72, 79, 87, 151, 162, 166, 190
Genealogies of tenth-century Welsh, 31, 38

Subject Index

SUPPLEMENTARY BIBLIOGRAPHY

[The same abbreviations are used in the following pages as are seen in the Bibliography, pp. 283-94, with the addition of the following : *A.B. Annales Bretagne ; Ant. Antiquity ; Arch. Camb. Archaeologia Cambrensis ; Arth. Lit.* R. S. Loomis (ed.), *Arthurian Literature in the Middle Ages* (Oxford, 1959) ; *Arth. Trad.* R. S. Loomis, *Arthurian Tradition and Chrétien de Troyes* (New York, 1949) ; *B.B.C.S. The Bulletin of the Board of Celtic Studies ; B.B.S.I.A. Bulletin Bibliographique de la Société Internationale Arthurienne ; Bull.J.R. The Bulletin of the John Ryland Library ; E.C. Études Celtiques ; J.C.S. The Journal of Celtic Studies ; J.N.L.W. The Journal of the National Library of Wales ; L.G.,* R. Nelli, *Lumière du Graal* (Paris, 1951) ; *L.H.E.B.* K. H. Jackson, *Language and History in Early Britain* (Edinburgh, 1953) ; *Ll.C. Llên Cymru ; M.A. Moyen Âge ; M.Ae. Medium Aevum ; M.L.Q. Modern Language Quarterly ; Proc. B.A. The Proceedings of the British Academy ; Q.B.P.I. The Quarterly Bulletin of the Polish Institute of Arts and Sciences in America ; R.F. Romanische Forschungen ; R.G. Les Romans du Graal dans la littérature des XIIe et XIIIe siècles* (Paris, 1956) ; *R.P. Romance Philology ; S.E.B.C.* N. K. Chadwick, (ed.), *Studies in the Early British Church* (Cambridge, 1958) ; *S.E.B.H.* N. K. Chadwick, (ed.), *Studies in Early British History* (Cambridge, 1954) ; *Sp. Speculum ; T.H.S.C. The Transactions of the Honourable Society of Cymmrodorion ; W.A.L.* R. S. Loomis, *Wales and the Arthurian Legend* (Cardiff, 1956).]

This re-issue of Sir E. K. Chambers' *Arthur of Britain* is sufficient proof of the continued usefulness of the book and of its value as an introduction to modern Arthurian studies. It is a survey of the salient features of the Arthurian legend in the light of what was known in 1927. But since that date research on the problems of the legend has greatly progressed ; much new knowledge has been gained and new light thrown on many problems, new theories have been propounded and texts re-edited. A steady stream of papers and studies flows from the press. All this makes necessary a revaluation of the old evidence and a consideration of the new. The purpose of this note is briefly to mention some of the studies which have appeared since the first publication of *Arthur of Britain* and to supplement the Bibliography which Chambers

himself wrote. Naturally some of these later works are in disagreement
with the views expressed in the book, but it was decided that it would
be better to leave Chambers' opinions to stand unaltered, even where
they are manifestly wrong, and to allow the reader to form his own
ideas after reading the later literature. Some reviews of *Arthur of Britain*
can be found in *P.Q.*VII, 411-2, *Ant.* II, 114-6, *Sp.* III, 259-62, *M.L.N.*
XLIII, 481-4, *History*, XIII, 346-8, *R.R.* XIX, 161-2.

The complexity of Arthurian problems, the great number of texts in
various languages and the ever increasing flow of publications make it
impossible to mention all the studies which have appeared. However,
bibliographies have been published which are essential for anyone who
wishes to read in this field, viz. J. J. Parry, *Arthurian Bibliography*, *1922-29*
(Mod. Lang. Ass. of America, 1931), and J. J. Parry and Margaret
Schlauch, *Arthurian Bibliography*, *1930-35* (Mod. Lang. Ass. of America,
1936). The June number of *M.L.Q.* has contained a Bibliography of
Critical Arthuriana since 1940 (the first list included literature published
in the period 1936-40) and in 1949 appeared the first volume of the
Bulletin Bibliographique de la Société Internationale Arthurienne which is
published annually. In his Bibliographical Note Chambers referred to
J. D. Bruce, *The Evolution of Arthurian Romance from the Beginnings down
to the year 1300* as an invaluable aid and as 'the most complete survey
of the whole Arthurian theme'. But as a re-examination has proved
necessary with *Arthur of Britain*, so too with Bruce's book. This is
ably fulfilled by R. S. Loomis, (ed.), *Arthurian Literature in the Middle
Ages : A Collaborative History* (Oxford, 1959) which is designed as 'a
new survey of a vast field'. As Bruce was the starting point for any
excursion into that field forty years ago, so must this book be today.
It is wider in scope that the earlier book and examines most aspects of
the theme. The treatment is more even as it is the work, not of one
man, but of some thirty specialists. An obvious gain from the collabora-
tion is that the editor has been able to call on modern Welsh scholars
to discuss early Welsh literature and to make use of those critical works
which are themselves published in Welsh. Other works of general
range are R. H. Fletcher, *The Arthurian Material in the Chronicles* (re-issued
Burt Franklin Bibliographical Series x, New York, 1958), J. Marx, *La
Légende arthurienne et le Graal* (Paris, 1952), A. D. Brodeur, *Arthur Dux
Bellorum* (University of California Studies in English, III, 1939). Arthurian

origins are discussed in E. Faral, *La Légende Arthurienne* (3 parts, Paris, 1929 : I, *Des Origines à Geoffroy de Monmouth*, II, *Geoffroy de Monmouth, La Légende arthurienne à Glastonbury*, III, *Documents*), W. F. Schirmer, *Die frühen Darstellungen des Arthurstoffes* (Köln, 1958), D. W. Barber, *Arthur of Albion* (London, 1961), which is, however, more concerned with Arthur in English literature, M. Hanoset, 'Des origines de la Matière de Bretagne', *Marche Romane*, x, 25-38, 67-78.

CHAPTER I

The *Historia Brittonum* of Nennius has been re-edited by F. Lot, *Nennius et l'Historia Brittonum* (Paris, 1934). This is a critical edition with variant readings and notes, but the Chartres text is given separately, 227-31. In his introduction Lot discusses the MSS., sources and authorship of the work and holds that it was for the most part written by Nennius. Faral, op. cit. III, 4-62 prints the Harleian and Chartres MSS : his study of the text is in I, 56-220. The Harleian text of the *Historia* is translated by A. W. Wade-Evans, *Nennius' History of the Britons* (London, 1937), and he translates and discusses the Chartres text in *Arch. Camb.* XCII, 64-85. The Irish Nennius is edited by A. G. van Hamel, *Lebor Bretnach* (Dublin, 1933), who attempts, by an examination of the Irish and Latin MSS., to show the gradual development of the text from a Latin *Liber Britannicus*, a *Liber Sancti Germani* and other British material. The *Historia* is again studied by. H. M. Chadwick, *S.E.B.H.* 23-6, N. K. Chadwick, *S.E.B.C.* 37-46, 91-3. On the name Nennius and possible connections see Sir Ifor Williams, *B.B.C.S.* VIII, 380-9. Other papers are I. Williams, *B.B.C.S.* III, 59-62, IX, 342-4, XI, 42-8 ; J. Loth, *R.C.* XLI, 150-65, LI, 1-31 ; R. Thurneysen, *Z.C.P.* XX, 97-137 ; K. H. Jackson, *Ant.* XII, 44-45 ; D. de Séchelles, *A.B.* LXIV, 145-62. Sir Ifor Williams' views on the story of Vortigern as an oral saga are in 'Hen Chwedlau' *T.H.S.C.* 1946-7, 28 f. and cf. N. K. Chadwick, *S.E.B.H.* 34-46. On Vortigern see H. M. Chadwick, ibid., 21-33 ; P. K. Johnstone, *Ant.* XX, 16-20 ; C. A. Ralegh Radford, XXXII, 19-24 ; J. D. Bu'lock, XXXIV, 49-53 ; N. K. Chadwick, *B.B.C.S.* XIX, 225-30. The Arthurian section of Nennius and the twelve battles are discussed and the evidence variously evaluated by A. D. Brodeur, op. cit.; W. A. Nitze, *M.P.* XXXIX, 1-14, *M.L.N.* LVII, 64-8, LVIII, 1-8 ; P. K. Johnstone, *Notes and Queries*, CLXVI, 381-2 ; R. G. Collingwood, *Ant.* III, 292-8, *Ant.* V,

236-9 ; O. G. S. Crawford, IX, 277-91 ; N. Tolstoi, *B.B.C.S.* XIX, 118-162 ; K. H. Jackson, *M.P.* XLIII, 44-57. The attempts to locate these battles cannot be said to be truly successful and the names do not appear to contribute a great deal to solving the problem of Arthur's historicity. It has been suggested (e.g. H. M. and N. K. Chadwick, *The Growth of Literature*, I, 155, R. Bromwich, *S.E.B.H.* 124) that they may have been taken from an early Welsh heroic poem which enumerated the victories (whether historically his or not) attributed to the hero. For the Battle of Breguoin see *Ant.* XXIII, 48-9. The Battle of Badon has frequently been discussed and variously sited, R. Birley, *Ant.* VI, 459-63 ; P. K. Johnstone, XIII, 92-6, XX, 159-60 ; D. P. Dobson, XXII, 43-5, and more recently K. H. Jackson, *J.C.S.* II, 152-5.

Assessments of the value as an historical tract of Gildas' *De Excidio Britanniae* are to be found in C. E. Stevens, *E.H.R.* LVI, 353-73, LII, 193-203 ; F. Lot, *Mediaeval Studies in Memory of G. S. Loomis* (Paris, 1927) 229-64 ; P. H. Blair, *The Origins of Northumberland* (Newcastle-on-Tyne, 1947) and see Faral, op. cit., I, 1-39. A. W. Wade-Evans' views on the authorship and structure of the *De Excidio* were known to Chambers who refers to the relevant articles. More recent are *Arch. Camb.* XCVIII, 113-28, *T.H.S.C.* 1943-4, 19-34, D. Myrddin Lloyd (ed.), *The Historical Basis of Welsh Nationalism*, chap. I, and *The Emergence of England and Wales* (2nd ed., Cambridge, Heffer, 1958). Chronological problems loom large in these studies as in *Ant.* VI, 82-4 and in the studies cited in chap. 6. Unfortunately there is still no satisfactory text of the *Annales Cambriae*. Faral, op. cit., III, 44-57 prints the chronicle and the genealogies in their proper place in the Harleian Nennius : his study is in I, 221-24. Wade-Evans gives a translation in his *Nennius' History of the Britons ;* but some work has been done on the contents and background, e.g. H. M. and N. K. Chadwick, op. cit., I, 146-9, 158 etc.; N. K. Chadwick, *S.E.B.C.* 46-65 ; J. Carney, *Studies in Irish Literature and History* (Dublin, 1955), 324-73 ; J. E. Lloyd, 'The Welsh Chronicles', *Proc. B.A.* XIV, 379-82. M. Watkin, *J.N.L.W.* XI, 181-226 offers new suggestions regarding the date of the MS.

CHAPTER II

When Chambers wrote there was no adequate text of Geoffrey of Monmouth's *Historia Regum Britanniae*. This deficiency is yet to be rectified although there are signs that a critical text is in the offing. E. Faral attempted such a text in *La Légende arthurienne*, III, 71-303, but this cannot be regarded as a success being based, as it is, on too few MSS., and having been adversely criticised. In 1929, too, was published A. Griscom's *The Historia Regum Britanniae of Geoffrey of Monmouth* (New York) which contains a diplomatic edition of the Cambridge MS. 1706 with variant readings from the Berne and Harlech MSS. These two books are the only recent editions of the *Historia*. The late Prof. Jacob Hammer spent a life-time examining and collating MSS. of Geoffrey of Monmouth (the MSS. listed by Griscom, op. cit., 551-82 are supplemented by Hammer, *M.L.Q.* III, 235-42) but he did not live to publish the full results of his research. He did, however, show the existence of more than one version of the *Historia*. One such variant he published, *The Historia Regum Britanniae of Geoffrey of Monmouth, a variant version* (Cambridge, Mass., 1951)—cf. J. J. Parry, *A Miscellany of Studies in Romance Languages and Literatures presented to Leon E. Kastner* (1932), 364-69—and he referred to another in his 'Remarks on the sources and textual history of the *Historia Regum Britanniae*', *Q.B.P.I.* II, 500-64, see p. 527. For another possible variant see A. G. van Hamel, 'The Old Norse version of the *Historia Regum Britanniae* and the text of Geoffrey of Monmouth', *E.C.* I, 197-247. The relationship of these variant texts, particularly the first published by Hammer, and the Vulgate (standard) version of the *Historia* is not wholly clear and their significance is in some doubt. For recent views, conflicting with those of Hammer in the introduction to his edition, see R. A. Caldwell, 'Wace and the Variant Version of Geoffrey of Monmouth', *Sp.* XXXI, 675-82, *B.B.S.I.A.* IX, 123-4, and *Arth. Lit.*, 86-7. The question of the date, the revisions and even possibly the authorship of the *Historia* will have to be re-examined on the basis of these variants. Hammer's comments on the value (or otherwise) of the dedications are in 'Remarks . . .' op. cit., 525-530.

The fullest studies of the *Historia* are Hammer 'Remarks . . .', J. J. Parry and R. A. Caldwell, *Arth. Lit.* chap. 8, Fletcher, op. cit., J. S. P. Tatlock, *The Legendary History of Britain* (Berkely and Los Angelos,

1950), and Faral, op. cit. Together they form a complete study of the work of Geoffrey of Monmouth, the last two being extremely detailed and valuable. Other discussions, among many more, are W. F. Schirmer, op. cit., 7-40; A. E. Hutson, *British Personal Names in the Historia Regum Britanniae* (University of California Publications in English IV, 1941); S. Piggott, *Ant.* XV, 269-86; 305-19; J. J. Parry, *Sp.* IV, 316-22; J. Hammer, *Latomus* V, 299-301, *Bull. J.R.* XXX, 293-311; L. H. Loomis, *P.M.L.A.* XLV, 400-15; N. Lukman, *Classica et Mediaevila*, XX, 170-212; J. S. P. Tatlock, *Sp.* VI, 206-24. Sebastian Evans' translation has now been revised by Charles W. Dunn (New York, 1958).

The main facts of Geoffrey's life and some inferences are in E. Faral, *Rom.* LIII, 1-42; J. E. Lloyd, *E.H.R.* LVII, 460-68; Tatlock, *Leg. Hist.* chap. 20. The 'Gwentian Brut' is rightly disregarded by Chambers as a late unhistorical work. It has no authority and is largely an eighteenth century compilation, but it is not to be confused with the authentic and valuable *Brut y Tywysogion* (The Chronicle of the Princes). See *Proc. B.A.* XIV, 376-7; G. J. Williams, *Iolo Morganwg a Chywyddau'r Ychwanegiad* (London, 1926), 198, 208, 214; T. Jones, *The Chronicle of the Princes, Peniarth MS.* 20 (Cardiff, 1953), xxxiv. The *Liber Landavensis* has been linked with Geoffrey of Monmouth, e.g. J. Loth, *R.C.* XV, 101-5, and cf. C. L. Brooks, *S.E.B.C.* 201-42. The Book of Llandaf is studied in papers by E. D. Jones, *J.N.L.W.* IV, 123-57; J. W. Jones, *Journal Hist. Soc. of the Church in Wales*, V, 23-37, IX, 5-22; C. W. Lewis, *Morgannwg*, IV, 50-65; Morgan Watkin, *J.N.L.W.* XI, 181-226. The *Prophetia Merlini* has long been claimed as the first of Geoffrey's works and most scholars have been of the opinion that this section of the *Historia* was published and was in circulation before the rest of the book. H. G. Leach, *M.P.* VIII, 607-10, attempts to prove this from the Islandic version, but see J. S. Eysteinsson, *Saga Book of the Viking Club*, XIV, 95-111 Tatlock, op. cit., 418-20, argues that the only independent version was a presentation copy to Bishop Alexander, but this view is not accepted, e.g., in *Arth. Lit.* 76. Commentaries on the *Prophetia* seem to have been more common than has been thought and J. Hammer published several in *Sp.* X, 3-30, XV, 409-31, *Q.B.P.I.* 1, 589-601, *Hommages à Joseph Bidez et à Franz Cumont* (Brussels, 1949), 111-19, *Charisteria Thaddaeo Sinko . . . Oblata* (Warsaw, 1951), 81-89, and cf. G. H. Gerould, *Sp.* XXVI, 102-3. That attributed to Alanus de Insulis

(Alain de Lille) remains the most elaborate : for a recent study see G. Raynaude Lage, *Alain de Lille*, (Montreal, Paris, 1951). The *Vita Merlini* is printed by Faral, op. cit., III, 307-52 ; studies are H. M. and N. K. Chadwick, *The Growth of Literature*, I, 123-32 ; Schirmer, op. cit., 32-5 ; J. J. Parry, *Sp.* v, 216-17 (cf. K. H. Jackson, *Féilsgríbhinn Eóin Mhic Néill*, Dublin, 1940, 535-50), and J. S. P. Tatlock, *Sp.* XVIII, 265-87.

CHAPTER III

The *Historia Regum Britanniae* is minutely examined and analysed in the studies mentioned above, where much will be found on Geoffrey's sources. Griscom, op. cit. and in *YC.* XXXV, 49-116, XXXVI, 1-33, attempts to prove the existence of the *liber vetustissimus* largely by a study of the variations between the Welsh versions and Geoffrey. His theories have not met with general approval and are not wholly acceptable ; see, e.g., J. E. Lloyd, *E.H.R.* XLVII, 490-1, J. J. Parry, *J.G.P.* XXX, 95-8. Earlier attempts along the same lines are discussed by A. O. H. Jarman, *Ll.C.* II, 161-83. It is too early to be definite regarding the contents of the Welsh texts as they have not all been published and as the textual history of the sixty or so MSS. is not known (Griscom, op. cit., 586-99, lists the majority of them). One Welsh version is in J. G. Evans, *The Texts of the Bruts from the Red Book of Hergest* (1890) and there are two others (one being the so-called *Brut Tysilio*) in the *Myvyrian Archaiology of Wales* (1870). More modern and better editions of two other versions are Henry Lewis, *Brut Dingestow* (Cardiff, 1940), and J. J. Parry, *Brut y Brenhinedd, Cotton Cleopatra Version* (Cambridge, Mass., 1937). A start has been made on the classification of the Welsh MSS. in the introductions to these two editions and also by Parry, *Sp.* v., 424-31, T. Chotzen, *E.C.* IV, 221-54. There is no adequate text or study of the *Brut Tysilio* to which adherents of the *liber vetustissimus* attached so much importance. This theory which accepts Geoffrey's remarks regarding his source more or less literally has been generally disregarded and the element of fraud and collusion between Geoffrey and Walter of Oxford which worried scholars is not taken so seriously, e.g. Tatlock, *Legendary History*, 424-5. There is no agreement as to how much traditional Welsh material underlies the *Historia* : the pendulum swings from an uncritical belief in a completely Welsh basis to a negation of any Welsh influence. Welsh

scholarship has made great advances since Chambers wrote and many
of the relevant texts have been edited so that this question can now be
more fully examined. However, as most of the studies and the critical
apparatus of these editions are themselves in Welsh, some scholars
have been forced to use the older faulty texts and translations. A fine
examination and summary of the material available is R. Bromwich,
'The Character of the Early Welsh Tradition', *S.E.B.H.* 83-136, also
I. Williams, *Lectures on Early Welsh Poetry* (Dublin, 1944). The
authenticity of part of the work attributed to the sixth century *cynfeirdd*
is no longer in any doubt, cf. I. Williams, *Canu Aneirin* (Cardiff 1938);
summaries in English are C. H. Gresham, *Ant.* XIII, 237-57 and K. H.
Jackson, *Ant.* XVI, 25-34; I. Williams, *Canu Taliesin* (Cardiff 1960).
References to Arthur in Welsh bardic poetry and elsewhere are collected
by T. G. Jones, *Aberystwyth Studies*, VIII, 37-93, and T. Jones, *B.B.C.S.*
XVII, 235-52 (review in *M.Ae.* XXVIII, 115-19); see also N. K. Chadwick,
Scot. Gael. Studies, VII, 115-83. Welsh Arthurian poems are discussed by
I. Williams, *B.B.C.S.* II, 269-86; E. D. Jones, *B.B.C.S.* VIII, 203-8;
M. Williams, *Sp.* XIII, 38-51: the poem 'The Spoils of Annwn' is studied
and translated by R. S. Loomis, *W.A.L.* chap. 9 (*P.M.L.A.* LVI, 887-
936). K. H. Jackson collects and discusses the evidence in *Arth. Lit.*
chap. 2. For the Arthurian legend before Geoffrey of Monmouth see
W.A.L. chap. 10 (*R.R.* XXXII, 3-38) and Tatlock, 'The Journey of the
Laon Canons', *Sp.* VIII, 454-65. The title Mabinogion, although it is a
ghost word having no real meaning, is used to refer to a group of
mediaeval Welsh tales, five of which are native while three are somehow
connected with three of Chrétien de Troyes' poems: the word should
properly be applied to 'The Four Branches of the Mabinogi' only (where
mabinogi means 'enfances'). Two of the five native tales are Arthurian,
viz. The Dream of Rhonabwy (ed. M. G. Richards, *Breudwyt Ronabwy*
(Cardiff, 1948)) and Kulhwch and Olwen; a critical edition of this
early (second half of XIc) and important story is soon to appear. The
best translation of all these tales is that by Thomas Jones and Gwyn
Jones, *The Mabinogion* (Everyman's Library). Specialist studies are: on
the Four Branches, W. J. Gruffydd, *Math vab Mathonwy* (Cardiff, 1928),
Rhiannon (Cardiff, 1953), *YC.* XLII, 129-47, *R.C.* XXXIII, 452-61 (both
papers on Mabon son of Modron); P. MacCana, *Branwen daughter of
Llyr* (Cardiff, 1959); A. O. H. Jarman, *Ll.C.* IV, 129-34. On the Dream

of Rhonabwy, M. Giffin, *T.H.S.C.* 1958, 33-40; N. Lukman, *Classica et Mediaevila*, XIX, 133-51 : on Kulhwch, I. Ll. Foster, *Féilsgribhinn Eóin Mhic Néill* (Dublin, 1940), 28-36, *Arth. Lit.* chap. 4. The Welsh Triads have been edited by R. Bromwich, *Trioedd Ynys Prydein* (Cardiff, 1961) : see also *B.B.C.S.* XII, 1-15, *T.H.S.C.* 1957, 116-32, *Arth. Lit.* chap. 5 and *S.E.B.H.* 113-18. The texts of many *Vitae Sanctorum* are printed by A. W. Wade-Evans, *Vitae Sanctorum Britanniae et Genealogiae* (Cardiff, 1944), and see Kathleen Hughes, *S.E.B.C.* 182-200; *Arch. Camb.* CI, 91-105. Those in which Arthur appears are studied by L. H. Loomis, *Sp.* VIII, 478-82; Tatlock, XIV, 345-65; Faral, op. cit. I, 236-44; N. K. Chadwick, *Scot. Gaelic Studies*, VII, 115-83; *W.A.L.* 214-6. Studies of individual saints are G. H. Doble, *Saint Cadoc in Cornwall and Brittany* (1937); W. J. Watson, *Scot. Gaelic Studies*, II, 1-12; P. Grosjean, *Analecta Bollandiana*, LX, 35-67; H. D. Emmanuel, *J.N.L.W.*, VII, 217-27; G. H. Doble, *Saint Iltut* (1944); *St. Carantoc* (1928); Caradoc of Llancarvan, author of the Life of Gildas (for which see *W.A.L.* 182-3, *Revue Historique*, CLX, 7-16) is discussed by Tatlock, *Sp.* XIII, 139-52; G. H. Doble, *Ant.* XIX, 94-5; see also Grosjean, op. cit., J. A. Robinson, *Journal of Theological Studies*, XXIII, 15-22.

The origins of Arthur, the various accounts of his family and attempts to fit him into existing genealogies are discussed by H. M. Chadwick, *S.E.B.H.* 51-60; M. Blaess, *B.B.S.I.A.* VIII, 69-77; J. J. Parry, *Sp.* XIII, 271-7; J. D. Bruce, *G.S. Loomis Studies*, 197-208. Chambers' statement (86-7) that Geoffrey of Monmouth was the first to make Arthur the son of Uther Pendragon is shown to be doubtful by A. O. H. Jarman, *Ll.C.* II, 127-8. The Arthurian legend and Cornwall is studied by R. S. Loomis, *W.A.L.* 181-2, *Arth. Trad.* 14-16, 214-9, and see A. E. Hutson, *British Personal Names . . .* passim; Tatlock, *Sp.* VIII, 455-65. On Kelliwic see *Ant.* XIX, 156, *T.H.S.C.* 1959, 64 and contrast *S.E.B.H.* 125. The best study of the emigration to Brittany is K. H. Jackson, *L.H.E.B.* 12-30.

Chambers' comments on Merlin (95-9) are in need of revision. He is probably correct in attributing the idea of two Merlins—Merlin Silvestris and Merlin Ambrosius—to a misunderstanding and misinterpretation of the Merlins found in the *Historia* and the *Vita Merlini*, a mistake which seems to be due to Giraldus Cambrensis, but his view that Merlin is 'wholly a creation of Geoffrey's active brain' is now untenable. Although some of the Welsh Myrddin poems are post-Galfridian, it is clear that the nucleus is early and that the legend of Myrddin is to be found in Welsh tradition prior to the appearance of the Historia. Tatlock's views on Myrddin are in *Leg. Hist.*, chap. 5. For a study of the growth of the legend see A. O. H. Jarman, *The Legend of Merlin* (Cardiff, 1960), and *Arth. Lit.* chap. 3 on the Merlin poems. Other studies on Myrddin, with a suggested explanation of Geoffrey's differing portrayals of him, are M. E. Griffiths, *Early Vaticination in Welsh* (Cardiff, 1937) chaps. 2, 3 ; H. M. and N. K. Chadwick, *The Growth of Literature*, I, 105-32 ; J. J. Parry, *Vita Merlini*, (Urbana, 1925) ; K. H. Jackson, *Féilsgríbhinn Eóin Mhic Néill*, 535-50 ; J. Carney, op cit., 129-64, 385-93 : also I. Williams, *B.B.C.S.* IV, 112-29 ; A. O. H. Jarman, *B.B.C.S.* IX, 8-27, XIV, 104-8, XVI, 71-6, *Ll.C.* III, 115-8. The Dialogue of Myrddin and Taliesin has been edited from the Black Book of Carmarthen by A. O. H. Jarman, *Ymddiddan Myrddin a Thaliesin* (Cardiff 1951), who dates the poem 1050-1100. The Prophecy of the Eagle, which is inserted into some Welsh versions of the *Historia*, is printed in Parry, *Brut y Brenhinedd*, 225-6, (in Latin) and H. Lewis, *B.B.C.S.* IX, 112-5 (in Welsh).

CHAPTER IV

Geoffrey of Monmouth's *Historia Regum Britanniae* seems to have had an immediate effect and versions in the vernaculars and in Latin verse soon appeared. The most elaborate of the latter type is the *Gesta Regum Britanniae* of the pseudo-Gildas which F. Lot examines in *Rom.* XXVIII, 329-33. Other Latin verse summaries are discussed by Hammer, *Latomus* II, 131-51, *Sp.* VI, 114-23, *P.Q.* XII, 225-34, *M.P.* XXXIV, 119-32. Tatlock, *Leg. Hist. of Britain*, chap. 21, examines the early and often fragmentary vernacular Bruts, and in the two subsequent chapters discusses the work of Wace and Laymon. See also *Arth. Lit.*, chaps. 9, 10. The most recent editor of Wace is I. Arnold, *Le Roman du Brut* (Paris, 1938, 1940) : for the sources see M. Houck, *The Sources of the Roman du Brut of Wace* (University of California Publications in English V, 1941). R. A. Caldwell's remarks on the variant version of Geoffrey of Monmouth, cited above, supplement a study of Wace's use of the *Historia*. Other dissertations are M. Pelan, *L'Influence du Brut de Wace sur les romanciers français de son temps* (Paris, 1931) ; M. Delbouille, *Rom.*

LXXIV, 172-99; R. A. Caldwell, *M.L.N.* LXIX, 237-9; I. Arnold, *Rom.* LVIII, 1-12; B. Woledge, *M.L.R.* XLVI, 16-30; H. Pilch, *Z.C.P.* XXVII, 1-9. There is no new edition of Laymon's Brut, but studies are G. J. Visser, *Laȝamon : An attempt at Vindication* (1935); R. Blenner-Hasset, *A Study of the Place-Names in Lawman's Brut* (Stanford Un. Publications . . . Language and Literature, IX, 1950); *M.L.N.* LV, 373-8; H. Pilch, *Layomons Brut : eine literarische Studie* (Heidelberg, 1960); P. J. Heather *F.L.* XLVIII, 339-65, LIII, 57-71; H. C. Wyld, *R.E.S.* VI, 1-30; R. S. Loomis, X, 79-82; J. S. P. Tatlock, *P.M.L.A.* XXXVIII, 494-529, *M.P.* XLIII, 72-6; W. J. Keith, *M.Ae.* XXIX, 161-172; The Welsh versions of Geoffrey (the earliest of which date from the early XIIIc.) have already been mentioned : for the Arthurian legend in other European countries see the relevant chapters in *Arth. Lit.*

The influence of the *Historia* on chronicles and on historical thought has been the subject of special studies, e.g. L. Keeler, *Geoffrey of Monmouth and the later Latin Chroniclers, 1300-1500* (Un. of California, 1946), *Sp.* XXI, 24-37; E. Jones, *Geoffrey of Monmouth, 1640-1800* (Un. of California, 1944); R. F. Brinkley, *The Arthurian Legend in the Eighteenth Century* (Baltimore, 1932); J. S. P. Tatlock, *Sp.* IX, 135-9; R. S. Loomis, *Sp.* XXVIII, 114-27; T. D. Kendrick, *British Antiquity* (London, 1950). The later controversy on the authenticity of the *Historia* is discussed by Kendrick, ibid.; A. O. H. Jarman, *Ll.C.* II, 1-18; J. F. Houseman, *R.E.S.* XXIII, 209-77. The Welsh 'continuation' of the *Historia*, The Chronicle of the Princes, is a sober chronicle of Welsh history from 682 to 1282, which owes little or nothing to Geoffrey. Two of the three versions have been edited and translated by T. Jones, *Brut y Tywysogion or The Chronicle of the Princes, Peniarth MS.* 20 (Cardiff, 1953), *Brut y Tywysogion . . . Red Book of Hergest* (Cardiff, 1955). Studies are J. E. Lloyd, *Proc. B.A.* XIV, 369-91; T. Jones, *Brut y Tywysogion* (Cardiff, 1953). On the basis of Geoffrey's colophon, the text has been attributed to Caradoc of Llancarvan, but as is shown in the above studies, and by Tatlock, *Sp.* XIII, 139-52, this is impossible.

There is no full discussion of the legend of Arthur's survival and ultimate return apart from *Arth. Lit.* chap. 7, but aspects of the theme are discussed in J. E. Lloyd, *B.B.C.S.* XI, 158-60; *W.A.L.* 61-76 (*M.P.* XXXVIII, 289-304), *F.L.* LXIX, 10-17; Tatlock, *M.L.N.* XXXI, 1-18, 113-25 (on Normanicus Draco). Glastonbury and Avalon, naturally, have been more fully treated. The history of the abbey is studied in Dom Aelred Watkins, *The Great Chartulary of Glastonbury* (Somerset Rec. Soc., vols. 59, 63, 64) ; G. Ashe, *King Arthur's Avalon* (London, 1957) is a convenient introduction both to the history and to the traditions, but should be used with care. Papers and studies are L. H. Gray, *Sp.* x, 46-53 ; C. H. Slover, *Sp.* x, 147-60, xi, 129-32, ii, 268-83 ; W. A. Nitze, *Sp.* ix, 355-61 ; E. Faral, op. cit., ii, 299-308, 402-60, *Revue Historique*, clx, 1-49 ; W. A. Nitze and T. A. Jenkins, *Le Haut Livre du Graal*, *Perlesvaus*, ii, 47-72 ; M. Williams, *Sp.* xiv, 199-208 ; L. Cons, *M.P.* xxviii, 385-94 ; A. H. Krappe, *Sp.* xviii, 303-22 ; R. S. Loomis, *R.R.* xxix, 175-7 ; C. H. Slover, *M.P.* xxviii, 395-99 ; T. Chotzen, *E.C.* iv, 255-74. L. M. Paton, *The Fairy Mythology of the Arthurian Romances*, first published 1903, is re-issued by Burt Franklin, New York, 1959

CHAPTER V

The Arthurian Legend proper consists of a large number of tales, some independent of one another, others linked in a series or connected by their subject matter. The principal texts are in French, German, English, Dutch and Latin. The field bristles with problems, questions of origin, diffusion, meaning and relationships, to mention but a few. A full bibliographical list is impossible but once again *Arth. Lit.* is a sure guide. R. S. Loomis, *W.A.L.*, chap. 10, examines the evidence for the existence of Arthurian tales before the appearance of the *Historia Regum Britanniae* and answers points raised by Tatlock in *Sp.* xiv, 345-65, and his *Leg. Hist.*, chap. 6. See also *Sp.* iii, 16-33. More particularly Welsh evidence is collected in *B.B.C.S.* xvii, 235-52, and *Aberystwyth Studies*, viii, 37-93 as noted above. On the testimony and date of the Modena sculptures see G. H. Gerould, *Sp.* x, 353-76 ; R. S. Loomis, *Sp.* xiii, 221-31, *Mediaeval Studies in memory of G. S. Loomis*, 209-28, *W.A.L.* 198-208 ; R. S. and L. H. Loomis, *The Arthurian Legend in Mediaeval Art*, 32-6. There seems to be no doubt that stories about Arthur were in circulation before the flowering of French romance in the XII and XIII centuries ; the points of controversy are the relationship of the later tales and poems with the Celtic stories and whether such stories are in fact the nucleus and source of the Arthurian legend as the term is generally understood. Celtic sources are examined by R. S. Loomis, *R.C.* xlvii, 39-62 ; M. Dillon, *Lettres Romanes*, ix, 143-59 ;

T F. O'Rahilly, *Ériu*, XVI, 7-20; J. W. Thompson, *T.H.S.C.* 1956, 137-42; T. P. Cross, *The Malone Anniversary Studies*, 1949, 110-14; J. Fourquet, *R.P.* IX, 298-312; H. Newstead, *P.M.L.A.* LXIII, 803-30; R. S. Loomis, *P.M.L.A.* LVIII, 1000-35: *Arth. Trad* has full discussions on these and many other topics. Linked with the problem of Celtic sources is the question of the diffusion of the tales and their passage from Wales (and Ireland) to France. This is discussed in the studies listed above and in *Arth. Lit.* chap. 6, *W.A.L.* 183-5, *Arth. Trad.* 15-18, 21-3, 27-32, *F.L.* LXIX, 1-25, *M.P.* XXXIII, 225-38; J. Marx, *La Légende Arthurienne et le Graal*, 55-8; K. Voret (trans. F. Dumont), *Introduction to the study of Old French Literature* (1931), 309-19. Non-Celtic sources are postulated by C. B. Lewis, *Classical Mythology and Arthurian Romance* (Oxford, 1932). R. S. Loomis answers criticisms of the Celtic source theory in *Rom.* LXXIX, 47-77.

Bleheris is again studied by M. Williams, *E.C.* II, 219-45; F. Lot, *Rom.* LI, 397-408; R. S. Loomis, *Rom.* LIII, 82-92; J. van Dam, *Neophilologus*, XV, 30-34; W. Kellerman, *R.G.* 137-48 and see *M.P.* XXII, 123, n.8.

The *lais* of Marie de France are edited by A. Ewert (Oxford, 1947) and discussed by E. Hoepffner, *Les Lais de Marie de France* (Paris, 1935), *Rom.* LVI, 1-32, 212-35 and in *Arth. Lit.* chap. 11. Papers are E. Brugger, *Z.F.L.* XLIX, 116-55, 201 f., 381 f.; S. Hoffer, *Z.R.P.* LXVI, 409-21; E. A. Francis, *Rom.* LXXII, 78-99; L. Spitzer, *M.P.* XLI, 96-102; G. E. Brereton, *M.L.R.* XLV, 40-5; G. V. Smithers, *M.Ae.* XXII, 61-92; R. Bromwich, *M.Ae.* XXVI, 36-8; *E.C.* IX, 439-74; C. Foulon, *A.B.* LX, 243-59; T. P. Cross, *R.C.* XXXI, 413-71, *M.P.* XII, 585-644; A. Adler, *B.B.S.I.A.* IX, 127-8; R. N. Illingworth, *E.C.* IX, 501-20.

Recent editions of Chrétien de Troyes are the C.F.M.A. Series (from the Guiot MS.), *Erec*, ed. M. Roques (1952), *Cliges*, ed. A. Micha (1957), *Le Chevalier de la Charette*, ed. M. Roques (1958), *Le Chevalier au Lion*, ed. M. Roques (1960), *Le Conte du Graal*, ed. M. Roques (forthcoming). Other editions are *Le Chevalier au Lion*, R. W. Linker (1940), and T. B. Reid (Manchester, 1943), *Le Roman de Perceval ou le Conte du Graal*, W. Roach (Grenoble-Lille, 1956), and A. Hilka (Halle, 1932). The poems (excluding *Perceval*) are translated by W. W. Comfort in the Everyman's Library. General studies are G. Cohen, *Un grand romancier d'amour et d'aventure au XIIIe siècle, Chrétien de Troyes et son oeuvre* (Paris, 1931, 1948);

Supplementary Bibliography

J. Frappier, *Chrétien de Troyes, l'homme et l'oeuvre* (Paris, 1957); S. Hoffer, *Chrétien de Troyes, Leben und Werke des altfranzösichen Epikers* (Graz-Köln, 1954); J. Frappier, *Le Roman Breton* (Cours de Sorbonne), *Introduction: Des Origins à Ch. de T.* (1950), *Cligés* (1951), *Yvain* (1952), *Perceval* (1953); A. Pauphilet, *Legs du Moyen Âge*, (Melun, 1950), 143-67, 170-209. *Arth. Trad.* gives a detailed analysis of the poems and discusses the sources. The following are discussions of individual poems and topics: J. Frappier's chapter (15) in *Arth. Lit.* contains many more. On the chronology of Chrétien's work see *B.B.S.I.A.* II, 70-88, VII, 89-103, *M.A.* LX, 51-79, *B.B.S.I.A.* IX, 85-100, X, 73-85, XI, 89-120, *Z.R.P.* LX, 246-61, LXII, 19-32. On the poems: T. P. Cross and W. A. Nitze, *Lancelot and Guenevere* (Chicago, 1930); K. G. T. Webster, *Guinevere: A Study of her Abductions* (Milton, 1951), which is, as the sub-title suggests, more than a study of Chrétien only; A. Micha, *Rom.* LXXI, 345-58; M. Roques, *Cahiers de Civilisation Médiévale* (1958), 141-52; A. Adler, *M.L.R.* XLV, 33-9; E. Philipot, *Rom.* XXV, 258-94; H. Newstead, *P.M.L.A.* LI, 13-75; W. A. Nitze, *R.R.* X, 26-37, *Sp.* XXIX, 691-701; C. Foulon, *A.B.* LXV, 147-58; P. Jonin, *Prolégomènes à une édition d'Yvain* (1958); M. Roques, *Rom.* LXXX, 1-18; E. Philipot, *A.B.* VIII, 33-83, &c.; T. Chotzen, *Neophilologus*, XVIII, 51-8, 131-6; A. G. Brodeur, *P.M.L.A.* XXXIX, 485-524; A. Adler, LXII, 287-305; J. Harris, LXIV, 1143-63; W. A. Nitze, *Sp.* XXX, 170-9; E. Brugger, *M.P.* XXXVIII, 267-87; W. A. Nitze, *Perceval and the Holy Grail* (Un. of California, 1949); W. A. Nitze and H. F. Williams, *Arthurian Names in the Perceval of Chrétien de Troyes* (Un. of California, 1955); J. Frappier, *M.A.* LXIV, 67-102; D. D. R. Owen, *Rom.* LXXX, 473-92; M. Roques, *Rom.* LXXXI, 1-36; and studies on the Grail cited below. The continuations of the *Perceval* have been edited by M. Williams (Gerbert de Montreuil, Paris, 1922, 1925) and others by W. Roach in three vols., Philadelphia, 1949, 1950, 1952-5. For discussions see *Arth. Lit.* chap. 17 and *R.G.* 5-14.

Three mediaeval Welsh romances have obviously a connection with three of Chrétien's poems, viz. *Erec, Yvain, Perceval.* There are no critical editions of these stories but the texts are diplomatically published by J. G. Evans, *The White Book Mabinogion* (Pwllheli, 1907). Their precise relationship to the poems is still not settled but reference may be made to the views of Zenker, *R.F.* XL, 251-329, *Z.F.L.* XLVIII, 1-82; Weisgerber, *R.F.* xl, 483-93 ; Mülhausen, *Z.R.P.* xliv, 465-543 : see also M. Williams, *Jour. of the Welsh Bibliographical Society*, iii, 73-81 ; R. M. Jones, *B.B.C.S.* xv, 109-16 ; R. Bromwich, xvii, 181-2 ; R. Harris, *M.Ae.* xxvii, 32-5 (answered by R. S. Loomis, xxvii, 175-8). The position is reviewed by Loomis, *Arth. Trad.* 32-8, and I. Ll. Foster, *Arth. Lit.* chap. 16. The general view that Chrétien and the Welsh romances derive from a common source in French based on Welsh stories taken to France by Breton *conteurs* is challenged by R. M. Jones, *Ll.C.* iv, 208-27, who claims that the Welsh tales are purely native and show few traces or none of French influence.

Books, papers and studies on the Grail legends are numerous and a brief selection only can be given here, but see *L.G.* 328-32. On the word Grail (Graal) see R. S. Loomis, *P.M.L.A.* lxxi, 846-9, L. Spitzer, *American Journal of Philology*, lxv, 354-63, W. A. Nitze, lxvi, 279-81, *M.P.* xiii, 681-84, J. Marx, *La Légende Arthurienne et le Graal*, 241-3. General studies on a variety of aspects are Marx, op. cit., A. Pauphilet, *Rom.* lxvi, 289-321, 481-504 (cf. *Legs du Moyen Age*, 170-209) ; *L.G.* and *R.G.* contain essays on various themes by a number of scholars. Theories on the origin and development of the legends are reviewed by Loomis, *Arth. Lit.* chap. 21, U. T. Holmes, *History of Old French Literature* (New York, 1948), 288 f., J. Frappier, *Chrétien de Troyes* (1957), 186-206. The Celtic origin theory has many adherents, e.g. Loomis, *Arth. Trad.* chaps. 67, 69, 71, 75, *W.A.L.* chap. 2 (*Sp.* viii, 415-31) ; A. C. L. Brown, *The Origin of the Grail Legend* (Cambridge, Mass., 1943) ; H. Newstead, *Bran the Blessed in Arthurian Romance* (New York, 1939) ; Marx, op. cit.; A. G. van Hamel, *R.C.* xlvii, 340-82 ; J. Vendryes, *E.C.* v, 1-50 ; M. Dillon, *Lettres Romanes*, ix, 143-59. Texts of the Thirteen Treasures of the Island of Britain (one of which is the *dysgl* of Rhydderch) are published by E. I. Rowlands, *Ll.C.* v, 33-69 ; R. Bromwich, *Trioedd Ynys Prydein* (Cardiff, 1961) 240-49 ; see also *W.A.L.* 39-41, *R.F.* xlv, 68-71. K. H. Jackson, *R.G.* 213-31, criticizes some of the proposed Celtic analogues, but see Loomis, *Rom.* lxxxix, 69-77. The attempts to derive the Grail from Byzantine ritual are discussed by Bruce, i, 257-9 ; more recent are R. Burdach, *Der Gral* (Stuttgart, 1938) ; E. Anitchkof, *Rom.* lv, 174-94. Cf. again M. Lot-Borodine, *Rom.* lvii, 147-205 ; J. Marx, op. cit., 235-40 ; W. A. Nitze, *M.P.* xxviii, 315-20, stresses the Celtic origin of the legends but admits later borrowing

Supplementary Bibliography

from Byzantine sources ; cf. his *Perceval and the Holy Grail*, 308-10, 316-25. See also M. Williams, *F.L.* LXXI, 85-103. U. T. Holmes and Sister M. A. Klenke, *Chrétien, Troyes and the Grail* (Chaple Hill, 1954) see in the *Conte del Graal* an allegory of the conversion of the Jews : (cf. U. T. Holmes, *A New Interpretation of Chrétien's Conte del Graal*, Un. of North Carolina Studies in Romance Languages and Literatures, VIII, *S.P.* XLIV, 453-76 ; M. A. Klenke, *Liturgy and Allegory in Chrétien's Perceval*, Un. of North Carolina Studies . . ., XIV, *S.P.* LIII, 1-21). There are criticisms by Loomis, *P.M.L.A.* LXXI, 840-52 ; R. Levy, *Medievalia et Humanistica*, VI, 76-83, *P.M.L.A.* LXXI, 853-62. On the theory which finds the origin of the Grail in a fertility cult see J. Weston, *From Ritual to Romance* (Cambridge, 1920) : rev. by W. A. Nitze *M.L.N.*, 352-60, and see *M.P.* XLIII, 58-62, *Arth. Lit.* 278-80. Chambers' own views on the Grail are in his *Sir Thomas Wyatt and some collected studies* (London, 1933), 1-20. Other views and theories are in D. de Séchelles, *L'Origine du Graal* (1954), *Rom.* LXXVIII, 182-98 ; M. Roques, *Rom.* LXXVI, 1-27 ; M. Lot-Borodine, LXXVII, 235-88 ; A. A. Barb, *Jour. of the Worburg and Courtauld Institutes*, XIX, 40-67 and see J. Marx, *M.A.* LXIII, 469-80.

H. Newstead discusses the origin and growth of the Tristan story in *Arth. Lit.*, chap. 12, where reference is made (p. 122) to the Tristan Bibliography in *Deutsche Arbeiten der Universität Köln*, XVII ; the early Tristan poems are treated by F. Whitehead, chap. 13. Béroul is edited by A. Ewert (Oxford, 1939) and E. Muret (C.F.M.A., 1913, 1947) : Bédier's edition of Thomas has not been superseded, but see also B. H. Wind, *Les Fragments du Roman de Tristan . . . par Thomas* (Leiden, 1950, 1960). E. Hoepffner edits *La Folie Tristan de Berne* (Paris, 1934) and *La Folie Tristan d'Oxford* (Paris, 1938) : see A. Adler, *Symposium*, VI, 349-58. Some discussions are B. Mergell, *Tristan und Isolde: Ursprung und Entwicklung der Tristansage des Mittelalters* (Mainz, 1949) ; J. Bédier, *Littérature française* (1948), 30-32, A. Pauphilet, *Legs du Moyen Age*, 107-41 ; J. Carney, *Studies in Irish Literature and History*, 189-242 ; R. Bromwich, *T.H.S.C.* 1953, 32-60 ; H. Newstead, *R.P.* IX, 269-84, XI, 240-53, *P.M.L.A.* LXV, 290-315 ; J. J. Jones, *Aberystwyth Studies*, XII, 21-33 ; R. S. Loomis, *A.B.* LVI, 203-27 ; P. Le Gentil, *R.P.* VII, 111-29 ; R. S. Loomis, *Rom.* LIII, 92-102 ; F. J. Tanqueray, LVI, 115-22, *M. Ae.* VI, 1-20. For the date of Béroul see *B.B.S.I.A.* IX, 134-6 ; G. Whitteridge, *M.Ae.* XXVIII, 167-71 ; R. de Lage *M.A.* LXIV, 249-70 :

and for Thomas, *B.B.S.I.A.* VI, 95-6. There are summaries on a number of points on the legend in *B.B.S.I.A.* VI, 95-101. G. S. Loomis, *Tristan and Isolt* (1913) has been re-issued by Burt Franklin, New York, 1959.

The growth of the Arthurian Legend and its textual ramifications are fully dealt with in a series of independent chapters in *Arth. Lit*. Robert de Boron's *Roman de l' Estoire dou Graal* is edited by W. A. Nitze (Paris, 1927): discussions are Nitze, *Sp.* XXVIII, 279-96 ; A. Micha, *Rom.* LXXV, 316-52, *R.P.* IX, 173-7 ; Becker, *Z.R.P.* LV, 260-9 ; Marx, *M.A.* LIX, 69-86 ; Hoepffner, *L.G.* 139-50, *R.G.* 93-105. W. A. Roach has edited the Modena MS. of the Prose *Joseph* in *R.P.* IX, 313-42, and the *Didot Perceval* (Philadelphia, 1941) which is discussed by Brugger, *Z.S.L.* LIII, 389-459 ,. Nitze, *M.P.* XLI, 1-5 ; Tieman, *R.F.* LXIII, 306-28 ; Micha, *Rom.* LXXV; 334-52 ; Loomis, *R.R.* XXXIII, 168-74. *Perlesvaus* is edited by W. A. Nitze and T. A. Jenkins, *Le Haut Livre du Graal — Perlesvaus* (2 vols., Chicago, 1932, 1937) and studied in *S.P.* XLII, 723-40 ; *Z.R.P.* LIX, 10-56 ; *Sp.* XIV, 199-208 ; *P.M.L.A.* L, 25-35, LXI, 42-83 ; *W.A.L.* 168-74 ; *R.P.* VI, 179-86 ; *Miscellany of Studies . . . presented to Leon E. Kastner*, 560-7 ; *F.L.* XLVIII, 263-6 ; *Rom.* LXXXI, 492-99 ; J. N. Carman, *The Relationship of the Perlesvaus and the Queste del Saint Graal* (Un. of Kansas, Humanistic Studies V, 1936). Recent editions of two of the Vulgate texts are A. Pauphilet, *La Queste del Saint Graal* (C.F.M.A., 1923, 1949), J. Frappier, *Étude sur la Mort le roi Artu* (Paris, 1936, 1954). Papers and dissertations are : Micha, *Z.R.P.* LXVI, 369-71, *M.A.* LVIII, 299-345, *Rom.* LXXII, 310-23, LXXIV, 200-20, LXXVI, 334-41, LXXIX, 79-94, 145-74, LXXXI, 145-87 ; Speyer, *R.R.* XXVIII, 195-203 ; R. S. Loomis, *M.L.R.* XXIV, 416-36 ; Kennedy, *M.Ae.* XXVI, 90-106 ; Adler, *P.M.L.A.* LXV, 930-43 ; Tanqueray, *M.Ae.* XII, 1-17 ; W.E.M.C. Hamilton, *Neophilologus*, XXVII, 94-110 ; M. Lot-Borodine, XXXIV, 65-79 ; P. Imbs, *Mélanges . . . offerts à E. Hoepffner* (Paris, 1949), 279-93 ; J. Frappier, ibid., 269-78 ; M. B. Fox, *La Mort le roi Artu* (Paris, 1933) ; G. Hutchings, *Le Roman en Prose de Lancelot du Lac* (Paris, 1938) ; P. Zumthor, *Merlin le Prophet* (Lausanne, 1943) ; F. W. Locke, *The Quest for the Holy Grail* (Stanford, 1960). F. Lot's *Étude sur le Lancelot en Prose* has been re-issued with additional matter (Paris, 1954). The *Suite du Merlin* is discussed by F. Bogdanow in *Arth. Lit.*, chap. 24, and see *Rom.* LXXXI, 188-98 ; E. Vinaver, *Mélanges . . . Hoepffner*, 295-300 ; M. D. Legge, *Le Roman de*

317

Supplementary Bibliography

Balain (Manchester, 1942). On the 'pseudo-Boron cycle' (so called) see *Arth. Lit.* 326-32 and the references given there.

Ulrich von Zatzikhoven's *Lanzelet* is translated with notes by K. G. T. Webster and R. S. Loomis (New York, 1951) and discussed by W. Richter, *Der Lanzelet des Ulrich von Zatzikhoven* (Frankfurt, 1934); R. Zenker, *Z.S.L.* XLVIII, 92-102 and see *Arth. Lit.* 436-9.

E. Vinaver's editions of Malory, *The Works of Sir Thomas Malory* (3 vols., Oxford, 1947), *The Tale of the Death of King Arthur* (Oxford, 1955) make further references superfluous. A bibliography is given in *The Works . . .*, 1652-8 and supplemented in *Arth. Lit.* 552.

CHAPTER VI

The historical Arthur remains a shadowy figure. Although there is much agreement that such a leader did exist in dark-age Britain, attempts to determine his place and background are various. Some discussions are K. Malone, *M.P.* XXII, 367-74, R. Thurneysen, *Z.C.P.* XX, 132-7; W. A. Nitze has taken up and developed the possibilities raised by the existence of a Roman commander named Lucius Artorius Castus stationed at York, in *M.P.* XXXIX, 1-14, *P.M.L.A.* LXIV, 590-6, *B.B.I.S.A.* V, 69-74: see also J. C. Russell, *M.P.* XLVIII, 145-53. For other views on the historical Arthur see J. J. Parry, *J.G.P.* LVIII, 365-79; A. D. Brodeur, *Arthur Dux Bellorum;* R. G. Collingwood and J. N. L. Myres, *Roman Britain and the English Settlements*, 320 f. The most recent survey is that by K. H. Jackson, *Arth. Lit.*, chap. I, who comes to the conclusion that although there is no direct proof of an historical Arthur, the weight of the evidence makes the hypothesis probable. References have already been given in chap. I to the battles named by Nennius and to Badon, and to the historical tracts, Nennius, Gildas, *Annales Cambriae.*

Background studies of the end of Roman Britain and the Saxon settlement are I. A. Richmond, *Roman and Native in North Britain* (Edinburgh, 1958); H. M. Chadwick, 'The End of Roman Britain', 'The Foundation of the British Kingdoms', *S.E.B.H.*, 47-60; E. A. Thompson, 'Zosimus on the end of Roman Britain', *Ant.* XXX, 163-7; C. E. Stevens, 'The British Sections of the Notitia Dignitatum', *Archaeological Journal*, XCVII, 125 f.; G. Sheldon, *The Transition from Roman Britain to Christian England* (London, 1932); T. C. Lethbridge, *Merlin's Island* (London, 1948); A. W. Wade-Evans, *The Emergence of*

England and Wales (2nd ed., Cambridge, Heffer, 1958) ; T. D. Reed, *The Battle for Britain in the Fifth Century* (London, 1944) : J. N. L. Myres, 'The Adventus Saxonum', *Aspects of Archaeology in Britain and Beyond* (ed. W. F. Grimes, London, 1951), 221-41 ; C. F. C. Hawkes, 'The Jutes of Kent', *Dark Age Britain*, 91-111 ; J. F. Turville-Petre, 'Hengist and Horsa', *Saga-Book of the Viking Club*, xiv, 273-90 : R. H. Hodgkin, *A History of the Anglo-Saxons* (Oxford, 1952) ; F. Stenton, *Anglo-Saxon England* (Oxford, 1943) ; P. Hunter-Blair, *An Introduction to Anglo-Saxon England* (Cambridge, 1956) ; M. Charlesworth and M. D. Knowles, *The Heritage of Early Britain* (London, 1950). Other papers are J. N. L. Myres, *Ant.* ix, 455-64 ; F. Lot, *Proc. B.A.* xvi, 327-44 ; C. L. Wrenn, *T.H.S.C.* 1959, 38-75 ; N. K. Chadwick, *Yorkshire Celtic Studies*, iii, 13-32. D. B. Harden (ed.), *Dark Age Britain* (London, 1956) is mainly concerned with the archaeological evidence, while K. H. Jackson, *L.H.E.B.* chap. 6, studies the linguistic evidence for the Saxon settlements. The Anglo-Saxon chronicle is translated by G. N. Garmonsway, Everyman's Library, 1953.

CHAPTER VII

For views on Arthur as a folk-hero and for his mythological associations see A. G. van Hamel, *Proc. B.A.* xx, 219-34 ; A. H. Krappe, *Sp.* xx, 405-14 ; W. J. Gruffydd, *The Welsh Review*, vi, 244-8 ; Lord Raglan, *The Hero* (London, 1936), 73-81. R. S. Loomis, *Celtic Myth and Arthurian Romance* (New York, 1927) attempts to find analogues in Celtic myth for Arthurian themes but the book should be read in the light of the author's later work (see *Arth. Trad.* ix). For Avalon, see chap. 4 above : Morgain la Fée is discussed in *W.A.L.* 105-30 (*Sp.* xx, 183-203) ; *Rom.* lxxx, 337-67 ; *R.R.* xxix, 176-7 ; *P.M.L.A.* lxi, 923-44 ; *Z.S.L.* xlviii, 82-92. For the legend of Arthur's survival see chap. 4 above : Welsh cave-legends are given by T. G. Jones, *Welsh Folklore and Folk Custom* (London, 1930), and in *W.A.L.* 69-71. The Wild Hunt is discussed by K. Meisen, *Die Sagen vom Wütenden Heer* (Münster, 1935) and see *W.A.L.* 71f., 82f. ; *R.R.* xii, 286-9 ; *Anglia*, lxi, 225-340. Recent views on the origin and meaning of the Round Table are in *Arth. Trad.* 61-8 ; Tatlock, *Legendary History . . .*, 471-5 ; *M.L.Q.* xiv, 131-2 (cf. xiii, 99-101) ; *R.P.* ix, 173-7 ; *M.L.N.* xliv, 511-9 ; *M.Ae.* xix, 39-42 ; *Med. Studies*, xiv, 143-9 ; *Z.R.P.* lxii, 87-91 ; *Rom.* lxxiv, 185-92.

Supplementary Bibliography

The *Pèlerinage de Charlemagne* is studied by R. N. Walpole, *R.P.* VII, 173-86 ; L. H. Loomis, *M.P.* XXV, 331-49 ; R. S. Loomis, *Sp.* III, 24-5 ; J. Horrent, *Le Pèlinerage de Charlemagne* (Un. de Liège, 1961). The Scottish localities in the Arthurian legend are discussed by R. L. G. Ritchie, *Chrétien de Troyes and Scotland* (Oxford, 1952) ; R. S. Loomis, *Proc. of the Soc. of Antiquaries of Scotland*, LXXXIX, 1-21. Some local Welsh traditions are in *B.B.C.S.* VIII, 124-5, XI, 12-14. J. R. Reinhard, *The Survival of Geis in Mediaeval Romance* (Halle, 1933), J. V. Harward, *The Dwarfs of Arthurian and Celtic Romance* (Leiden, 1957), R. Bernheimer, *Wild Men in the Middle Ages* (Cambridge, Mass., 1953) cite Celtic and other analogues for incidents and characters in Arthurian romance.

For opinions (necessarily tentative) on Celtic religion and mythology see A. G. van Hamel, 'Aspects of Celtic Mythology', *Proc. B.A.* XX, 207-48 ; M.-L. Sjoestedt, *Gods and Heroes of the Celts* (trans. M. Dillon, London, 1949) ; P. Lambrechts, *Contributions à l'étude des divinités celtiques* (Bruges, 1942), A. Rees and B. Rees, *Celtic Heritage* (London, 1961), J. Vendryes, *La Religion des Celtes*, vol. III of A. Grenier's *Les Religions de l' Europe ancienne* (Paris, 1948). The Irish heroic tales and sagas are discussed by R. Thurneysen, *Die irische Helden- und Königsage* (Halle, 1921) ; M. Dillon, *The Cycles of the Kings* (Oxford, 1946) ; *Early Irish Literature* (Chicago, 1948). T. P. Cross and C. H. Slover, *Ancient Irish Tales* (London, 1936) give translations and T. P. Cross, *Motif-Index of Early Irish Literature* (Un. of Indiana, 1952), is very useful.

University College of Wales,   BRYN F. ROBERTS.
        Aberystwyth.